VINCENT PRICE
The British Connection

VINCENT PRICE
The British Connection

Mark Iveson

First published in 2020 by Telos Publishing Ltd
139 Whitstable Road, Canterbury, Kent CT2 8EQ

www.telos.co.uk

Telos Publishing Ltd values feedback. Please e-mail us with any comments you
may have about this book to: feedback@telos.co.uk

ISBN: 978-1-84583-136-3

British Library Cataloguing in Publication Data. A catalogue record for this book
is available from the British Library.

Contents

Dedication

Dedicated to the memory of Vincent Price.
Great actor, cultural icon, and above all, boyhood hero.

And to the memory of Chris Phipps.
An amazing racounteur and above all, a dear friend.
I treasure the wonderful memories we shared together.

Acknowledgements

I have been blessed with so many friends who have stood by me while I was writing this book. As with my previous work *Cursed Horror Stars*, I have to limit my lasting gratitude to a chosen few.

First, to my mother Inga, who is brilliant as always. To my resident Girl Friday Carolyn Eastgate, whose endless support at my various book talks, coupled with a solid supply of red wine is always appreciated! And to my dear friend and fellow writer Sally Franz for doing her bit with her valuable book suggestions.

My thanks to friend and author Daniela Norris for her belief in me ('I bloody well told you so!'), to Peter Cumisky of *New Writing North* for getting me started with my book talks at the Castle Keep in Newcastle, and to Marcus Brooks of the *Peter Cushing Appreciation Society* (I'm the longest serving member) for just being a top man.

Also my thanks to Steve Walker and David Howe at Telos. Once again it is an amazing opportunity to which I owe them a great debt of gratitude. Thanks to Ian Pritchard for the indexes. And to the Swanwick Writers Retreat for continuing to inspire me with its magic.

I reserve a special thanks to dear friend and fellow author Chris Phipps for getting me involved in the 2016 *Whitley Bay Film Festival* and the 2016 *Newcastle Book Festival*. Sadly Chris passed away prior to publication. The book is dedicated to his memory. Also a big thanks to David Hepworth, organiser of the *Newcastle Book Festival*. Taking part in the event remains one of the highlights of my life as a writer.

Introduction

'What's important about an actor is his acting, not his life.' – Vincent Price

It was the death of Vincent Price that indirectly inspired me to write my first book, *Cursed Horror Stars*. I was visiting a childhood pen-pal in Columbus, Ohio, during that fateful October of 1993 when they announced the actor's death on American TV. Naturally, I was shocked by the news. Price represented an important part of my childhood, and his passing took it all away in one sudden swoop.

Being Halloween a few days after his death, not surprisingly, his films were broadcast on TV all over the States as a tribute to this iconic figure of American horror. It was a Halloween I'll never forget. It was also the time I made the decision to write a book on the genre.

Price had the unique distinction of being equally influential in British horror. When American International Pictures, who Price was under contract with, established a London base in the sixties, most of his subsequent movies were made in the UK. His British output not only consolidated his popularity among fans, it provided him with four career defining performances. An Anglophile through and through, Price loved the UK.

Prior to the publication of *Cursed Horror Stars*, I was writing articles for the movie webmag *Shadowlocked*. One of my pieces, *Vincent Price: The British Connection*, focused on his UK horror films. I decided to expand it into book form – and here it is! In addition to covering his British chillers in more detail, this book also examines the strong links he held with the country.

Vincent Price is an incredible individual: actor; art connoisseur; lecturer; gourmet; raconteur; a remarkable all-rounder. I hope my book stands as a valuable tribute to a man who can never be equalled or replaced.

Long live Vinnie!

Mark Iveson
December 2019

The Early Years (1911 – 1935)

'A man who limits his interests, limits his life.' – Vincent Price

Vincent Price: A graduate student in 1939

The undisputed king of American horror, Vincent Price holds a special place in the hearts of many fans for his successful association with English gothic. It comes as no surprise that Price was often mistaken for being British, a by-product of his upper-middle class upbringing, his time in London as an art student and his early theatre years, all of which contributes to his impeccable mid-Atlantic diction that allowed him to alternate from English to American with comparative ease, and further enhanced by an unmistakable voice that was as famous as the man himself.

But, 'the Englishman from St Louis,' as he once described himself, was as American as they came.

Vincent Leonard Price Junior was born in St Louis, Missouri on 27 May 1911. There were strong family links to the UK via Price's grandfather, New Jersey born Dr Vincent Clarence Price, who was of Welsh descent and colourfully described as a 'wonderfully, black-haired, black-moustached, "black" Welshman.' Another part of Price's British ancestry dates back to 1620 with Peregrine White, allegedly the first child to be born on *The Mayflower* as the ship arrived from Plymouth to dock in the New World.

In researching her father's biography, Price's daughter Victoria cast her own doubts about this tenuous family link: 'The Price account of the distinguished White lineage appears to be flawed,' she wrote. 'The purported family genealogy leading back to Peregrine White cannot be confirmed by *Mayflower* records.' There was a second ship called *Mayflower* that sailed from London to the newly established Plymouth Harbour, Massachusetts in 1629, so it is possible that the White family sailed on that ship instead.

Whether or not the link can be verified, Peregrine White's descendent, Dr Russell White, an eminent physician from Buffalo, New Jersey, met Vincent Clarence Price, a young working class student who had just graduated from medical school in 1852 as a newly qualified druggist. White took to Price immediately, and encouraged his new protégé to further his medical studies at New York College. The relationship took an important step forward when Price married Dr White's daughter, Harriet Elizabeth, in 1855. The following year he graduated with a Medical Diploma in pharmaceutical chemistry.

Dr Price set up a medical practice but struggled for a few years. His skills as a chemist enabled him to create baking powder using his mother's recipe for biscuits. After taking out a patent on his invention, Price and his wife joined the many 19th Century Americans and European immigrants heading out West to seek their fortune. Arriving in Waukegan, a bustling Illinois port city situated on the Great Lake, Dr Price established a thriving medical practice and rose to prominence within the city's social circle.

Dr Price pursued his dream of turning his baking powder formula into a success. Entering into a partnership with banker Charles Steele and setting up a factory in Chicago, the dream took shape after several early struggles. The demand for baking powder quickly increased, making Dr Price an extremely wealthy man.

Thanks to his new found wealth and social standing, the Price family moved to a large mansion in the city. They had five children, the youngest being the actor's father, Vincent Leonard Price, who was born in 1871. The children were educated at prominent public schools with Vincent Leonard attending Racine College Grammar School in Wisconsin. Deeply interested in drama during his college years, he met Richard Head Welles, whose son Orson worked with Vincent's son many years later.

'By his 50th birthday, Dr V C Price was a multimillionaire,' said Victoria. After buying out his partner in 1884, Dr Price appointed his oldest son, Russell, vice president of the Price Baking Powder Company with the intention of selling his interests and retiring. 'It would appear that his skill at invention was not matched by his skill at investment,' Victoria added, 'and the Panic of 1893 virtually wiped him out.' The downturn in the family fortunes forced Vincent Leonard Price to drop out of Yale University and abandon his career in the arts. He returned to Waukegan looking for work.

Retaining some of his business holdings, Dr Price used his influence to get his son a position as manager of the Pan Confection Company. Despite harbouring a deep regret at not following his chosen path in life, Vincent Leonard Price was a better businessman than his father, and the country's love for sweets turned the Pan Confection Company into a growing concern, its success making Price and his beloved wife, Marguerite Cobb Wilcox, financially secure for the rest of their lives.

'My mother and father fell in love when they were nine and never saw anyone else,' said Vincent Price of his parents. Coming from a long line of fiercely independent women, Marguerite Cobb Wilcox showed those strong willed qualities when she changed her birth name from Daisy, which she despised, to Marguerite. Her ancestry was equally colourful. She descended from the French Desnoyers family, who arrived in the Midwest from Paris to become America's first silversmiths. Her mother, Harriet Louise Cobb, married Henry Cole Wilcox, who drowned five months after the wedding leaving Harriet pregnant with Marguerite.

Marguerite's lineage had strong UK links (Price described her as 'French, Dutch and English, but American through and through'). She was 11 years old, when her mother married the aristocratic Anglo-Irish seafarer Captain Hans Mortimer Oliver. She adored her new stepfather, impressed by his English ancestry and fanciful tales of the high seas. When she married Vincent Leonard Price in October 1894, Captain Oliver took them on a trip around the world as a honeymoon present.

The marriage between the strong willed Marguerite and the easy going Vincent Leonard was a happy one as their actor son observed. 'If ever there was a woman who knew what she wanted, it was my mother. Father was beautified by her the day she set eyes on him, and he became a full-fledged saint as the years rolled by. They were married for 53 years, until death did them part, and he sat back to wait out the few years until he could join her.'

Vincent Leonard Price's financial fortunes increased further when he merged the Pan Confection Company with two smaller candy manufacturers. Renamed the National Candy Company, it went from strength to strength with jellybeans, jawbreakers and gob stoppers, becoming part of America's sweet culture. The Prices moved with their two children, Harriet (born 1887) and Mortimer (born 1899), to St Louis, now Missouri's fastest growing commercial city, and where their youngest son Vincent Leonard Price Junior was born.

Thanks to his father's financial success and the family's social prominence, Price enjoyed a secure, upper middle class childhood. According to Victoria: 'The St Louis in which Vincent Leonard Price was raised was one of country clubs and ladies' groups, private schools and summer homes. Upper middle class St Louis society was a world to which young Vincent was perfectly suited, yet one from which he always seek to distance himself.' Price had his own down-to-earth view of his family upbringing, 'Not rich enough to evoke envy and just successful enough to demand respect. It is the ultimate plateau in American life and is only reached by hard work, just enough ambition, and the guidance of a good woman.'

With the National Candy Company becoming a major part of St Louis' commercial centre, Vincent Leonard Price's prominence increased further with his appointment as vice-president and director of the St Louis Chamber of Commerce. The family also increased with the birth of Laralouise in 1904 and Vincent Leonard Junior in 1911. His birth coincided with an honour his father received at the annual convention of the National Candy Association. Not surprisingly, Vincent Leonard Junior became known as 'The Candy Kid' although his more familiar family nickname was 'Bink'.

Bink's stage career began in 1914 when the three year old performed in a play at his sister's school. Despite his young age, he made an impression thanks to his natural talent for drama, and armed with a new love for theatre, he often staged his own plays at home.

Bink had a happy childhood despite a number of contradictions regarding his relationship with Marguerite, who, being in her late thirties at the time of his birth, had settled into the busy lifestyle of social gatherings and parties. 'My mother was a truly delightful creature,' he recalled with great affection, 'and it is to her I owe much of my love of the beautiful and also my desire to share it with other people.' He further added that, 'Women can be dull, but she wasn't. She was fun for her children and fortunate for her husband.'

Victoria Price paints a slightly different picture of the mother/son relationship. Although there was never any ill feeling between them, Bink's arrival limited Marguerite's busy social life leaving the boy somewhat neglected. 'When I think of her, if I think of her,' he added, 'it's mostly with regret that I knew her so little, so briefly. I was, as she joked, the child of her old age. She was in her late thirties when I "came along". I never really thought I was born, she was so fond of saying "came along". Come to think of it, its sounds a little unwelcoming, as though I was a stranger at a late supper after a show, I dropped in and her manners, being polished enough, she said, "Hello. Sit down. Have something to eat."'

Marguerite was a formidable woman. Dissatisfied at the level of local public education in St Louis, she and several neighbourhood women founded the St Louis Community School, which was dedicated to giving affluent young children a progressive education that included free expression and creativity.

Bink attended the school, and he expressed himself through poetry, art, and

11

of course acting in the school plays, which included lead roles in *Robin Hood* and the *Pied Piper of Hamlin*. It was also the place where he met his first girlfriend, future actress Barbara O'Neil. They continued their on/off relationship for the next 20 years.

Marguerite ruled the family with an iron but fair hand and Bink, being the youngest, had more of a free reign over his older siblings, all of whom adored their baby brother.

Of his father, there was always great love and affection. Vincent Leonard Price Senior remained a devoted family man to which happiness was a way of life. Being denied the chance to follow his intended career in art, he encouraged his family to follow their own path; he had the money, the social stranding and the popularity of his friends and associates to do this. Thanks to his business connections, there were always chocolates and other goodies for the children at Christmas. Not surprisingly, Bink became a massive fan of the festive season.

Bink's next seat of learning was the St Louis Country Day School. Founded by the wealthy local farmers that wanted to improve the quality of education, the school developed a reputation for athletic and academic excellence. It also provided a springboard for students to move onto Harvard or Yale. Bink's father was also on the school's Board of Trustees.

Bink did not take his studies seriously although he excelled in art and sports. Being tall and well built – thanks to his mother's cooking and his father's endless supply of sweets – he towered over all his classmates as well as his father and older brother. Eventually buckling down to study and achieving decent grades, his love of performing did not diminish; he joined the school's musical group The Troubadours.

The family's home life was completely immersed in all forms of art, especially music. Bink's siblings could sing, play piano, and appreciate opera. The youngster admitted that when it came to piano, his right hand, 'never seemed to figure out what the left hand was doing.' Bink's musical strengths veered towards singing; he had an excellent baritone voice. 'But my musical instinct was more for caricature. I might have been a good singer if I hadn't felt that the orchestra or accompanist was bound to win.'

There were two other passions that became synonymous with Bink's life. The first was cooking. 'My family were very adventurous in the kitchen,' he recalled as he watched his mother perform the art of pancake making. From this small start, he became a gourmet of some distinction.

The second was art. Bink discovered a book on the subject at home and studied the reproductions illustrated inside with great interest and enthusiasm. He became a regular visitor at St Louis' City Art Museum where he immersed himself with the classics on display. But his interest wasn't just confined to the great artists.

During a summer trip with school friends to a ranch in south Colorado, Bink, while horse riding, discovered some pottery in a patch of ground. Investigating further, he discovered a wood etching and a skull. As it turned out, he had stumbled upon an Indian burial ground. Eventually opened up by archaeologists, the 12 year old featured in the local newspapers in both Colorado and Missouri.

Bink's hobby took a step further when he visited the only art dealer in St Louis. Occasionally the dealer held exhibitions consisting of etchings and engravings. 'It was one of these daring exhibitions that I fell financially in love with a work of art for the first time.' It was Rembrandt's *Two Nude Models, One Standing* at a cost of $37.50. Saving up his allowance and working a variety of summer jobs, he purchased the engraving, and this began his successful second career as an art expert.

Cinema was equally important to Bink, and his first taste of horror was watching the German expressionist classic *Der Golem* (1920), starring Paul Wegener as the clay man of Jewish folklore. 'I wet my pants!' he exclaimed at his reaction to the movie. Like many children, he became enthralled by this new world of entertainment.

Bink's parents finally built a dream home that reflected their eclectic artistic tastes. The family's financial security enabled them to pursue leisure interests such as baseball and football; St Louis having teams of both. For Bink, childhood was an enjoyable and busy time as he immersed himself with everything and anything.

And that included travel. Despite many family vacations across America and Canada, Bink's ambition was to visit Europe – and on his own! Now 17, the tall, handsome and unusually mature teenager lobbied hard for his parents' permission to travel across the Atlantic. Marguerite was naturally horrified at the thought of her little boy venturing into the unknown, but Bink was adamant. Using his own money, a donation from his much loved grandmother and funds provided by his always understanding father following the sale of the family summerhouse in Canada, he would achieve his wish.

Bink arrived in New York with his father, and on 6 July 1928, he began his journey with Tour 22 – a five-week tour of the seven capital cities in Europe. One destination was a city he became closely associated with for the rest of his life – London.

And London agreed with him. After seven days crossing the Atlantic, his ship arrived in Plymouth and the tour group checked into a hotel in South Kensington. The city made an impact on Bink as he travelled the London Underground and visited St Paul's Cathedral, Hampton Court, Windsor Castle and the many famous art galleries. One famous venue that Bink was completely enthralled by was the British Museum. 'Nothing can touch it for clutter, for atmosphere, for gravity of purpose, that purpose being to collect civilisations complete under one roof. It is the home of discovery.'

Tour 22 continued onto Belgium, Germany, Switzerland, Italy and France. Travelling through Cologne, Milan, Rome and Paris, he revelled in German architecture, admired the Swiss scenery, Italian renaissance and French nightlife. This fantastic tour marked the end of his childhood and the beginning of his new journey as an adult. Bink would now be known as Vincent Price.

Returning home, Price needed to work hard at school if he was to follow his father's footsteps into Yale. Aware that he had slipped in his studies, his parents sent him to Milford School, New Haven for an intensive two-week course in Plane Geometry. In June 1929 he graduated from St Louis Country Day School and took his College Board examinations. A letter of acceptance from Yale quickly followed and in September he embarked on the next phase of his amazing life.

After experiencing the delights of Europe, Price found his freshman year at Yale disappointing as the courses were basically a repeat of his high school studies. His roommate at Yale was old friend Ted Thomas so it lifted the gloom of his first impression. October 1929 was a bad year. The infamous Wall Street Crash forced many students to drop out of university when their once wealthy fathers encountered financial problems; in some cases they dropped off buildings and bridges rather than face a life of poverty.

Price remained philosophical about the hardships that swept America. 'I've always believed the Great Depression was the best thing that happened to all of us children of affluent parents. Entering Yale that year with its wellborn, often extremely rich scions of old and new rich parents was no joke. People were hurling themselves out of windows at an alarming rate and oddly enough jumpers included some of the boys about to enter Ivy League colleges. I guess the thought of being poor or comparatively so was more than they could face. It seemed to me and most of the survivors ridiculous.'

Price need not have worried about his future at Yale. The constant demand for sweets meant the National Candy Company remained unaffected by the economic downturn. The obvious financial restrictions brought out 'the bohemian' in Price, especially when he could take frequent trips to New York. 'If you couldn't afford to take your girl to a classy restaurant and show, the Village was cheap and so were movies, especially art movies. There was always a Nadick's nutbread and cream cheese sandwich, or Horn and Hardart's palatial slot machine, food vending marble rooms to get a nosh, and it didn't take long for the college crowd to make them more than acceptable, even chic.'

Price initially considered Sheffield Scientific School, but his desire to follow an artistic career influenced his decision to enrol at Academic School. For his return to Yale the following year, he immersed himself in Shakespeare and the poetry of Shelley and Tennyson. He continued his love for art and remained an avid movie fan.

Harbouring what he called, 'My two secret ambitions – to be an artist or an actor,' it comes as a surprise that he showed no interest in the Yale University Dramatic Association, even though his girlfriend Barbara O'Neil, who lived nearby, had joined a nearby drama academy. Instead he opted for the Yale Glee Club, where his singing voice was put to good use. The Glee Club made regular tours across America, but the main attraction for Price was a proposed tour of Europe, which took place towards the end of his junior year.

Price was among the sixty strong Glee Club men that sailed from New York to Boulogne. They performed in Paris and then Zurich before travelling to Hungary. When the Glee Club returned to the States, Price remained in France with the intention of seeing Europe again. 'I found out how little I had learned in college, which I think an awful lot of us do. Continued learning is the true key to all existence.' Travelling to Vienna to brush up on his German, Price met a female cabaret singer who got him work as a singer and dancer at the nightclub she performed in.

Returning to Yale, Price did well enough in his studies to get a place on the art history course he coveted. His time at university remained a cocoon in the face of the harsh realities brought on by the Depression. 'I don't think I would have been determined to make something of myself if it hadn't been for the Depression,' he said of his situation as a well-educated man facing possible unemployment. 'When I graduated, there were no jobs. I realised you have to seize every opportunity.'

During his final year at Yale, Price became friendly with several writers and artists living around Connecticut, among them James Thurber. Graduating in June 1933, he was determined to make a career in art. 'I knew that in my adult life had to be in the arts, but how, I hadn't the slightest inkling. In some way I wanted to apply my education, self-taught and school taught, to making a life and a livelihood as an artist.' Price decided against working for his father, who presented him with a $1,100 cheque to help finance two more years of further education.

His mother also found an opening for an apprentice teacher at Riverdale Country School in New York. Price was accepted, and although he viewed it as a temporary solution, it allowed him to think about his next career move without having to worry about money. Being in New York also meant he could pursue his artistic and social interests.

Price's links to Britain were at their most influential during his time at Riverdale. The Latin master Marc Baldwin, who originally came from England, saw great potential in the young man. Acting as Price's mentor during his time at school, Baldwin and his wife Cecile took their protégé under their wing and encouraged his artistic skills.

Price described his spell at Riverdale as, 'wet-nursing some of the richest delinquents on the Eastern seaboard.' He taught English language, coached the soccer team, acted in the school plays and worked as counsellor at the school's summer camp. His main goal was teaching visual arts, but it proved to be hard work. 'Vincent found his first year out in 'the real world' quite difficult,' said Victoria. 'He realised that his Yale education had given him the basic tools with which he had to make something of himself, but still he felt unprepared.' Worse still was the realisation that he wasn't a good enough artist. 'Periods of discovery about yourself is seldom fun,' he lamented. 'My year of teaching taught me that whatever I was going to do or be, I had to know more.' One way to express his love of art was through education as a teacher.

Price's love for the theatre never left him. He played Captain Corcoran in three performances of Gilbert and Sullivan's *HMS Pinafore* for the Riverdale Players. 'I do love the stage, and never before have I realised how much at home I am on it. I simply must try it some day and prove myself that I can't do it or can do it.'

Price needed to join a stock company if he wanted to continue acting. He visited several theatrical agencies without any success, and even his friends felt that teaching was a better career move. With a graduation present from his father, encouragement from Marc Baldwin, and a desire to travel again, he successfully applied for admission to an exclusive art history programme at the Courtauld Institute at London University.

On 14 September 1934, Vincent Price sailed once more to England. It was a journey that defined his future.

'London of 1934 was one of the glories of the civilised world. What was left of the Empire was considerably less than in its Victorian heyday; it was an atmosphere rather than a climate and for an American, still glamorous. Above all, it was still more for your money than anywhere else in the English-speaking world. London! My God what a city. Established, stolid, cold and warm, wet but never dry – maybe of modern cities the greatest, the most entertaining.' Price's vivid feelings of the city reflected a happy period in his life. Unlike his fun loving years at Yale, he took his studies at Courtauld very seriously, and of course London had its fair share of art galleries, museums, and theatres for him to visit during his free time.

Being tall, handsome and flamboyant by nature, Price made friends with everyone, including Florence Stoker, widow of *Dracula* author Bram Stoker. Like many Americans, he held a deep fascination for the British aristocracy and the Royal Family. His time in London introduced him to many actors and writers, among them Sir John Gielgud, who was the toast of the West End following his performance as the title character in *Hamlet*. 'Gielgud cautioned me to see his Hamlet many times and he was so right,' Price recalled. 'As the enormity of his performance grew on me in the eleven times I saw it, so did the mind-blowing, overwhelming genius of Shakespeare.' It was Gielgud who initially encouraged Price to take up acting, having already given him a copy of Konstantin Stanislavski's *An Actor Prepares*.

Spending Christmas with friends in Graz, Austria, Price's trip to Nuremberg coincided with the National Party Day rally. Hearing Adolf Hitler speak, he was disturbingly taken in by the charm and charisma of Germany's newly appointed chancellor, although politically, Price was naïve about the tense situation in Europe.

Returning to London, he grew disenchanted with Courtauld. With most of his lecturers away on vacation, there were few classes to attend, so he concentrated on this thesis, and used his free time to visit the theatre whenever he could. This included a production of *Romeo and Juliet* starring John Gielgud, Laurence Olivier, Edith Evans and Peggy Ashcroft.

Price also saw a low key production of *Basalik* at a small, private theatre club. The play starred American opera singer Paul Robeson and Australian actress Coral Browne. Price and Robeson became good friends, but their friendship would have negative repercussions years later.

The increased theatre activities went a stage further. In a letter to his parents in February 1935, Price admitted that, 'My lectures are slowly becoming very dull as three of the best men are sick. So I have been museuming and gallerying a lot. I have just gotten a small part in a play at the Gate Theatre, which is a very famous little theatre company here, and so you know (or don't you!) how happy I am. There is nothing in the world like the profession to me, but don't worry dearests I am not slacking my work. But please don't be angry, as I can no more leave it alone than I can give up my love of life for it is so wonderful. Pray I make a go of it.'

Price did make a go of it. The British connection of his amazing acting career began on the London stage.

The Theatre Years (1935 – 1938)

'Someone called actors "sculptures in snow".
Very apt. In the end it's all nothing.' – Vincent Price

Price in *Victoria Regina* (1935)

The timing was perfect! With Christmas coming, and lecturers taking their holidays, Price only had a few classes, leaving him plenty of time to follow his new vocation. 'I fell in love with the theatre, which was very easy to do in England, particularly at that time, because it was very cheap. You could go and see any play, or any concert for 50 cents.' He quickly became a part of that new world, thanks to a small role in a brand new production.

Price's friend and roommate David Babbington-Smith persuaded him to audition for a controversial new play called *Chicago*. Written by Maurice Watkins, the play was produced at the Gate, a small private theatre club situated just behind London's Charing Cross Station. 'It was a private, experimental theatre,' said Price, 'that only held 100 people.' Run by producer-director Norman Marshall, the Gate was far removed from London's West End because most of the patrons were younger than the average theatre goer. The costs were cheaper and the small intimate atmosphere of the Gate meant both the actors and the audience operated on the same wavelength.

Babbington-Smith took Price to the Gate where the casting of *Chicago* took pace. Thanks to his American accent, Price was offered two small roles, burly police sergeant Charles Murdock and a Judge. Joining the cast in February 1935, Price often said it was his ability to speak while chewing gum that got him the role of Murdock; this talent became useful when he taught the actresses playing the gangsters molls how to chew gum and speak at the same time.

Price was obviously thrilled to be on stage. 'I was getting very English when this so American part came along, now I'm complete mid-west and ever so tough. I am so tickled about the show. It is really very good and though my part is small, it is a start and the people are so grand. There are no people so much fun as theatre people. My how they do work and what experiences they have on tour and in town – a real life of ups and downs, excitement and dejection.'

Chicago opened on 13 March 1935 to a positive critical and audience response. It couldn't have come at a better time for Price even though he achieved it with some difficulty because he was still studying at Courtauld. With his fellow actors encouraging him to audition for further stage roles, his career as an art historian became a distant memory. 'If any chance comes to prove myself (as an actor), believe you me I'll take it, regardless of anyone's objections or reasons.'

Price's second acting role secured theatre stardom. The next Gate production was Laurence Houseman's *Victoria Regina*. The play was based on Queen Victoria's romance with Prince Albert of Saxe-Coburg. It was the first time a play about a member of the Royal Family would be premiered on stage, although a ruling by the Lord Chamberlain prohibited all plays depicting the British monarchy in any form. The Gate however, was private theatre club, and exempt from such restrictions. This enabled Norman Marshall to generate a great deal of publicity and press support, including the casting of the unknown Patricia Stanley, who was related to royalty, as Victoria.

Thanks to his resemblance to the prince, and the time he spent in Germany and Austria, Price successfully auditioned for the role of Albert. According to Marshall, 'The choice (of playing Prince Albert) was limited by physical appearance, as the Prince Consort was an exceptionally tall man. In the end I gave the part to a young and totally inexperienced American called Vincent Price, who had not only the height and looks for the part but was able to put on an extremely convincing German accent.' For added publicity, Marshall promoted his new star as, 'an English actor who played a great deal in Germany.'

There is always a risk in casting an unknown and inexperienced actor in a lead role, and the result can be disastrous for all concerned, but at least Price's time on *Chicago* gave him a head start. Playing a prominent part in a new stage production meant he had to work twice as hard, but his acting instincts paid off. 'When I played Prince Albert, I discovered that Albert, who was a German Prince, never really learned to think in English. He didn't like the English that much, and they didn't like him. He always thought in German, so I translated the whole part, and learned it in German, then learned it in English, but I thought in German. That was a method of preparation, a kind of reality I could give myself.'

'We should hear of him again,' the *Daily Mail* said of Price's performance. On 1 May 1935, the 24 year old experienced, 'the most exciting day of my life – my first taste of stardom.' The press were enthusiastic about his interpretation of Albert even though the play only achieved a modest success. With the situation between Germany and the rest of Europe worsening, interest in Victoria and Albert declined sharply. Most of the Gate's regulars were absent; the bulk of the audience being older people who remembered the Queen.

Victoria Regina closed after a month, but for Vincent Price is was an amazing start to a new career. Now the toast of London, he got invited to parties and social gatherings where he mixed with other actors. There were also several lucrative job offers, so not surprisingly his art studies fell by the wayside.

Price intended to make his career in London. Producer Sydney Carroll offered him Orsini in *Twelfth Night* and Orlando in *As You Like It* for Regent's Park's prestigious summer Shakespeare repertory season. Unfortunately, Price did not have a work permit because he was American and a student, and therefore unable to act in legitimate theatre. The Gate was a private club so these restrictions did not apply, but when it closed for the summer, Price, who had already quit Courtauld with an uncompleted master's degree in art history, was now at a loose end. Britain's newest stage star was in effect, unemployed and unemployable.

Price didn't stay depressed for too long. His extended break from acting allowed him to take his proud parents on a tour of the UK when they came to visit. On his return to London, he heard that Gilbert Miller, a major figure in British and American theatre, had secured the rights to *Victoria Regina* with the intention of making it a lavish Broadway vehicle for America's First Lady of Theatre, Helen Hayes. During the negotiations, Houseman made sure that the deal included Price as Prince Albert.

Coming over to London in September 1935, Hayes met her new co-star and despite her initial reservations about casting the unknown American, she was impressed by what she saw. 'I'm delighted about Mr Price,' she said to Laurence Houseman. 'Albert seemed such a problem to cast. You can't imagine what a relief it is to solve it so simply.'

Price was equally impressed by his new leading lady. 'I don't think she is

America's greatest actress, but I do think she's one of the kindest people I've ever met in my life.' After a beneficial few weeks in London, Price signed a contract to appear in the Broadway production. Hayes then returned to New York with Gilbert Miller to finalise the opening date.

In the meantime, the Gate reopened and Price played the role of Max in Arthur Schnitzler's comedy *Anatol*. Working once more with Patricia Stanley, he relished the chance to do something more comical. 'I do feel I need this part as it is straight and comedy both of which I need badly as it will take my mind of Albert for a while.'

The opening night for *Anatol* was a disaster. According to Price, 'One scene was a wild dinner party, and since the stage was right in the audience's lap, it was difficult to fake the food. Oysters were part of the dialogue and the menu, so real oysters they had to be. Oysters are terribly expensive in England, and since all the Gate productions were done on a shoestring, we were not given those delicious Ostend or Whitstable varieties, but the kind that are sold incognito by street vendors. Opening night, in the gusto of the first performance, the three of us involved in the scene ate two dozen oysters between us, and if the notices the next day were bad (which indeed they were), they had nothing on the oysters. We were all violently ill. Bad notices and bad oysters are guaranteed to build any actor up to a big let-down.'

It wasn't just the bad oysters. Price's performance suffered when his clipped English accent lapsed into his familiar St Louis voice. It was clear from his less than rave reviews that the actor had other things on his mind – playing Albert on Broadway.

When *Anatol* closing its disastrous run in October 1935, Price arrived in Southampton to board the *SS Aquitania*, but being broke he was reduced to steerage class. As the ship set sail and the English coastline faded from view, Price embarked on a new journey. The first phase of his British career was over. It would be thirty years before he returned.

When the *Aquitania* docked in New York on 5 November 1935, Gilbert Miller invited the press to greet the arrival of his new star. Unaware of the media attention, Price left steerage looking like a bedraggled hobo, with his cat Albert the Good under his arm (Price had a great love for animals and Albert was the first of his many pets). Instead of meeting the press (who had gone to the first-class disembarkation), he cleared customs and took a cab to his hotel.

When Price turned up for rehearsals the next day, Miller gave him a dressing down for his unintentional behaviour. Once things were sorted out, rehearsals went well. Because Price knew the part backwards, he could seamlessly fit in with the new cast and crew.

More importantly, he formed a close bond with Helen Hayes. 'I really owe so much to Helen. I had a wonderful experience with her. When we did *Victoria Regina*, she was 35 years old and I was 24. She could have made it very tough for me. You know as a young man coming in and doing his first play on Broadway, with the top star of the day. But she was so marvellous to me!' Hayes always felt her lead actors should establish a strong working relationship to enhance a play's success. She became Price's mentor, and her guidance proved most beneficial, especially when he jumped from gifted amateur to Broadway star overnight.

Victoria Regina premiered at Baltimore's Auditorium Theatre on 12 December 1935. The play proved an instant hit, with the New York press hailing Price as 'a talented new discovery.' He had a genuine chemistry with Hayes, and the two played off each other with great skill. The young man's inexperience performing in a larger theatre did not show and the audience reaction was positive.

Victoria Regina received a command performance at Washington's National Theatre on 16 December 1935 with First Lady Eleanor Roosevelt attending. Then came the Broadway opening at the Broadhurst Theatre on 26 December 1935, which received 22 curtain calls. Now the toast of Broadway, Price quickly befriended actors, producers and critics. Hayes also introduced him to several influential names in the American theatre and royalty in the shape of the Queen of Spain.

But like many young actors starting out, instant success could be just as much a negative as a positive. How can one follow such an amazing Broadway debut?

Hollywood quickly took interest in this new kid on the block, and when *Victoria Regina* closed for the summer, movie mogul David O'Selznick offered Price a screen test. Arriving in Hollywood in June 1936, he auditioned for the role of Ashley Wilkes in *Gone With the Wind*, which would eventually be made – without him – in 1939.

Taken in by the glitz and glamour of Tinsel Town, Price was guest of honour at a party hosted by Joan Crawford, an actress he once described as 'a star without trying.' The chance of instant movie success, and the financial rewards that came with it, was enough to temp any handsome young actor to make a go of it.

Thanks to Helen Hayes' influence, Price put Hollywood on hold so he could gain more experience in summer stock. 'It was Helen who taught me just how hard I had to work to learn the business after my beginner's luck. I realised the best training is just to keep acting, working with other actors. I also took acting classes. I learned the importance of moving gracefully and developing absolute ease on stage.'

Price gave his first summer stock performance in J M Barrie's *What Every Woman Knows* at the Westchester Theatre, New York with respected stage star Mildred Natwick. He worked with Natwick again when he played the Earl of Essex in *Elizabeth the Queen* at the Ridgeway Theatre, New York.

To round off this 'training' period prior to returning to Albert, Price played Irish leader Charles Stewart Parnell in Elise Schauffer's *Parnell* at the Suffern County Theatre. Playing the romantic interest was his childhood sweetheart Barbara O'Neil; the two resumed their on-off relationship.

Victoria Regina finally closed in the summer of 1937. Now tired of Albert, he declined the subsequent tour of the States as he needed to get the role out of his system, and with further encouragement from Helen Hayes, he was ready to move on.

His first post Albert role was Halmar Ekdal in Henrik Ibsen's drama *The Wild Duck* at the Lakewood Theatre, Maine. Opening in June 1937, it received excellent reviews confirming that there was more to Price than playing the Prince Consort. And as a serious drama, it increased his standing further. He remained at the theatre to repeat his role as *Parnell* with the highly respected Broadway actress Edith Barrett.

Although still romantically linked with Barbara O'Neil, Price quickly hit it off with Edith. The critical and audience response to *Parnell* was favourable, and when the play closed its run, they remained at the Lakewood Theatre for a weeklong production of J B Priestley's *Eden's End*. Once again the critics praised his performance.

Returning to the Westport Theatre, Price appeared alongside Anna May Wong in a dramatic adaptation of Puccini's opera *Turnabout*. Remaining at the Westport for the comedy *The Lady of La Plaza*, Price got lined up for a return to Broadway in the Ladisluas Bus-Fekete's romantic comedy *Jean*.

Renamed *The Lady Has a Heart*, the play opened at the Longacre Theatre on 25 September 1937, but the negative reaction towards Price's performance left a bitter taste in his mouth. 'When you are a big success in the beginning of your career, it is hard to swallow adverse criticisms. All actors are criticised from time to time, of course. But we still resent it. The problem it bothers you that someone didn't think you were as good as you thought you were. At other times you might think that you have not been very good but the critics rave about you. That's often harder to take because you want the critics to be honest.'

Price felt his work as a serious actor was being overshadowed by his new matinee idol image. Thanks to his good looks and easy going charm, he now had a solid female fan base so *The Lady Has a Heart* enjoyed a successful three-month run. 'I'm afraid the public likes me but not the critics,' he lamented. Any negativity the actor went through during this low period were uplifted by his relationship with Barbara O'Neil.

The depressive mood may have influenced Price's decision to give Hollywood another try. The play soldiered on until December 1937 and with no stage roles on the horizon, he successfully screen tested for the romantic lead in MGM's *Marie Antoinette* (1938). Still not ready to tackle film work, Price turned it down along with other lead roles until he 'felt sure of himself.' He also tested for the lead in *Juarez* (1938) but lost out the Brian Aherne.

Returning to New York, Price faced the start of a new year with no definite career plan.

'The Mercury was, at the time, really hotter than a pistol,' said Price when he received a remarkable offer to join The Mercury Theatre Company on a five-play contract. The company, long regarded as the 'Old Vic of the USA', specialised in revitalising the old classics, but in new and innovative ways, and the standard of production was incredibly high. Not surprising since John Houseman and America's greatest theatrical maverick, Orson Welles were the power behind this prestigious group.

Price joined without hesitation. He saw Mercury as a way to dump his despised matinee idol image and build a reputation as a serious actor. 'I felt that Orson and the company really were what I wanted out of the theatre, sort of a place to identify and learn my business,' Welles also knew Price's Broadway reputation generated welcome publicity for the company. 'We were not big theatre names with marquee values,' said Mercury director Norman Lloyd. 'So when Vincent arrived, it was an affirmation of the status of the Mercury, because he was a leading man who was hot on Broadway. I thought what the hell, all the ladies are going to see him.' Lloyd further added that, 'we were wild and nutty and full of great theatre energy and joy. Vincent was so elegant, and right, and we were so scruffy and dirty and awful.'

Like their distinguished fathers before them, Price and Welles got on famously; both were exceptionally mature young men who achieved early stage success. Price was also enthralled by this phenomenally talented individual with a (British sounding) voice that was equally as famous as his own. 'Orson was 21 years old, and to work with him was so exciting. He was fresh and new with wonderful ideas, and it was an exciting time in the theatre.' Welles scoured a massive coupe with his modern dress version of *Julius Caesar* and wanted to push the boundaries of Theatre in much the same way Bertolt Brecht had done so in Germany.

Price's first Mercury role was Master Hammon in the Elizabethan comedy *Shoemaker's Holiday*; critical reaction was far more positive following his lukewarm reviews in *The Lady Has a Heart*. Edith Barrett's presence in the cast further enhanced his performance. By this time things had cooled off with Barbara O'Neil.

On 23 April 1938 Vincent Price and Edith Barrett married at St Thomas Protestant Episcopal Church. *The Shoemaker's Holiday* had just closed its run and 48 hours after the wedding the couple appeared in George Bernard Shaw's *Heartbreak House*, an ambitious Mercury production with Welles playing the elderly Captain Shotover.

Heartbreak House turned out to be a troubled production that soured Price's working relationship with Welles. 'Orson was not very good in it because he never rehearsed with us. The company was marvellous; it was an all-star cast, as they call it. He was completely undisciplined.' Being this acclaimed maverick genius, Welles did what he wanted regardless of what other people felt, and this went against the grain of the ever professional Price.

'I never got to know Orson Welles better,' Price recalled. 'But he became a legend before his time. He could have been one of the greatest American theatrical and cinema directors, but he had to act. Whether he directed or acted, a play was his show and finally, for that reason and the fact he ignored contracts and gave no one else credit, that Mercury fell apart.' He further added that, 'Orson is a genius, and a grand guy, but I fear that the Mercury is his, and that all others are disregarded, even the actors working with him.'

Heartbreak House received mixed notices but Price was once again singled out for praise. When the play closed, Welles announced his next production would be Shakespeare's *Henry V* with Price in the title role. Playing Shakespeare held mass appeal to the actor, but he finally lost his patience with Welles. Turning down the role broke his contract with Mercury after two plays, not that it made any difference as Mercury lasted one full season before collapsing.

In any case Price had other things on his mind. With a new wife and a greater level of confidence in his abilities following his productive spell at the Mercury, he decided the time was right to give Hollywood another go. In June 1938, the couple arrived in California to start a next phase of Price's illustrious career.

Renting a chateau in Hollywood, Price negotiated a respectable film deal. He managed to get Universal and MGM to outbid their offers before signing with Universal on 30 June 1938. It was an exceptional contract for someone who only appeared in a couple of screen tests. In addition to a $1,000 salary, the contract allowed six months stage work on Broadway and six months work on at least two films. To increase his standing further as an A-list actor, he wisely inserted a clause preventing him from starring in second features. Thanks to his theatre reputation, Universal were happy to comply.

Price was initially unsure about his new life in Los Angeles, a city so different from his bohemian existence in London and New York. 'I am very enthusiastic about the possibilities, 'he said of the West Coast, 'but it will take time and a great effort culturally to make it what it should be. Bad taste is more apparent here than any other part of the country. They are years behind the times in architecture and what modern efforts they've made are too extreme.' Price loved the ocean and the beach, as did Edith. 'Oh this climate has limitless advantages. It should make things easy for culture to flourish.'

Although their romance was over, Price remained friends with Barbara O'Neil, who had since married. 'All is well, and she and Edi get along well and we are all great friends.'

After fulfilling his final summer stock obligation in New York, Price returned to Hollywood in August 1938. He was initially cast in *The Sun Never Sets* (1938), an epic drama about the Bengal Lancers. When that fell through he was slated to star in James Whale's *SOS* (1938). Eventually the studio decided on *Service de Luxe* (1938), a screwball comedy designed to revive the screen career of silent star Constance Bennett. With his wife on stage in New York, and after two months of hanging around, Price could now prove his worth in a major Hollywood movie.

So begins the next phase of his career, and one where his British links are evident.

The Hollywood Years (1938 – 1947)

'Doing a religious picture is a boring thing because everybody is on their best behaviour – hoping for the keys of the kingdom, I guess.' – Vincent Price.

Price in *The Tower of London* (1939)

Horror fans might have a hard time seeing Vincent Price as a romantic lead, but that's how his Hollywood career began.

When *Service De Luxe* commenced production in August 1938, the experienced stage actor was now an inexperienced film star who once again had to start from scratch. 'Everything is done by someone else,' he said. 'Even your voice is controlled by the soundman.'

With typical enthusiasm, Price observed the other actors working in this technical medium. Constance Bennett also gave him much needed support, and he held nothing but admiration for his co-star. 'Two things were in her favour, she could act and she was nice, and she accepted me as, if not an equal, a competent newcomer.'

It was just as well because Price became extremely nervous when he began filming. 'This is my first picture and naturally I pretty wound up in knots the first day I worked. Blew lines and all that. Miss Bennett was swell. Took take after take without a murmur until I calmed down.'

Price was also encouraged by Rowland V Lee, who he described as, 'a gentle and superb director who is very interested in me and will work to make my start as good as possible.' Thanks to Universal's advance publicity, Price was in constant demand for tabloid interviews. Edith was still in New York: the couple had been apart for two months so the press attention helped alleviate his loneliness. When she returned to Hollywood in September 1938, the couple rented a house in Beverley Hills.

Service De Luxe got its big cinema release in October 1938 and critical reaction was positive. Price was singled out for the kind of praise that fulfilled his potential as Hollywood's newest leading man. But despite good performances, Price did not have the 'ordinary Joe' quality of Robert Cummings. His effeminate looks went against the urban machismo of Clark Gable, and he lacked the athleticism of Errol Flynn. And while he could be very effective performing light romantic comedy, he lacked that sense of the absurd that marked the screen personas of Cary Grant and Ray Milland. In a nutshell, his looks, height, manner and deportment worked against him.

For Price to succeed in Hollywood, he needed to prove his versatility as an actor. 'I hope to make another picture and get a serious character role. That's when acting is fun, when you must convince an audience that you're someone else. Here everything is individuals and their personalities are never hidden for fear the general public won't take it.' Such was his determination, he asked Universal to cast him in supporting roles. 'I talked them into letting me do a smaller part in which there was a chance of establishing myself as a character. I really didn't fit in the mould of a leading man in terms of Hollywood.'

Putting the disappointment of *Service de Luxe* behind him, Price returned to Broadway in December 1938 as the Reverend William Duke in the fantasy *Outward Bound*. Directed by Otto Preminger, the play was a huge success; it even received a special performance the following month in Washington DC for President Theodore Roosevelt's birthday.

Edith Barrett's stage career was not progressing as well and palled considerably with her husband's Hollywood and Broadway success. When she starred as Cathy in the Broadway production of *Wuthering Heights*, the play suffered in comparison to the film version starring Merle Oberon. Her sense of frustration would have a negative impact on her marriage and subsequent mental health problems.

When *Outward Bound* closed in June 1939 after 255 performances, Price returned to Hollywood where Universal loaned him out to Warner Brothers for his next assignment. As well as being his first colour film, *The Private Lives of Elizabeth and Essex* (1939) had Price playing a British character for the first time on the big screen.

As the great adventurer Sir Walter Raleigh, Price doesn't have much to do, but he makes the most of his limited screen time and looks good in costume. The film itself plays second fiddle to the stormy relationship between the temperamental stars Bette Davis and Errol Flynn.

With Flynn constantly turning up late without knowing his lines, the increasingly frustrated director Michael Curtiz used Price to feed the dialogue to Flynn before every take. Price had played the Earl of Essex on stage, and Curtiz used it as a shock tactic when he threatened to fire Flynn and replace him with Price if he didn't get his act together. It worked and Flynn caused no further problems on the set. Price and Flynn remained friends; the two were reported to be seen playing tennis in full costume.

Released in September 1939, *The Private Lives of Elizabeth and Essex* was a typical Hollywood blockbuster – popular entertainment but complete rubbish historically. Despite the next to nothing part, Price's involvement in a high profile picture improved his career opportunities.

When production wrapped in August 1939, Price returned to Universal for his next 'British' movie, and his first chiller. Directed by Rowland V Lee, *The Tower of London* (1939) is a horror comic reworking of Shakespeare's classic play *Richard III* starring Basil Rathbone as Richard III and Boris Karloff as his loyal, beetle-browed executioner Mord. Price is on hand with a small but impressive role as Richard's snivelling brother Lionel, Duke of Clarence. 'I had what we call today a cameo part, which means very little money. I am a character actor; that's what I like to do,' explained Price. Also appearing (in their only film together) was Barbara O'Neil.

Price became lifelong friends with Rathbone and Karloff; he had previously met Rathbone when he began his career in London. 'Basil was an intelligent person and a brilliant actor. He was rather unhappy towards the end of his life about having been stuck in the *Sherlock Holmes* pictures. He had been this great Shakespearean actor in the theatre, but most people thought of him as Sherlock Holmes or a villain.'

Price's friendship with Karloff remained one of the highlights of his career. 'I worked with him right from the beginning of my career, up through both of our careers. I think one of the extraordinary things about Boris was his gratitude for *Frankenstein* (1931). It was something that plagued him all his life, as a good part plagues every actor, but he was so grateful for it, because it gave him enormous fame. He knew he had gotten stuck on something, but he had a great pride in it.'

Working with Karloff and Rathbone was fun, especially during Price's first movie death scene when Lionel and Richard take part in a drinking bout which leads to Lionel's demise. Price recounted the incident with great humour: 'We had this scene where Basil and I had to drink to the kingdom of England. Rowland Lee didn't like the dialogue, and neither did we, because the more we drank, the less we could remember. It was only Coca-Cola, but coke is stimulating too. Well, over in one corner was a huge vat of malmsey wine in which I had to be drowned.'

'Boris and Basil, knowing I was new to the business, thought it would be great fun to throw everything they could into that vat of wine, which was actually just water. You know: Coca-Cola bottles, cigarette butts, anything they could find to dirty it up, because they knew at the end of the scene I had to get into it. There was a handrail at the bottom of the vat, so I could dive down and hang onto it. I had to stay under for a full 10 counts, and then I was yanked out by my heels.'

'Well, when I came out I got a round of applause from the crew but was disappointed not to see Boris and Basil. Then a few minutes later they reappeared and they were nice to me. They congratulated me on playing the scene so well for a newcomer, and then presented me with a case of Coca-Cola!' Considering how nauseous he was after drinking the stuff, one wonders if Price ever touched the case afterwards!

The Tower of London is a lavishly mounted Universal production with excellent sets and a *tour-de-force* performance from Rathbone. Price makes the most of his limited screen time and completely looks the part, emphasising how ideally suited he was to costume pictures.

During the making of *The Tower of London*, Price landed a lemon of a role in the unintentionally hilarious jungle adventure *Green Hell* (1940). Directed by former horror maestro James Whale, Price described it as, 'One of the corniest pictures ever made.' The cast and crew had a lot of fun on the set, but for Price, he entered a new phase of his career that later became a future trademark – hamming it up! Although still a serious actor at the time, he lightened the mood with an over the top performance.

The horror and British links continued with the title role in *The Invisible Man Returns* (1940). Production began in October 1939 and although Price gets second billing after British actor Cedric Hardwick, he takes centre stage as fugitive nobleman Sir Geoffrey Radcliffe. Like Claude Rains in *The Invisible Man* (1933), Price's distinctive voice is put to good use. When he's not invisible, he's hiding under bandages. Full marks to John P Fulton's Oscar winning special effects.

The director of the film was German born Joe May. His limited English caused quite a few problems on the set. 'He really couldn't speak any English at all,' said Price. 'He was a charming man, but very volatile, really uptight. I don't think John Sutton understood a word he said, nor could Nan Grey. Cedric really hated him. Hated him! Fortunately I spoke German so I could understand him. He would give direction, and I'd say, "For God's sake Joe, tell me in German because I can get along better with you in German than I can in English."'

Shot for $250,000, the film did well at the box office. 'The only premier I really enjoyed,' Price said of the opening night. 'At the end of the film, I reappeared vein by vein, artery after artery, a weary drunk in the seat in the front of me said to his friends, "That'll teach me not to drink cheap whisky."'

Although enjoyable, *The Invisible Man Returns* is the kind of B-movie fodder that Price wanted to avoid. His next effort (and his last for Universal) was far more satisfactory. Reunited with Joe May, *House of Seven Gables* (1940) is a big budget adaptation of Nathaniel Hawthorn's brooding novel about a century old curse that haunts the Pyncheon family. Replacing Robert Cummings, Price has an effective dramatic role (that allows him to age) as composer Clifford Pyncheon.

House of Seven Gables is Price's first venture into American gothic, and one where his multi-layered performance finally eradicated his matinee idol image. The film is not as effective as it should have been, despite an excellent production and good acting. When the film premiered in San Francisco in February 1940, as part of a double bill with *Black Friday* (1940), Price was joined by *Black Friday* stars Boris Karloff and Bela Lugosi – a foretaste of things to come!

By December 1939, Edith Barrett, now pregnant with their first and only child, returned to Hollywood with the hope of establishing a film career. The overjoyed couple set up a new home in Beverley Hills and managed to spend the kind of quality time denied them when they were following their separate careers.

When production on *House of Seven Gables* wrapped in January 1940, Universal decided not to renew Price's contract. In many ways it was a godsend. With the exceptions of *The Tower of London* and *House of Seven Gables*, none of his film roles came close to the quality material he'd been searching for. It was obvious that the studio didn't know what to do with an actor too unconventional to be a romantic lead and too young to be a character player.

In the spring of 1940, Price signed a seven-year contract with 20th Century Fox. The contract also allowed six months off a year for stage work. With the remarkable Darryl F Zanuck in charge, the studio had a much higher profile than Universal, with films produced at a grander scale and featuring top stars, writers and directors. This was a step in the right direction for Price. Now approaching 30, this phase of his Hollywood career remains his best in terms of quality and performance.

Price's Fox career got off to an excellent start in May 1940 with a well-received performance as Joseph Smith, founder of the Mormon religion, in *Brigham Young* (1940). It was a small but important role that begins with Smith's trial for heresy and subsequent assassination (the real Smith was lynched) that prompts Brigham Young (Tyrone Power) to lead the dead prophet's followers to Utah. The film was released in August 1940 to critical acclaim.

Price took a break from film work to visit his family in St Louis (Edith's pregnancy prevented her from coming). During his time home he appeared in *The American Way* at the Municipal Opera House and returned to the Lakewood Theatre for a summer stock season of three plays: Owen Davis' *Mr and Mrs North*, reprising Essex in *Elizabeth the Queen* and *Poet's Corner*, an autobiographical piece written by Price who also played a small role in the production.

'Play writing is one of my ambitions,' he said, 'but I wrote this mainly to get it off my chest.' The reviews and audience response was very positive for the actor. 'At least I feel confident to go on and write.' Although there was interest from Broadway, *Poet's Corner* never went beyond its premier.

Price returned to Hollywood to work on his next film, *Hudson Bay* (1941). Although limited to two scenes as King Charles II, he is perfectly cast as England's most fashionable and flamboyant monarch.

But there was now a new role in Price's life – fatherhood.

On 30 August 1940, Vincent Barrett Price was born at the Good Samaritan Hospital in Hollywood. With *Hudson Bay* going into production in September 1940, the Prices bought a new house and the actor could now spend more time with his family.

Hudson Bay was Price's last film for three years, and for a man who needed to keep busy, Price found this period of inactivity extremely hard, not only because of the obvious financial obligations, but for the fact he had to make use of his of own time by himself. It would be another four months before he found any work, by which time Fox had stopped paying him.

Thankfully the stage saved him from losing his sanity with a three week run at the Del Monte Theatre, Los Angeles in *The Constant Wife*. He then joined a West Coast touring company for a production of *The Mamba's Daughter* starring Ethel Walters, one of the few major black Broadway stars. Price, who plays a white plantation superintendent, found the rewards of working with this fine actress as stimulating as the fact he was now earning again. He remained with the play for two successful openings in San Francisco and Seattle. It meant staying away from the family once more but at least the financial situation improved further with Edith playing a well-received supporting role in the film *Ladies in Retirement* (1940).

Edith's slowly rising film career must have influenced her decision to not appear with her husband in his next stage production. After seeing Patrick Hamilton's Victorian melodrama *Angel Street* in a small Hollywood theatre, the couple secured the Broadway rights.

For Price, this lurid slice of English gothic was a foretaste of the future screen villainy he would be associated with. He plays Manningham, a psychopathic killer who marries a wealthy woman then drives her insane. The couple found a producer and a scheduled opening for December 1941. However, at the last minute, Edith left the production reportedly due to illness although her real reason was to remain in Hollywood and secure further film work. Returning to New York in November 1941, Price was once again away from his family.

Angel Street opened on 5 December 1941 – two days before the bombing of Pearl Harbour – at the Golden Theatre, to huge Broadway success, running for nearly 13,000 performances. The critical notices were excellent and Price relished the opportunity to play outright villainy. 'The whole audience hissed. I have found my niche. The moment the hero loses his hair and gets bags under his eyes, he's through! But not the villain! The more crinkly and crevassed he gets, the better you like him.'

During his time on *Angel Street*, Price acted in several radio soap operas as well as entertaining American servicemen at the Stage Door Canteen. In October 1942, 20th Century Fox ordered him back to Hollywood because many of the male actors under contract were volunteering for military service.

After a wonderful year on Broadway, Price, with his confidence fully restored, felt the time was right to give Hollywood another try. He left *Angel Street* on 5 December 1942 and returned to Tinsel Town for his best film performance yet.

Fox had secured the rights to Franz Werfel's novel *Song of Bernadette* in April 1942. The Austrian born Werfel had already fled to France following the rise of Adolf Hitler, and prior to leaving Paris for America, he arrived in Lourdes where he heard the story about Bernadette Soubirous, a teenager who claimed to have seen a vision of the Virgin Mary in a nearby grotto. Persecuted by the authorities and spending her final young years in a convent, after her death in 1876 she was canonised in 1933. When he arrived in America, Werfel decided to preserve the memory of Bernadette by writing a book about her life.

Production began in November 1943 and Fox took a brave step by casting the unknown Jennifer Jones in the title role; fourth billed in the cast is Vincent Price as Imperial Prosecutor Vital Dutour, a government official (and supposed atheist although the real Dutour was catholic). Handsome, bearded and elegant, but cynical of religious dogma, Dutour is determined to prove Bernadette's story false. He also constantly complains about his influenza as he coughs into his handkerchief. As it turns out, it is the beginning of the throat cancer that will eventually kill him. The final scene has the pale, dying Dutour joining the long line of worshippers at Bernadette's grotto, but knowing his denial of God has condemned him to a lonely death. It is an excellent performance that shows Price's full acting range. 'One of my best roles. I felt at home with a cast of highly competent stage actors.'

During the making of *Bernadette*, Price and fellow actor and art expert George Macready opened The Little Gallery in Beverly Hills. It enabled Price to meet many of Los Angeles' great artists as well as several émigrés arriving from Europe. It proved a popular venture that included an exhibition of paintings (several of which Price bought) by controversial American writer Henry Miller. Busy day jobs, increasing rent payments and expensive overheads forced The Little Gallery to close the following year. But art would never be far away from Price's life.

Previewed in December 1943 to qualify for the Oscars, *Song of Bernadette* went on general release in January 1944 to great box office success and winning four of the eleven Oscar nominations. Price wasn't nominated, but his performance made Darryl Zanuck realise that the actor deserved good acting roles in good films.

That came about with *The Eve of St Mark* (1944), a wartime drama featuring Price as cynical southern poet turned soldier Private Francis Marion. 'One of the best parts I ever had and one of the best performances I ever gave. It was one of the first times I was allowed to play a contemporary person.' Next came a prominent supporting role as Secretary to the Treasurer William Gibbs McAdoo in *Wilson* (1944), a biography of President Woodrow Wilson (played by an Oscar winning Alexander Knox). He rounded things off with *Keys to the Kingdom* (1944), another religious drama where he turned in a brief but well played performance as Monsignor Angus Healy.

During the making of *Keys to the Kingdom*, Price received his call up papers to join the US Navy, but for unconfirmed reasons, he never enlisted. Claiming it was colour blindness that prevented him from joining, he actually passed the vision test to get in. The most likely reason had to do with 20th Century Fox intervening. With many of their star actors going against their contracts by joining up, leading men became scarce, and Fox had enough clout to intercede and prevent Price from enlisting. Zanuck had a high profile assignment lined up for the actor, and this would be one of the defining moments in his career.

Price described *Laura* (1944) as, 'one of those few pictures that is perfect. Not pretentious, very simple, just brilliant.' He is correct in his opinion because as *film noir* goes, *Laura* is perfect: an intriguing murder mystery that is not so much a 'who done it' as a 'who done what?' *Laura* is also a study of four despicable people, the most self-centred being radio personality and Laura's jealous mentor Waldo Lydecker – an unforgettable star turn by Broadway actor Clifton Webb. 'Clifton was the kindest man I ever knew in my life,' said Price. 'I first met him in New York what I was in *Victoria*. He said, 'you need publicity. You're a top young actor of New York today, and you need to be included in everything.' Clifton would always put me in any kind of benefit that he had a chance to.'

Price was in good company with Dana Andrews as Detective Mark McPherson, the policeman who falls in love with Gene Tierney's murdered career girl Laura Hunt, or rather her portrait, which dominates the proceedings, and makes the real Laura's appearance halfway through the film all the more shocking (if Laura wasn't murdered, who was?). What makes the film interesting is how Laura is described so glowingly pure by all who knew her, yet the actual person, when she finally appears, is a cynical, bitter individual.

Price rounds off the quartet as Laura's slimy fiancée Shelby Carpenter, a handsome, sharp-dressed ladies' man, every inch the southern gentleman from his immaculately groomed hair to his polished shoes. Shelby is also a penniless, sleazy gigolo: a weak-willed liar and cheat, more interested in looking good than being good. Completely flawed, he is the least threatening of the four (because he's so gutless). Price's performance is suitably oily, but not exactly villainous. He's simply a pathetic creep with nothing to offer but charm and lies. The actor's good looks and towering presence adds depth to the role.

The director of *Laura* was Otto Preminger. Although disliked by the actors on the set, Price enjoyed working with him. 'I know Otto has that reputation with actors, but I loved him. I did two pictures and a play with Otto, and I had a wonderful experience working with him. Now I may be one of the few people in the world who likes Otto Preminger, but I do.' Price also added that *Laura* was, 'the best thing that Otto Preminger ever did, and I think Otto thinks that as well.'

Released in October 1944, *Laura* did excellent business at the box office despite mixed reviews. It received five Oscar nominations but Price was not among the nominees, not that he was bothered. 'Every actor longs to be in a classic film, a film that is so well made, so well directed, photographed, written, everything. It remains a classic. And one of those films that I was in, and I am most proud of it, was *Laura.*'

Although Price's film career flourished, his marriage to Edith floundered. Despite her massive stage reputation, her film career was reduced to small supporting roles. In reality she hated the theatre and marrying a young, upcoming actor fuelled her desire to make it big in Hollywood. 'I think she got married to get out of the theatre,' Price said, 'and it was a terrible blow to me. It didn't do our marriage any good, I'll tell you that.' Not surprisingly, they separated.

There were other devastating factors, namely Edith's increasing alcohol consumption and deteriorating mental health. She also had little idea of money, even when her husband tried to make ends meet during his lean period: she once hired a limousine to go shopping and drove past her husband, in the unemployment line, much to his outrage. A generous man by nature, Price always tried to be careful with his money, a by-product of his upbringing.

Edith became increasingly reclusive, spending her time painting and drinking. 'You sensed that this was an extraordinary sensitive actress, fragile, volatile,' said old friend Bill Brice. 'She also projected a sense that she needed help, that she needed people around her to help her. She didn't seem strong.'

The couple reunited later that year following the advice of Price's father. They bought a new home and for a time they settled back into family life.

Price reunited with Otto Preminger for *A Royal Scandal* (1945), a troubled production about the life and loves of Catherine the Great. Sporting a misbegotten French accent, Price has a tiny role as the Marquis de Fleury, and he camps up to no real effect. It was a definite comedown for both actor and director after *Laura.* More satisfactory was *Leave Her to Heaven* (1945), which reunited him with Gene Tierney. Fourth billed, Price only has a few scenes as attorney Russell Quinton, but performs them with memorable gusto.

Price's next two films were early examples of how his career would develop. Based on Ann Seton's popular novel of the same name, *Dragonwyck* (1946) was on Fox's schedule for almost a year. Production began in February 1945 and Price desperately wanted to play the sadistic Nicholas Van Ryn. 'I had to fight tooth and nail like the devil to get this part.' He lobbied hard to win over director Joseph Mankiewicz and the studio executives, but it took some convincing. They wanted Laird Cregar, but he died in December 1944.

Any doubts Mankiewicz had about Price's ability to carry the role quickly evaporated. 'Joe was a very good director,' Price said. 'He had been a producer at Fox and he produced *Keys of the Kingdom* so I knew him. Joe gave me a marvellous piece of direction where I propose to Gene Tierney. I had lost a lot of weight because the character I was playing was a drug addict. Joe told me to stand very straight and erect, so I'd look as tall and thin as possible. Then Joe yelled at me. "Remember Vincent, nice erection!" It took quite a few takes to finish that scene because everyone on the set was so convulsed with laughter.'Price felt that, *'Dragonwyck* turned out to be a really marvellous film.' Seton's book is pure American gothic and this is reflected in the film's production design, especially Van Ryn's impressive mansion, created by art director Lyle Wheeler. 'It was a wonderful house,' Price recalled. 'You could have moved right in, except they tore it down a week after we finished shooting. The exterior was glass shot, but the interior was a complete house.'

Dragonwyck is excellent cinema, with first class production values and perfect acting. Price makes the film with an outstanding performance as the destructive aristocrat. As well as getting some of the best reviews of his career, he received a Box Office Blue Ribbon Award. On the negative side, his pitch-perfect flare for screen villainy turned into an image that slowly became his screen persona. But at this present moment in time he was still a handsome leading man, emerging as an actor of considerable repute.

With *Dragonwyck* scoring a huge box office hit, Price should have moved on to similar roles in high prestige films. Instead Fox took advantage of his newly found villainous status and cast him in the low budget thriller *Shock* (1946).

'*Shock* was an experiment, actually,' said Price. 'The studio was spending too much money making films and taking too long to make them. Something had to be done to boost output and they cut down on costs. So they asked me and Lynn Bari if we could make a film in 20 days and still have it look like a first-class production. I read the script and thought it was pretty good. I said, "Certainly we can do it, if you don't agree to change the script and louse it up for us." And they agreed, and we went ahead and shot it, in exactly 20 days.' *Shock* is an efficient potboiler that performed well at the box office.

Getting top billing for the first time in his career, Price plays Dr Richard Cross, a psychiatrist who murders his wife in a fit of rage. Witnessed by a woman who goes into a catatonic shock, Cross, who runs the sanatorium the woman is committed to, tries to convince her that she imagined the whole thing. Price is in good form and despite the speed of the production, carries the entire film.

Price's personal life took another bad turn with the death of his beloved mother in October 1946. Marguerite's death devastated the entire family. His father decided to sell the family home in St Louis and move to Tucson, Arizona where the climate was helpful to his arthritis. The death of the elder Price's wife and the disintegration of the younger Price's marriage brought both men closer together with the actor spending as much time as he could with the old man.

Price's final film for Fox was *Moss Rose* (1947). It was another gothic melodrama but not in the same league as *Dragonwyck*. It was also set in London with Price playing another English character, this time Scotland Yard detective Inspector Clinner. It also gave him an opportunity to work with the great Ethel Barrymore.

By 1947 the studio system started falling apart, and Price severed his own ties with Fox after turning down a villainous role in *Captain from Castile* (1947). As a free agent for the first time, it was a new phase in his career, and one he looked upon with a great deal of optimism. 'I liked it for a time,' he said of his studio years, 'but I felt that I would make the giant step into real parts if I left Fox and become a freelance actor, free to choose only the roles I wanted and be not be forced to go into picture after picture where I was part of the wallpaper.'

The Freelance Years (1947 – 1954)

'The best parts in the movies are the heavies.
The hero is usually someone who really has nothing to do.
He comes out on top, but it's the heavy who has all the fun.' – Vincent Price

Price and Ann Dvorak in *The Long Night* (1947)

There was always period of uncertainty for a freelance actor newly released from a studio. A contract player was guaranteed work; a regular salary and protection. A movie contract also meant the studio controlled every aspect of an actor's career.

Vincent Price was luckier than most of his contemporaries. His versatility, affability and reliability meant he would never be out of work for long periods of time.

Price knew that his future lay in character roles. Although still eligible enough at 36, he had realised long ago that he would never be a romantic lead. His aristocratic good looks hardened slightly with age, and his forthright acting style and impressive stage presence made him ideal for villainous roles, an image further enhanced by his (future) moustache. Playing supporting roles had many advantages because he didn't need to carry a picture; he could work solely on giving a good performance without the added pressure of being the star. Typecasting carried a double-edged sword for Price: the well-paid work was there, but financial necessity came at the expense of artistic freedom. At least rewarding theatre roles gave him the opportunity to sound off whenever movie villainy got tiresome.

Price kick-started his freelance career with a crime thriller for Universal called *The Web* (1947), which had him fourth-billed as suave villain Andrew Colby. The film is forgettable but at least it gave Anglo-Irish actor Edmund O'Brien the chance to play a hero, while Price steals the acting honours with a polished performance. RKO's *The Long Night* (1947) had the actor playing the Svengali-inspired magician Maximillian, whose controlling influence over screen newcomer Barbara Bel Geddes ends in him being gunned down by her lover Henry Fonda.

Back at Universal he was British again as Boss Tweed in *Up in Central Park* (1948). Perhaps miscast as the character was short and hardboiled in the stage version (played by Noah Beery Snr), Price was tall, handsome and elegant. The film was critically panned, and Price described by one reviewer as 'a more inappropriate choice could hardly be imagined'. But if there was one positive thing that came from the film was the actor's first meeting with Welsh born costume designer Mary Grant.

'She actually designed clothes that fit comfortably and allowed action,' Price said of Mary. 'She was the first designer I met who thought that actors, like movies, should move.' Mary herself had little time for actors but found that Price, 'seemed less troublesome than most men about the business of fitting. Usually most actors are either too nonchalant or too fussy. He was one of the first I had worked with who hit the happy medium.' The couple met again at a dinner party later that year where Price admitted he had never met anyone from Brooklyn before. Mary, who had studied design in New York, deliberately lost her Welsh accent to fit in with the crowd, so it came as a surprise to Price when she told him she was British.

During the making of *Up in Central Park*, Price returned to horror with an uncredited voice-only gag appearance in *Abbott and Costello Meet Frankenstein* (1948). This horror spoof has Universal's comic duo pitting their (half) wits against Dracula (Bela Lugosi), The Wolf Man (Lon Chaney Junior) and Frankenstein's Monster (Glenn Strange).

When the ghouls are destroyed, Bud & Lou escape from Dracula's castle in a boat with Abbott saying, 'There's no one to frighten us anymore.' Then Price's unmistakable voice (lighting a cigarette, which is all we see of him) replies, 'Oh, that's too bad. I was hoping to get in on the excitement.' 'Who said that?' asks Abbott to which Price replies, 'Allow me to introduce myself, I'm the Invisible Man,' to which the duo jump overboard to the sound of his manic laughter. His uncredited turn in *Abbott and Costello Meet Frankenstein* is the nearest Price ever got to making a film with Lugosi.

Price's voice remained a permanent fixture on radio during the golden age of Hollywood. 'Radio is a great teacher. Some of the best drama ever done in America was produced during the heyday of radio.' Around this time he retained another strong British link by playing Leslie Charteris' crime busting sleuth Simon Templar AKA *The Saint* on radio. He played the role for the next four years, first for CBS and later for NBC.

Price remained active on the stage by taking part in a series of one-act plays for the Actor's Lab at the Las Palmas Theatre. Unfortunately, the Actor's Lab had a very strong left wing following and although the plays he performed in had nothing to do with politics, his association with the group would come back to haunt him.

By December 1947, Price's marriage to Edith was over and the couple permanently separated with Edith suing for divorce. Without his family, a despondent Price faced Christmas alone. Wandering into a pet shop, he bought a mongrel, which he named Joe, who would be his closest non-human companion for the next sixteen years.

One bright spark for Price came with a New Year's Eve party at the home of old friend Deanna Durbin. It was memorable that his date for the evening was Mary Grant. With the start of another year, Price was starting a new life. With weekend visits from Barrett, his own visits to Tucson to see his increasingly frail father, and his beloved Joe by his side, Price joined acting colleagues and fellow art lovers Edward G Robinson and Sam Jaffe in the opening of The Modern Institute of Art in Los Angeles. But despite a solid membership, it closed after two years due to lack of funding.

After putting so much time and money into the project, the closure was a great disappointment to Price. He now felt it was his duty to bring art to the masses despite the mounting apathy from potential financiers. 'You can sell 'em sin and you can sell 'em sex but when you try to peddle "culture" you run smack into a solid wall of stupid ignorance.' His comments reflected more disgust than sadness but the event fuelled his lifelong ambition to make art an important part of LA's cultural heritage.

Professionally, 1948 kicked off with a lavish big budget MGM production of Alexander Dumas' classic tale *The Three Musketeers* (1948). Price was part of a cast that included Gene Kelly (playing against type as D'Artagnan), Lana Turner (Countess Milady de Winter), Angela Lansbury (Queen Anne), Van Heflin (Athos), Gig Young (Porthos) and Robert Coote (Aramis). His own role was that of scheming royal adviser Cardinal Richelieu. MGM decided not to offend religious groups by making Richelieu Prime Minister and dropping the familiar red robes of a high ranking member of the Roman Catholic Church.

Although brightly performed, with Kelly making the most of playing a character who wasn't an American serviceman on leave, the film is too slow thanks to an overkill of romantic scenes and too much cheesy dialogue getting in the way of the swashbuckling fun. Price brings his own suave menace to the proceedings, mixed with a bit of tongue-in-cheek relish. 'We laughed a lot,' recalled Angela Lansbury. 'I think Vincent and I took it all with a big grain of salt.'

Another routine wartime pot boiler came his way in *Rogues Regiment* (1948) playing Nazi gun runner Mark Van Ratten. Resplendent in his white suit, he provides solid support in a forgettable film.

By June 1948, Price's personal life took another tragic turn. With his divorce in the process of being finalised (although it dragged on for several months), his father's health deteriorated. He flew out to Tucson to stay with the old man for the last two days of his life, and later arranged for his funeral in St Louis. He was unable to attend due to his movie commitments on *The Bribe* (1949).

With a cast including Robert Taylor, Ava Gardiner and Charles Laughton, Price plays another villain. With his hair dyed grey and his facial features heavier than usual, a tired looking Price walks through his role with little enthusiasm, the pressures of his divorce and father's death affecting his performance. Although a box office success, *The Bribe* did not advance his career other than providing another entry in his increasing colourful portfolio of sophisticated bad guys.

The Bribe did provide the added joy of working with one of the screen's most enduring sex symbols – Ava Gardner. 'I wanna pay tribute to this woman. I have had the pleasure working with – I was going to say playing with, but it was working with – some of the most famous sex idols in the movie business, like Jane Russell, Lana Turner and Maureen O'Hara. But the only one that ever seemed to me to live up to her reputation as a sex object was this lady Ava Gardner … mmmm … Every time I think of her, I just go limp … No, I don't mean that. It's just a question of semantics, isn't it? But Ava Gardner, my God she was sexy, let me tell ya.'

Although he harboured a distant hope of getting back together with Barbara O'Neil, the new woman in his life was Mary Grant, who he had been seeing throughout the early part of 1948. Understandably, he kept the relationship secret to avoid causing any difficulty with Edith and Barrett, whose first meeting with his future stepmother took place in November 1948. The two got on immediately much to the actor's delight.

The acrimonious divorce proceedings dragged on with Edith constantly changing her demands regarding financial settlements and visitation rights. In January 1949, she filed another divorce suite, which Price did not contest, citing mental cruelty. Edith received $600 a month alimony and £330 in child support (Price retained full visitation rights for Barrett). She also demanded their Santa Monica home, several art works, a $25,000 life insurance and various bank accounts and bonds amounting to $20,000. It was a costly and bitter affair for all concerned but once things were finalised in June 1949, a relieved Price could move on with his life.

Ever the busy man about town, Price gave an art lecture at the East Los Angeles Junior College and travelled to Mexico and South America for the first time where his immersed himself with the art and culture of the continent. There was also another film to make.

Bagdad (1949) was a colourful costume picture starring Maureen O'Hara. As the sinister Turkish military governor Pasha Ali Nadim, Price excels in more well-dressed villainy with the added effect of playing the role with one drooping eye. This was not achieved solely for the film. During a fancy dress party at the Modern Institute of Art , Price and Mary turned up as a, 'space couple in long underwear, dyed black hair, with black stocking caps that fitted like helmets down into the neck. We were black from head to toe, with black masks over the eyes and, on top of our heads, a triple-tiered set of strobolite plastic propellers.' When one of the guests offered him a cigarette, the box of matches used to light the cigarette was held too close to Price. The matchbox burst into flames and flared up in his face.

Price continued through the evening in obvious pain. Later he was in too much agony to tolerate any light. Mary remained with him during his recovering as did the ever loyal Joe, who refused to leave his master's side.

Price continued working on *Bagdad* without a word of complaint. 'It was terribly painful,' said Maureen O'Hara.' He couldn't open his eye, so he had to play the role with it swollen closed. But halfway through the movie it started to get better, and he had a helluva time trying to keep it closed. He really should have put an eye-patch over it and then he wouldn't have had so much trouble. He was complaining and laughing. He made a big, big joke out of the whole thing.'

Ironically, the *Los Angeles Examiner*, in their review of *Bagdad*, commented that Price's drooping eye was, 'an annoying quirk.'

In August 1949 Price took Mary to San Diego where he was judge at an art show. Also attending was old friend Perry Rathbone, director of the St Louis City Art Museum. The three got together and after seeing the sights of California, they headed across the Mexican border to Tijuana where the couple tied the knot on 29 August 1949 with Rathbone acting as witness! 'Poor Perry was in a state of shock,' said Price, 'and especially when he was not allowed to tell anyone our secret, both of us feeling slightly guilty to have done this without telling our families, who incidentally couldn't have cared less one way of the other.'

Setting up home in Benedict Canyon, the Prices were true soul mates with their appreciation of the arts being of the upmost importance. Price's love of art went hand in hand with Mary's talent for design. More importantly, they made a second home for Barrett, whose relationship with his mother had deteriorated, while his own relationship with Mary continued to be close. Price eventually won custody of Barrett and with Mary's help, he created a stable and loving home for the boy.

A few weeks after the wedding, Price returned to work on the screwball comedy *Champagne for Caesar* (1950), starring his long time idol Ronald Colman. 'My favourite actor of all time was Ronald Colman. I really worship him.' So much so he got tongue-tied on their first meeting. Despite the embarrassment, he found Colman, 'one of the most charming men in the business.' They became good friends and enjoyed a happy working relationship on the film.

Moving away from villainy, Price relished the chance to play comedy, a medium that ideally suited his acting style. As eccentric soap tycoon Burnbridge Wells, Price livens up every scene with inspired hilarity. '*Champagne for Caesar* was one of the funniest scripts I'd ever read,' he recalled as he got to camp things up with a madcap performance. Despite good reviews, *Champagne of Caesar* did not do well at the box office, which disappointed Price as he hoped the film's success would have enabled him to escape typecasting. When production wrapped in October 1949, he surprised the press by announcing he'd been married to Mary Grant – for over a month!

Shortly after completing *Champagne for Caesar*, Price was given top billing for the second time as James Addison Reaves AKA *The Baron of Arizona* (1950), one of his favourite films. Directed by the formidable Samuel Fuller, it's a semi fictional account of a former clerk with the Santa Fe Land Office trying to swindle the US Government out of the territory of Arizona. He does this by using forged Spanish land grants and insisting that his wife is a descendant of King Ferdinand VI.

Posing as a monk, Price gets a rare chance to seduce several women. He enjoyed working with 'Colonel' Fuller, who he described as, 'a very flamboyant director character, very much like an old time director. He wore puttees and a megaphone and everything. But I thought he was very good.' Thanks to Fuller, Price stretches himself once more as an actor with an excellent multi-layered performance.

Returning to comedy in *Curtain Call at Cactus Creek* (1950) starring Donald O'Connor, Price hams it up as the superbly theatrical Tracy Holland, forever spouting Shakespeare and going completely over the top. The highlight of the film is his brilliantly overplayed rendition of the sketch *Ruined by Drink*, which deserves some kind of cinema immortality.

Once again the stage provided a welcome change from his screen antics when he returned to the Las Palmas Theatre to play Sir Robert Morton in Terence Rattigan's *The Wilmslow Boy*. The play was a huge success and secured Price further roles in theatre.

Price's next film cast him alongside Robert Mitchum and the statuesque Jane Russell in RKO's *His Kind of Woman* (1951). During the making of *Curtain Call at Cactus Creek*, Price received an offer to play Mark Cardigan from studio head Howard Hughes. 'I was one of three actors under a personal contract to the great eccentric. I have a tender place in my heart for Howard Hughes. For all the jokes and barbs, he was quite a fellow.'

Shooting of the film took over a year, but being on a steady income, Price had no complaints and enjoyed working with Jane Russell. 'I fell in love with Vinnie,' she recalled. 'He could charm the birds out of the trees. How amazed I was meeting him and finding out what a marvellous sense of humour he had, because he had always played the "proper" young man, and if they wanted a "proper" young man, sophisticated, almost British, they got him. Then his wild humour comes out and you think, "Why aren't they using some of that?" that's why we had a lot of fun at the end of *His Kind of Woman*, because he got to play the ham actor with the cape and all that.'

Flamboyant throughout, Price goes over the top without teetering into caricature. His antics rubbed off on the cast and crew making it a very happy shoot for all concerned. 'He had great charm,' said Robert Mitchum. 'He was totally free of any affectation at all, really, personally. He was a very caring person. He was very versatile and demonstrated it. Vincent was a pleasure to know.'

Price's next film took him to the South of France. The shooting of *The Adventures of Captain Fabian* (1951) began in August 1950 and reunited him with Errol Flynn. Production was put on hold when the French authorities withheld work permits for the American actors, a situation further complicated by Warner Brothers claiming that Flynn's involvement in the film, produced by Republic, was a breach of contract. Since he was co-producer and co-writer, the film could not start without him, and production was suspended for a month.

Still on full salary, and with Mary, who designed the costumes, by his side, Price made the most of his paid vacation. They toured Paris and began collecting rare drawings and other art works; it was more fun than the movie itself. Flynn's excessive lifestyle had finally caught up with him and he suffered badly in comparison to Price. Although adequate enough, it's a far cry from the commercial highs of *The Private Lives of Elizabeth and Essex*.

Returning to RKO, Price reunited with Jane Russell for *The Las Vegas Story* (1952), a routine thriller also starring Victor Mature and featuring third-billed Price as crooked promoter Lloyd Collins. For once the actor wasn't thrilled with his underdeveloped part. 'He didn't play the star,' recalled Russell, 'but he was a little unhappy. But he wouldn't go fight for it. He wanted to get along, just get along. He wanted to please the director.' Price still rises above it with his trademark villainy and caused no problems on the set. 'Vinnie was a consummate actor,' Russell added.

Following a documentary film *Pictura – Adventure in Art* (1951), Price returned to the theatre. In 1952 he played Sir Henry Harcourt-Reilly in T S Elliot's *The Cocktail Party*, another strong British connection, and directed by old friend Norman Lloyd. After a successful run at the La Jolla Playhouse, the production was taken to the Curran Theatre in San Francisco.

While touring with the play along the Northwest coast, Price collapsed in Tacoma. Rushed to hospital, he was diagnosed with a duodenal ulcer, the first of his many stomach problems. With Reginald Denny replacing him for the rest of the tour, Price returned home to recuperate.

Fully recovered, Price returned to the La Jolla Playhouse to appear in Christopher Fry's *The Lady's Not for Burning* with Norman Lloyd directing once more. This also had a successful run in San Francisco. Returning to St Louis, Price appeared in *Death Takes a Holiday*. It was followed by a tour of Boston and Newport with the farce *Goodbye Again*.

Returning to the La Jolla Playhouse, Price worked with Norman Lloyd in a revival of *The Wilmslow Boy*, which was followed by an ambitious production of *Billy Budd* with Price as Captain Vere (the cast included an unknown James Coburn). These successful productions brought him great satisfaction. 'He was totally immersed in the theatre,' said Lloyd. 'He loved the theatre. I know he had his whole art world out there, but as an artist, he really cared. He never mocked anything in the theatre.'

Later in 1952, Price played the Devil in George Bernard Shaw's *Don Juan in Hell*. Directed by Charles Laughton, the tour was a success and the following year he received an offer to play the Duke of Buckingham in a Broadway production of *Richard III*, directed by Jose Ferrer, who played the title role. Although the play ran for a month to mediocre reviews, Price was thrilled to be performing Shakespeare on Broadway.

He was due to work once more with Jose Ferrer in a Broadway production of Albert Husson's comedy *My Three Angels* but it clashed with the offer of a starring role in a new film produced by Warners. After much consideration, plus the obvious financial rewards, Price opted for the film. It was a decision that changed the course of his career and cemented his future reputation as America's king of horror.

The film was called *The House of Wax* (1954).

The Horror Years (1953 – 1960)

'The horror thriller offers the serious actor unique opportunities to test his ability to make the unbelievable believable.' – Vincent Price

Price in *The House on Haunted Hill* (1959)

'I would have loved to have done that play,' Price said about his decision to turn down *My Three Angels*. 'It was an enormous success, but so was the film.' Accepting the starring role in *House of Wax* was, at the time at least, the right career move; horror films weren't fashionable in Hollywood compared to the popularity of science fiction. And it was a rare chance to play lead after years of solid supporting roles. Price also added that, 'the people who did the play – it didn't mean anything to them at all. It was a great hit but it didn't help them in their careers, whereas *House of Wax* changed my life.'

House of Wax was a profitable albatross around Price's neck because it secured his cinematic reputation as the Merchant of Menace. It also undermined his serious work in the theatre; he aspired to play Shakespeare but seldom had the opportunity to. Villainy was now the order of the day.

House of Wax is a remake of *Mystery of the Wax Museum* (1933) with Price playing Professor Henry Jarrod (previously played by Lionel Atwill), a famous sculpture who ends up disfigured after his business partner burns down their wax museum to claim the insurance. Resurfacing in New York years later, the wax figures, recreated from his previously destroyed work, are people he has murdered and subsequently dipped in wax. Jarrod's face is also made from the stuff, his real face being burned beyond recognition.

Mystery of the Wax Museum was memorable for the pioneering three-colour Technicolor process. *House of Wax* went a stage further by using 3-D. What made it interesting is the fact that director Andre de Toth couldn't see the effects because he was blind in one eye! 'Jack Warner called me and said, "Listen, do you want to make this film?" I said, "Yes sir." He said. "Take that goddam black patch off your fucking eye, because I don't want to be the butt of a joke. You understand?" So I put my black patch in my pocket, and I suffered because it hurt.'

For Price, the 3-D process and the discomforts caused by the make-up had their own drawbacks. '*The House of Wax* was very demanding, as I had to get to the studio every morning at 5:30 am to put that makeup on. It took three hours to put on and it was agony, absolute agony! Because it was a 3-D film, it was made with two enormous cameras photographing in a mirror, so that you could get two tracks, and because of that unwieldy camera I had to do my own stunts. They couldn't do a close up of me and then cut to a double. The most difficult stunt was at the very beginning when the fire starts in the museum, and I run under this balcony that's in flames just before it falls. I actually did that. I worked it out with a stuntman. Anything on the floor that I might trip over or slide on was moved away and we figured out a course for me to take around these burning figures so that I could get into a little tiny closet when this 3,000 lbs of burning balcony fell. It was scary.'

'The makeup director (George Bau) spent three weeks studying people who had been burned, then stuck pieces of rubber on my face with pure alcohol. Two doctors supervised it to be sure the burns were as real as could be. It took almost three hours to put on and as long to take off, and both processes were very painful. I couldn't eat because my mouth was partially "scar tissue," so I drank many liquids and because of the running around in makeup, I fainted one day from lack of oxygen. It took my face months to heal because it was raw from peeling off wax each night.' The makeup was effective enough when he turned up at the studio canteen. 'The girl at the cash register turned green and almost fainted. Then the patrons got up and headed for the door.'

Price always had great affection for the film. 'I loved *House of Wax*. It was great fun to make. And it was fun to be part of the growing technology of the motion picture industry.'

House of Wax didn't revive the dormant horror genre, nor did it establish 3-D as a successful gimmick.

Thanks to the advance publicity that included Bela Lugosi in full Dracula costume turning up for the New York premier, the film did great business across the States. More importantly it introduced Price to a new generation of teenage fans – an important factor in his future horror career.

Shortly after completing *House of Wax*, Price landed a similar role as Don Gallico in *The Mad Magician* (1953), a threadbare 3-D effort for the Edwin Small Studios. Price rises above the weak material with customary relish.

His next film was RKO's *Dangerous Mission* (1954), starring Victor Mature and Piper Laurie. Once again he assumes the bad guy duties as Paul Adams, although he adopts a more casual look. A big budget Irwin Allen spectacular, much of the $45,000 budget was spent converting two massive sound stages into a replica of Montana's northern glaciers, complete with wind machines that produced 50 tons of ice a day. At least the spectacle compensated for the mundane plot. Price also has a brilliant death scene when buried in an avalanche. Also filmed in 3-D, the process had become passé to cinema goers and the film bombed at the box office.

There was much more fun with his next effort. Long considered one of his best 'worst' films, *Son of Sinbad* (1954) is an absolute hoot from start to finish with Price in his element as downtrodden tent maker and would-be poet Omar Khayyam. '(RKO) sent me the script and asked if I liked it. I said, "I think it's the worst script I've ever read." They said "It is, isn't it?"' Being contracted to RKO, he had to do the film, but at least he had a whale of a time making it, especially when he was surrounded by 250 beautiful young women. 'The script called for girls, girls, girls!' he added. 'Instead of the 40 thieves, we had their daughters. Every marketplace was wriggling with girls selling their wares. 20 girls had just won a Midwest (Howard) Hughes inspired beauty contest. The prize had been a part in the movie. I was asked to pose with them and got their stories first hand: most of them couldn't wait to get back home!'

Price completely steals the show with a splendid comic performance. Not only does he get the girl, he's far more heroic than Dale Robertson's Southern-accented Sinbad, who is incapable of helping anyone, and often gets his poet friend into trouble. Logic was not the film's strongest point and watched in the right frame of mind, it makes for enjoyable viewing.

Less amusing was a situation in Price's life that may have permanently swayed his decision to become entrenched in horror. Midway through 1953, the movie offers stopped coming in. The Hollywood blacklisting had begun.

In 1947 the House Committee on Un-American Activities (HUAC) began to step up their communist-hunting efforts by extending their search to Los Angeles with the blacklisting of ten writers and directors (known as the

Hollywood Ten). Although Humphrey Bogart, Frank Sinatra and other major stars gave their support to the Ten, they never had the backing of the studios and during the next eight years the community was divided into 'friendly' and 'unfriendly' witnesses. After the Ten were suspended without pay, the studios refused to hire known or even presumed communists or those linked in any way to communism or these people. It didn't matter if that person was a close friend; family member or drinking buddy.

By 1953, Senator Joseph McCarthy, with support from the studios, stepped things up with a full-scale witch-hunt. Hollywood became suspicious of everyone. Even Humphrey Bogart, Edward G Robinson, Peter Lorre, Orson Welles, Paul Robeson and Charlie Chaplin were targeted for their communist affiliations. 'Everyone was so full of fear,' said Eddie Albert, himself a blacklisted actor. 'Many people couldn't support their families, or worse, their lives were ruined and they had to go out and do menial jobs. Some even killed themselves.' Others, like actor Sam Wanamaker and director Joseph Losey, moved to England to pursue their careers.

The process of alienation happened when Price and Mary had to sign an oath of loyalty to the State Department when they renewed their passports. Then Price was dropped from CBS TV's *The Pantomime Quiz* without explanation, and his burgeoning horror career came to a halt when Karl Malden replaced him in Warners' second 3-D chiller *The Phantom of the Rue Morgue* (1954).

Price did appear as Casanova in the Bob Hope comedy *Casanova's Big Night* (1954) only to have his name removed from the credits, a decision made by Paramount in response to his blacklisting. It was just as well since Price, and a good cast of Basil Rathbone, Joan Fontaine, John Carradine and Lon Chaney Junior all look ill at ease with the mistimed laughs from an off-form Hope.

It came as no surprise that Price was treated this way. He had a close friend in Paul Robeson, whose anti-American comments were well known. Friendships with art lovers Edward G Robinson and Sam Jaffe also fuelled government suspicions. His work at the La Jolla Playhouse and links to the American-Russian Institute and the Hollywood Independent Citizen Committee of Arts, Sciences and Professions, where he gave many speeches, were considered un-American by McCarthy.

Price may have despised staunchly right-wing actors such as John Wayne, but he wasn't a communist. If anything his affability towards his fellow man proved his undoing in the face of mounting suspicions. It was enough to keep him out of film acting for almost a year. Although he was more greylisted than blacklisted, he received no visits from HUAC or the FBI.

Price was at his wit's end, but thankfully the ever supportive Mary rushed to his side with several writing projects to keep his mind active. Fortunately, television had distanced itself from HUAC so he kept busy with appearances in the drama anthologies *Climax* and *Science Fiction Theatre*. Art projects and lectures were also on hand, but with acting being his main source of income, he needed to clear his name straight away.

On the advice of former Assistant Attorney General Mabel Walker

Hildebrandt, Price contacted the FBI directly to arrange an interview that took place with Mrs Hildebrandt as witness. The agents who questioned Price were suitably impressed by his answers and once the extremely long interview had finished, they were satisfied that Price had no communist connections. He did sign a document for the agents refuting all allegations. This did not exonerate him as far as Hollywood was concerned, the FBI having no direct links to the studios. Price sent the document with a letter to CBS confirming that his name had been cleared and he was now available for work.

Ironically, only months after the interview, Senator McCarthy was discredited. But the damage had been done. Lives were ruined and friendships ended bitterly. For Price, it was a betrayal of his principles. Professionally he became more worried about his financial future. A generous man by nature, and one who had never lived in poverty, he constantly fretted about money. Thanks to McCarthy, the desire to act got replaced by the need to work. Price now accepted anything and everything regardless of quality.

Price returned to the big screen in March 1956 as Svengali-inspired agent Charles Winthrope in *Serenade* (1956), another Mario Lanza vehicle about a local boy making it big as an opera singer. Looking tired from the pressures of his blacklisting, Price performs with an air of world-weariness about him. At least he had some excellent dialogue to compensate. An uncredited narration in *The Vagabond King* (1956) also filled the void.

There was also a welcome career boost with a trio of big budget epics. *The Ten Commandments* (1956) is a typical Hollywood spectacle from the legendary Cecil B DeMille. Following the blacklisting, Price lobbied hard for the role of Baka, the sadistic, whip-cracking architect of Pharaoh's Golden City, who later meets his doom at the hands of Moses (Charlton Heston at his most Biblical) for cracking one whip too many. It's a small role but Price was in good company with a stellar cast of Yul Brynner, Edward G Robinson (also recovering from the blacklisting), Cedric Hardwick Yvonne De Carlo and John Carradine. Being a DeMille extravaganza ensured the kind of box office receipts that could only enhance the actor's dented profile.

'DeMille was a wonderful director to work with,' said Price. 'He was 100% visually minded. Really, his stories were very thin, but the visual effects he pulled off were marvellous. The script was of secondary importance to him. What he was interested in was what was on the screen, the use of crowds, particularly. He was really fond of putting hundreds, even thousands, of people in a shot and then pulling it off. Spectacle! That was DeMille.' Price enjoyed the experience and responded with a good performance despite not looking remotely Egyptian!

Charlton Heston had nothing but admiration for Price. 'Vincent was a good actor. I had great respect for him, and great admiration for his abilities, which were considerable. There's no question about that.'

Price's next effort was the Fritz Lang thriller *While the City Sleeps* (1956). Once again the actor was part of an ensemble cast that included Dana Andrews, Rhonda Fleming, Ida Lupino and George Sanders. Set in New York in the midst of the notorious Lipstick Killings, Price is in fine manipulative form as playboy Walter Kyne. When he takes control of his wealthy father's newspaper business, he offers a top executive job to the reporter that can bring in a scoop on the killings.

It's typical *film noir* with greed, blackmail, deception, back stabbing, unsympathetic characters (apart from the killer oddly enough) and lots of gorgeous women. Although well staged, it lacks the intimacy of Lang's early work. Price gives a solid performance as Kyne: although a pampered and nasty piece of work, he proves to be more honourable than the reporters in his charge.

While the City Sleeps provided good box office takings but Lang biographer Paul H Jenson thought the film was 'Profoundly ordinary.'

Lang had a reputation for being a hard task-master and with RKO producer Bert Friedlob allowing him a free hand, the director pulled out all stops as Price observed with great respect. 'When somebody knows that much about making movies, you go along with it, because (Lang) knew what he was doing, and he knew what he wanted. He was a wonderful man, and I had a great friendship with him. *While the City Sleeps* came at the end of his career, but he was still a marvellous director.'

Irwin Allen's *The Story of Mankind* (1957) is the worst of Price's three big budget efforts, but at least he was working once more with Robert Colman. Both actors take centre stage to the main story where the Spirit of Mankind (Colman) argues before a heavenly court about the salvation of the human race against Mr Scratch (Price), who is all for destroying the world.

The film has its fair share of guest stars in bizarre and unsuitable roles – Peter Lorre's Nero looks so ill it's unlikely he could pick up a fiddle while Rome burned, let alone play it. Bad boy Dennis Hopper is an improbable Napoleon, and to call Harpo Marx's casting as Sir Isaac Newton weird is an understatement. Also included were Groucho Marx, Chico Marx, Cesar Romero, John Carradine and Henry Daniel, all of whom give bad performances. *The Story of Mankind* is valuable as a record for fans to spot their favourite actors and wince at how dreadful there are.

Taking the main roles, the sinister and goateed Price manages to emerge from this mess with some dignity. Sadly Colman looks ill and embarrassed. It seems the actors only took part in the film so they could work together once more. It was the last time too; Colman died a few months later.

Price's sterling work in all three movies didn't lead to a permanent revival in his screen career, and the commercial failure of *The Story of Mankind* left him in a weak position when it came to future film assignments. Price proved difficult to cast even if he could act many of his contemporaries off the screen without trying. While John Wayne seemed unaffected by age and was able to continue his career without any problems, others like Errol Flynn were out on a limb. Price wasn't as badly affected as Flynn; but away from villainy, there were few good film roles on offer.

There were other factors to consider. A new generation of independent filmmakers were emerging from the staid shadows of old Hollywood. Drive-ins were attracting younger audiences and new acting talent, mainly from television, rose to prominence. These intense young juveniles were inspired by 'The Method', a new and radical style of acting synonymous with Lee Strasberg and his New York's Actor's Studio.

Soon naturalistic mumblers such as James Dean, Marlon Brando, Rod Steiger and Paul Newman brought a new form of realism that made Price's classical style redundant. 'When Jimmy Dean and Marlon Brando and those people came out,' he recalled, 'there was a kind of speaking in the vernacular. And all of us with trained accents and trained English and theatrically we were different in our approach to acting – that if you wanted to stay in the business, you bloody well went into costume pictures!'

Costume pictures were unfashionable in the wake of this contemporary realism, and British cinema also embraced the new style a few years later with kitchen sink dramas that made stars out of Laurence Harvey, Albert Finney, Tom Courtney, Richard Harris and Alan Bates. Even musicals took a radical turn with the introduction of rock and roll, and a certain Elvis Presley. Popular low budget science fiction movies ran alongside *On the Waterfront* (1954) and *Rebel Without a Cause* (1955). Price still needed to work, but this new style of cinema simply wasn't his style.

And Price had little time for this new style. 'I really hate acting that is "true to life". Marlon Brando is a superb actor, but he is more baroque than I will be. In *Sayonara* (1957) he used an accent that was not southern, it was coloured – a complete phoney from beginning to end.'

The success of Hammer Films' *The Curse of Frankenstein* (1956) revived the dormant horror genre and established classically trained actors Peter Cushing and Christopher Lee as big stars. With horror slowly making a comeback in America, it looked certain that Price, who had the same versatility as Cushing, could take a natural step into the genre, where his acting style was ideally suited.

Away from films, he wasn't exactly idle. His prominence in the art world enabled him to go on lucrative lecture tours, after dinner speaking engagements, gallery openings and extensive work for the UCLA Arts Council. More importantly he still pursued his lifelong dream of establishing a museum in Los Angeles. He joined the board of the Los Angeles County Museum and used his influence to achieve funding. The museum moved to larger premises where it became one of America's most prominent art centres. Price remained on the board until his death.

Stage roles still came his way, and the burgeoning influence of television providing many opportunities. Most big film stars considered television a third rate medium and avoided it like the plague. Price on the other hand embraced it without complaint. It was well paid work and being a name actor, he was often in demand.

In addition to an unsold pilot for a series called *The Left Fist of David* starring Price and Peter Lorre as feuding antique dealers, there were many memorable appearances in the CBS TV quiz shows *$64,000 Dollar Question* and *$64,000 Challenge*, both of which provided much needed income for the actor.

Price also starred in an episode of *Alfred Hitchcock Presents* called 'The Perfect Crime', where he played a Sherlock Holmes-inspired detective who murders a district attorney after he finds out the detective had previously sent an innocent man to the electric chair. Other TV efforts included another unsold pilot for the quiz show *Key Witness* and the detective series *Double Indemnity*.

Price still needed a particular image if he was to stop his film career grinding to a complete halt. Now in his late forties, it looked like he would fade away in movie cameos that grew smaller as he got older. Salvation of sorts came with a quintet of horror films. While they were not considered brilliant, they were forerunners to the next phase of his career, and one that would keep him in starring roles for over a decade.

The Fly (1958) is the first and best known. A higher than usual $50,000 budget gave the film a lavish look. Unusually for a chiller, it was made in colour and filmed in wide-screen. Published by *Playboy Magazine* in 1957, George Langelaan's short story had been optioned by 20th Century Fox, and keen to capitalise on Hammer's gothic revival, took advantage of the changing cinematic scene. Price's villainous image proved useful when he appeared on various movie posters (looking suitably sinister) as well as introducing the trailer with typically creepy relish. In the mind of director Kurt Neuman, Price's new found horror reputation would draw in the crowds.Price is actually third billed in the cast, and his role isn't villainous. 'I've done only three horror films prior to *The Fly* and in this my role is straight.' Nor does he play the title monster, making it all the more baffling that *The Fly* helped establish Price's horror image. More surprising is the fact that the actor wasn't first choice. After Michael Rennie turned it down, Neuman lobbied for Price despite objections from Fox's executive producer Buddy Adler who felt the actor didn't have enough marquee value to promote the film. Thanks to the success of *House of Wax*, he was brought in.

Price can't have been happy about being cast in *The Fly* on the strength of a film he did five years previously. '*House of Wax* was a tremendous success, and I played this outlandish character and people remember me in it. I've given better performances in a number of better films, but no one remembers that. I don't want to be identified with any specific type of characterisation, certainly not villainy. Shakespeare was right, I must admit, when he wrote: "The evil men do live after them, the good is oft interred with their bones." But I wish he weren't so precise.'

Other than transferring the location from France to Quebec (and keeping the French character names), James Clavell's script follows Langelaan's story. Although pivotal to the narrative, Price's role as Francois Delambre is secondary, and pretty thankless; he's hardly seen in the second half. The real star is Al Hedison as Francois' brother Andre, a scientist whose experiments in matter transference goes badly wrong when his atoms are mixed with a passing fly, leaving him with the insect's head and leg. The story is told in flashback with Andre's wife Helene (Patricia Owens) being arrested by Inspector Charias (Herbert Marshall) for killing Andre by crushing his head with a steam hammer!

The Fly grossed over $3 million at the box office, making it Kurt Neuman's best known work as director. It was also his last film; he died shortly after its release. Although well received at the time, *The Fly* has dated badly. Al Hedison became so embarrassed by his participation he used his middle name David for the rest of his career in order to distance himself from the movie.

Even the unforgettable climax featuring Price and Herbert Marshall catching sight of the fly, with Hedison's head and arm, in the spider's web crying 'Help meeeee!' has been undermined by Price's famous story about how he and Marshall found it impossible to keep straight faces during the scene. 'I must confess that it's hard not to break up with laughter when we're doing some of these pictures. Once during *The Fly*, Herbert Marshall and I had to examine a spider's web which held a small fly which was supposed to be my brother – and it took a whole day to film it. We kept laughing ourselves sick. In the end we had to film back to back – we couldn't even look at each other's face!'

If *The Fly* offered an interesting taster regarding his future horror career, then his starring role in *The House on Haunted Hill* (1958) sealed his fate. Price is in his element, taking centre stage as Frederick Loren, a sleazy millionaire who invites five strangers (with the tempting offer of $10,000) to spend the night with him and his wife at a notorious haunted house. With the possibility of ghosts, ghouls and skeletons lurking around every dark passageway, there is more to this creepy night out than Loren lets on.

For the first time, Price gets to play the kind of barnstorming melodrama often associated with his horror work. Still handsome and impeccably dressed (the moustache now a permanent feature), his grandiloquent presence and flamboyant personality, coupled with his wonderful voice, is vintage Vinnie all the way. Nor did Price act the diva like many other stars. 'He knew his lines,' recalled screenwriter Robb White, 'he knew what to do, he didn't need much direction, and he gave nobody any trouble.'

But Loren is a far more complex character and Price takes it a stage further. Behind his sardonic bonhomie hides a darker persona as he tries to expose (or maybe murder) his unfaithful wife, although that may not even be the case as the film has enough red herrings to sink a ship!

The House on Haunted Hill was directed and produced by one of the great cinematic showmen, William Castle. Castle first met Price in a coffee shop, where the producer pitched the idea of the film. Price loved it and took in instant liking to Castle who he described as, 'one of the last great characters in the movies. A witty man who loved a gimmick and knew how to make them work. The movies might be better off if there were more producers like Bill Castle. Castle is not only a producer, he's a showman.'

'Bill Castle was a great fellow for gags,' Price added. 'For *The House on Haunted Hill* Bill had this idea, which he called "Emergo". I throw my wife into a vat of acid. Then, when I bring her out she's "clean". She's a skeleton and I wind her up on the wires. Well "Emergo" was a thing where they rigged the theatre with a real skeleton on it. So when I start to wind her up, the skeleton goes out over the audience. It opened (December 1958) at a theatre in San Francisco, and they stampeded on the opening night. They knocked out the first eight rows of seats. It was a big success.'

To a modern audience, the thought of a 12-foot plastic skeleton flying over a cinema would generate more laughs than scares. But this was 1958 and picture goers were perhaps less sophisticated. Made for $150,000, *The House on Haunted Hill* grossed over $4 million at the box office. More importantly, the film consolidated Price's popularity with his younger fans. Thanks to Castle, 'The world can never grow old for me as long as there are young people, seeing it differently, every second of the day, for all my days.'

Price moved away from horror with a supporting role in Irwin Allen's big budget drama *The Big Circus* (1959). Production began in February 1959 with Price playing circus ringmaster Hans Hagenfield. Decked out in the standard ringmaster's uniform of scarlet frockcoat, black boots and top hat, the actor looks magnificent, and adds class to a role that only requires him to introduce the circus acts.

Horror continued when he played Francois Delambre again in *Return of the Fly* (1959). Initially Price was ecstatic about the script and the expansion of his original role. 'It was actually a better script than *The Fly*,' he recalled, as he signed on the dotted line without realising the direction it was heading.

'What Vincent read was a first draft,' said producer Edward L Bernds, 'and like many first drafts it was overlong, and some cuts were made to trim it down, and some changes were made to bring about budget economies. Vincent liked some of the scenes we had cut and he objected. If I recall correctly they were scenes with Danielle de Metz, scenes of warmth and charm, but when you're pressed for footage, not truly essential to the story.'

The situation wasn't helped by the fact that 20th Century Fox, who produced *The Fly*, showed no interest in the sequel and farmed it out to Associated Producers. This messy effort is the least interesting of Price's quintet of chillers.

Price also has surprisingly limited screen time. Looking older and greyer, he gives a low key performance. He doesn't completely walk through the film, but it's clear his heart wasn't in it. *Return of the Fly* has the hallmarks of a poverty row chiller and proved a step down for the actor.

Despite the disappointment of the assignment, Price remained affable with the cast and crew. 'Price was always a gentleman,' said producer Bernard Glasser, 'always ready and prepared, but as I recall he was not overly enthusiastic about the screenplay.' Edward L Bernds concurs. 'Working with Price was a real delight, thoroughly professional, always prepared, giving his best to every scene. His wasn't even the biggest part in *Return of the Fly*, but his star status and the strength he brought to his performance lifted it out of the B movie category it might have fallen into.'

Return of the Fly did reasonable business, so the horror ascendancy continued with *The Bat* (1959), an adaptation of Mary Roberts Rinehart's 1908 crime novella *The Circular Staircase*. The story has a celebrated history. In 1920 Rinehart and playwright Avery Kemper completed the stage version, re-titled *The Bat*, which played on Broadway for 867 performances and made $9 million at the box office.

There were several film versions, the most recent being *The Bat Whispers* (1930) starring Chester Morris.

Production began in April 1959 and once again Price found himself at odds with the script. 'I thought they would revive it and bring it up to date, because, when I was a little kid, I had seen *The Bat* on stage and it frightened me to death. I thought it would have that same kind of hold on an audience. It didn't because it wasn't a good script.'

Despite his sinister appearance on the movie posters posing next to a bat, Price does not play the title role. Nor is he a vampire as the poster led audiences to believe. *The Bat* is actually a masked killer/cat burglar with a clawed glove, who is out to locate a stash of loot embezzled by a bank manager and hidden in a creaky old mansion. Even Price's top billing is misleading; the real star is Agnes Moorehead as Cornelia van Gorder, a crime writer and amateur detective who rents the mansion unaware of the hidden loot and the intentions of the masked killer.

Price consoled himself with the red herring role of Dr Malcolm Wells, a physician who studies the behaviour of vampire bats. Wells murders the bank manager when he learns of the hidden fortune and sets about looking for it himself, before coming to a fatal end when he locks horns with *The Bat* during the climax. But for the most part he is side-lined throughout the film.

The Bat is a cranky whodunit complete with thunderstorms, secret panels and dodgy murder suspects, none of which can compare to the creaky dialogue, dramatic clichés, and a scenery chewing cast on an off day. Price was strictly there for the marquee value. Small wonder he returned to welcoming arms of William Castle, who at least could offer him something to work with. While *The Tingler* (1959) lacks the fun of *The House on Haunted Hill*, it is far superior to *Return of the Fly* and *The Bat*, and Price is once again in his element as Dr William Chapin, a loopy scientist whose aim is to – literally – scare people to death, especially his unfaithful wife (Patricia Cutts). Researching into the concept of fear, he learns that it can create on the spinal column a slug like parasite – the Tingler – that can be removed only by screaming.

In order to isolate the parasite, Chapin takes LSD in an attempt to frighten himself. When that fails the drug-fuelled doctor ends up scaring his wife to death before removing the parasite from her corpse. But in true horror tradition, the rubber-looking Tingler escapes and runs amok in a nearby cinema.

Being a William Castle movie, the gimmick is the focal point. 'On *The Tingler*,' recalled Price, 'Bill came up with an idea called "Percepto", where the seats in the theatre were supposed to be wired for electric shocks. Well we opened at a theatre in Boston, and it didn't work at all. They couldn't rig the seats. It didn't work nearly as well as "Emergo".'

Because Price had never taken drugs before, being on an LSD trip in the film posed a problem. 'I wasn't much good at that because I didn't know what the effect was meant to be.' Not that he needed to do any research on the subject. 'Even the people who do take LSD, they don't remember what happens to them, so what good would it do to take it to learn how to play the part?'

Price wasn't keen to accept the role, but Castle was undeterred. 'Vinnie, you got to play the doctor in it. You'll be perfect!' he exclaimed to his reluctant star. 'Bill, I don't want to be typecast,' replied Price, only for Castle to say, 'Vinnie, with the success of *The House on Haunted Hill*, I think it'll open a whole new career for you.'

Castle's observations proved correct. At a time when many well established actors were fading into increasingly smaller and sporadic film appearances as they approached middle aged, Price could remain in starring roles. And the all-important teenage market kept his profile remarkably high. Naturally the money he made for starring in these chillers allowed him to pursue more interesting theatre assignments and art projects.

Made for $1 million, *The Tingler* scored a box office hit. The film's success also increased Price's standing in the art world, where his expertise became useful on TV with *The $64,000 Challenge*, although a Congressional investigation into the rigging of certain quiz shows brought further scandal. Price was not implicated, and half the money he won on the quiz he donated to the UCLA for the purchase of art works.

The new found celebrity status proved useful when he penned his 'visual autobiography', *I Know What I Like*. Although less about his life and career and more about his love of art, the book sold extremely well, and this led to a new career writing books, periodicals and newspaper articles. As 1959 drew to a close, Price embarked on a 55 city lecture and book-signing tour.

William Castle wanted Price for his next film *13 Ghosts* (1960), but the actor received an interesting offer from Samuel Z Arkoff and James H Nicholson of American International Pictures. This new film would catapult him into major horror stardom.

The Corman Years (1960 – 1964)

'I don't play monsters. I play men besieged by fate or out for revenge.' – Vincent Price

Price in *House of Usher* (1960)

Throughout the fifties, Low budget science fiction films became the staple of teenage America's drive-in cinemas, and leading the way was a small independent company called American International Pictures. The men behind AIP were Samuel Z Arkoff and James H Nicholson. A former lawyer, the Iowa born Arkoff headed for Hollywood after World War II to make his name in the movies. He started out representing several low budget producers before going into filmmaking himself.

By contrast James H Nicholson was a general manager for the movie distribution company Realart. Arkoff represented Nicholson on an infringement case against the company, and both men became friends and business partners, setting up American Releasing Corporation in 1954.

The partnership had their specific roles. According to actor Robert Quarry, 'Jim was the artistic supervisor. Sam was money and promotions – God knows he was clever.' Unlike the shy retiring Nicholson, the extrovert, cigar chomping Arkoff looked every inch a Hollywood producer and played it to the hilt with his own brand of showmanship. The company changed its name to American International Pictures two years later when the duo decided to go into film production.

The company quickly expanded, and the timing was perfect in view of the economic downturn affecting Hollywood. With television becoming the most popular form of entertainment for the average American household, the studios struggled to attract cinema audiences.

To get people off their backsides and into the cinemas again, the major studios produced big budget epics alongside lesser efforts that mainly relied on gimmicks (3-D, Cinemascope). AIP, being a small independent company, had the drive-ins. Teenagers still went to the cinema and with science fiction replacing horror as the youngsters' main source of movie fun, Arkoff and Nicholson capitalised on this new market. 'There are some unkind people who say we made films aimed directly at the youth,' said Arkoff. 'That's a matter of semantics. We did make pictures that appealed to youth and didn't moralize'.

Arkoff and Nicholson produced low budget quickies that could turn over a fast profit within a few days while the Hollywood majors took several months to a year to recoup their production costs. AIP's best known efforts were *I Was a Teenage Werewolf* (1957) and *I Was a Teenage Frankenstein* (1958), both of which appealed to youngsters because of the teenage cast, the only adult being the main villain played in both films by character actor Whit Bissell.

Unlike Hammer, AIP was not a production company. Arkoff arranged finance and distribution deals with independent producers as well as buying up foreign language films cheaply for American distribution. AIP produced movies at a breakneck speed: 22 were completed in 1958 alone.

AIP became so successful that Arkoff took a leasehold on one of Charlie Chaplin's old studios on Sunset Boulevard. Unfortunately this was a financial disaster. To recover costs, Arkoff produced a low budget Italian sword and sandal epic, which grossed $1 million in America. Returning to the States, he received an offer from comedian Red Skelton to buy up the lease; Chaplin was his hero and he wanted the studio for that very reason.

'We would have gladly given him the studio,' said Arkoff, 'but he bought the whole lot. So we got all our money back plus a three-year lease out of the deal, so we could use a little studio there as well as keep our offices. We never had a studio since. You don't need studios to make pictures. As a matter of fact you're really better off without one with today's audiences that are visual-minded. They want it realistically done, not against cardboard backgrounds and papier-mache sets.'

AIP continued arranging finance and distribution for their producers, one of whom influenced the future careers of nearly every leading American filmmaker over the next forty years. Francis Ford Coppola, Jonathan Demme, John Sayles and Ron Howard began their careers with this remarkable man, who once told them, 'Work for me like a dog for very little money and I will give you a chance in the movies.' This man was Roger Corman.

The son of a successful commercial engineer, Corman was born in Detroit in 1926. The family moved to Los Angeles when he was a teenager, and it was mixing with the Hollywood kids at Beverly Hills High School that ignited his love for cinema. He was set to follow his father's footsteps into engineering but quit Stanford University after just four days. Following a stint in the US Navy, he returned to Los Angeles to work as a messenger boy for 20th Century Fox. After graduating from Oxford University with a degree in Modern English Literature (he spent his spare time writing scripts), he returned to LA and with the financial help from his parents and his brother Gene (who worked as an agent), he produced *Monster from the Ocean Floor* (1954).

Directed by Wyott Ordung, the film is awful beyond belief but with help from his brother, Corman sold the film to Robert Lippert for $110,000. He then put his money into another film, and thanks to his conveyor belt approach, churned out eight films that year, which included the original *The Fast and the Furious* (1954), which was remade in 2001 starring Vin Diesel.

The Fast and the Furious was the first film to be distributed by Arkoff and Nicholson's American Releasing Company and its success led to several lucrative job offers from the major studios. Happy with his own brand of guerrilla filmmaking, Corman signed a three-picture deal with ARC, who provided the kind of fast capital the director needed to get his movies completed as quickly as possible.

Arkoff returned his production costs to Corman with each film he made, giving him the required cash to start his next production. '(ARC) wanted to take my picture, and I said that I would let them have it if they would give me an advance against the release of the picture, and also make a deal for a series of subsequent pictures in which they would give me advances in every one. That way I could make a series of pictures and get at least a portion of the negative costs back and not have to go through the wait.' In return Arkoff arranged distribution around the various drive-ins and made deals with smaller distributors so the profits coming in would advance the costs further. ARC also struck up a long term deal with film lab Pathe to defer payments on prints and advance money on future projects.

Making his directorial debut with the western *Five Guns West* (1955), Corman moved into science fiction with *The Day the World Ended* (1956). With ARC becoming AIP, the trio of Corman, Arkoff and Nicholson embarked on an unbroken run of cheap and cheerful monster movies, each one turning in a healthy profit. Corman produced and directed as many as eight films a year, some of which were improvised over a weekend.

AIP's success began to slow in the late fifties with independent producers Herman Cohen and Bert I Gordon starting to take their own bite from the monster movie cherry. Other low budget film companies such as Republic and Allied Artists also muscled in, and even the Hollywood majors took notice. AIP quickly moved into teenage delinquent movies with later forms of exploitation consisting of biker, beach party and LSD pictures.

Arkoff knew AIP had to invest in more expensive productions, and the timing was right for Roger Corman, who also wanted to change direction. 'I was starting to think that (AIP) had been selling their double bills a bit too long. Although the profits were good, they weren't as big as they once were. I was also getting very restless with this format, partially because of the financial restrictions, and, partially because I simply wanted to make bigger pictures.'

Taking into account Hammer's success, and the fact that Herman Cohen had abandoned low budget quickies in favour of more expensive colour productions, the restless Corman approached Arkoff with the ambitious idea of adapting to the big screen (and in colour) the horror stories of American writer Edgar Allan Poe. 'At the time there was a system that was doing well,' Corman recalled, 'doing two low budget pictures and sending them out as a combination – two science fiction films or two teen films and so forth. I had done a number of them for AIP and other companies. Then AIP asked me to do ten-day black and white horror films but, frankly, I was getting tired of this and wanted to do something better. Also I thought that the idea had been repeated so much it was losing some of the impact at the box office.'

'I said (to Arkoff), let me do one fifteen-day picture in colour on a slightly bigger budget, and they asked what I wanted to do, and I said *The Fall of the House of Usher*, which I read when I was a junior at high school and I had always loved. After some discussion, it was agreed that they would let me make the film.'

It was an incredible risk, but the ever astute Arkoff gambled on a $270,000 budget (large by AIP's standard) to produce Corman's project. But a lavish looking colour production wasn't enough. One sure sell was the addition of a name actor, and one who had to be on par with Hammer's Peter Cushing and Christopher Lee.

'Vincent Price was my first and only choice for the lead role of Roderick Usher,' said Corman. 'It wasn't one of those things where you had a list and he was on top of the list. He was simply the person I wanted and Jim Nicholson, who was more involved with the casting and that end than Sam Arkoff – Sam was more at the business end – agreed with me. It was the fact I knew he was a very fine actor, that he had done one or two pictures in the horror bracket, he had a solid career in other types of films, and also I felt he was right for the role. We sent the script to Vincent. He liked it and we had a meeting and got along very well.' Like many well-read men, Price was a great admirer of Poe.

Money proved a problem when it came to hiring Price. He may not have been a big Hollywood star anymore, but he was still in demand and wouldn't come cheap. According to Sam Arkoff, 'We paid Vincent Price $50,000 for *House of Usher*. That was a lot of money for AIP and I wasn't sure if we could afford Vincent. We were a very young company at the time and we didn't have the money and we couldn't afford to buy Vincent. So we worked out a deal with him whereby we could pay him more, but we would only pay over a period of time. And I sold him on the idea, which was true, that this was for his future. This was laying money aside for the future. I know his agent didn't want him to take the deal, but Vincent took it.'

Arkoff further added that, 'we negotiated an agreement that we both could live with. I guaranteed him a series of pictures and we deferred his payments. That made him affordable to us, and we clearly got our money's worth.'

Signing a three-picture deal, Price got paid $3,000 in monthly instalments. 'It was a gamble,' he said of the arrangement. 'I think there comes a time in everybody's career when you suddenly say money isn't everything: I wanted to take a gamble on something I believe in.'

Price found a kindred spirit in Roger Corman. 'Roger was a wonderful director. He was very intelligent and very well organised. He had a genius hiring wonderful people, which is the secret to all these great directors. He showed people how to make pictures fast and on a small budget, and they made money! Working with Roger was a gamble. I believed that the works of Edgar Allan Poe hadn't been done properly on the screen. What Roger tried to do was express some of the psychology of Poe's characters, and imbue our movie versions with the spirit of Poe. I always tried to base my characters as much as I could on what Poe had written because it was a sharper clue to the character.'

'Vincent was the consummate professional,' said Corman. 'He had been trained in a classical manner, but he also worked a little bit with the Method. He and I would discuss the role before shooting. We had no problems whatsoever. It was congenial and friendly and as professional a method of working with an actor I have ever had.'

The chemistry between actor and director reflected the way Roderick Usher would be portrayed. '(Price) had some ideas; I had some ideas,' Corman added. 'I saw Roderick Usher then, and still do, as an extremely intelligent, extremely sensitive and very complex person, and I believe Vincent Price was that person. He was able to access that sensitivity very well.'

With everything in place, Corman assembled a first rate crew. As art director and production designer, Daniel Haller created the Usher family's atmospheric and creepy home. 'The monster of the movie is the house itself,' said Arkoff, 'and that is courtesy of Haller's gothic designs.' Award winning cinematographer Floyd Crosby made striking use of visuals that complimented Haller's sets, and composer Les Baxter, who had a long career on the jazz circuit, especially with the Exotic Movement, provided an excellent score.

Brought in as screenwriter was novelist Richard Matheson, who regarded his work on *House of Usher* (1960) as one of his toughest assignments. 'I knew I would be working within a limited budget, but I tried not to let that affect my writing. The story was simple, anyhow. What could they spend the money on? Poe's story is very brooding and ruminating, and not too much plot, movement or dialogue, so I kind of faked the Poe touches.' This wasn't an easy thing to do because Matheson was hardly in awe of the story or the writer. 'I've never had a particular interest in Poe, nor did I develop one while working on the films.'

Matheson became good friends with Price and greatly admired him as an actor even if he felt the horror persona started taking over the artist. 'He's fallen into acting habits. The first time he ever snapped out of it was when I wrote *House of Usher* for him. He liked the script so much it shook him out of his usual style and as a result he did a commendable job on it. But as he did more and more Poe pictures he started sliding back into the same thing.'

Production began in January 1960 and the end result is a visually striking piece of American gothic that's not without its faults. Because the original story is short, it was difficult to expand it to feature length. The film is slow moving and the juvenile leads are weak. Despite the money at his disposal, Corman, who was more a technical director than an actor's director, focussed on getting the film finished on time and within budget, meaning the supporting performances suffered.

'Corman was very good with pace and giving things an interesting look,' said Matheson, 'but he didn't work with actors, and the actors in the Poe films were usually not very good. There were exceptions in each film – Price always did a professional job – but in *House of Usher* I think all three of the other people were not particularly good, and that was the whole cast!'

Matheson aimed much of his criticism towards Mark Damon, who played the handsome hero. 'Mark Damon was playing, I guess, at being a method actor, and before he went on the set he would run in place and huff and puff! Then he would walk in on a scene where Price would be chatting with somebody, and Price would out-act the hell out of him!'

'Vincent breathed plenty of life and gothic horror into all the lines and action,' said Corman. Clean shaven, with white hair and pale skin, Price's hyper sensitive, inbred Roderick Usher is the ultimate Poe anti-hero, full of chest thumping melodrama and quasi-philosophical speeches of dread, evil and death – a typical Poe/Price characterisation. There is always a woman involved too, in this case his sister (Myrna Fahey), a sickly girl whose relationship with her twin brother has incestuous overtones. Eventually she is buried alive only to come back and claim revenge in a spectacular climax. *House of Usher* sealed Price's fate once and for all; he was now America's king of horror.

House of Usher grossed over $2 million at the American box office, and its run turned out to be longer than previous AIP features. It did even better in Europe. 'We were a little surprised that the film was so successful,' said Corman. 'We had a sneak preview and the audience loved it. We anticipated that the movie would do well, but not half as well as it did.'

Matheson agrees. 'The funny thing was that, after the movie was completed, no one at AIP knew what to do with it. They were running it on a double bill with *Psycho* (1960). It made so much money that they couldn't believe their wallets!'

House of Usher had been seen as a one-off, but its success prompted the series of big screen Poe adaptations. After years of low budget schlock, AIP had gone partly legitimate. With a name actor under a personal contract, the time was right to revive the American gothic chiller.

Price's next film was a rip-roaring and moralistic adventure. Based on Jules Verne's novel of the same name, *Master of the World* (1961) is basically an aerial version of *20,000 Leagues Under the Sea* with Price playing the Nemo inspired inventor Robur the Conqueror. With his airship *The Albatross*, Robur and his crew travel from country to country threatening to destroy all weapons of mass destruction unless the world can bring about peace. The production consisted mainly of cheap sets padded out with stock footage from earlier films so the high aspirations were let down by the low budget, leaving Price, and the decent supporting cast of Charles Bronson, Henry Hull and David Frankham, to take on the dramatic weight. Some scenes do work and Price's performance adds a certain vigour to the proceedings.

'I loved *Master of the World*,' he said, 'because I thought it had marvellous moralising philosophy: a man who sees evil and says "Destroy it!" It's a great Jules Verne concept.'

Price worked once more with Charles Bronson, and Richard Matheson (who wrote the screenplay) recalled how unsociable the moody actor was towards Price, nor was he happy with his performance as the nominal hero. '(Bronson) was miscast, and he knew it. He was very unhappy. Testy is more the word. Vincent Price, who could make friends with a dead man, and very often has in the movies, said, "I can't get through to this guy. I cannot make friends with him." I guess Bronson's always been that way.'

Price returned to Poe with *The Pit and the Pendulum* (1961). Budgeted at $200,000, it is the weakest of the series but grossing over $2 million was enough to keep everyone happy. It's a reworking of *House of Usher* with different sets, again brilliantly designed by Daniel Haller. The script was provided by Richard Matheson, who had less to work with this time around. 'I think *Usher* turned out to be the best of the ones I wrote. It was the only one that was pure Poe. The rest of them had less Poe to build on. *The Pit and the Pendulum* had one little scene from Poe from which I had to make up the whole story.'

Playing another tormented soul, Price is Don Nicholas Medina, a Spanish nobleman whose father Sebastian (played by Price in flashback) was one of the instigators of the Spanish Inquisition. Living in seclusion with his sister at his castle, he mourns the death of his English wife Elizabeth (Italian cinema's first lady of horror Barbara Steele). As it turns out Elizabeth is alive and plotting with her lover to despatch Nicholas by driving him mad. Of course the tables are turned and Nicholas ends up giving them both a taste of their own medicine, while putting Elizabeth's brother on the rack to face the pendulum of the title.

Although beautifully shot with the pendulum climax being the high point (despite being a rubber blade, actor John Kerr looked absolutely terrified as the pendulum swung towards him), the film fails to do justice to an excellent production. Price is hammy, Kerr's nominal hero is wooden, but the biggest crime of all is an underused Barbara Steele having her voice redubbed, as was the case in most of her Italian films. Corman felt her thick working class accent, 'didn't blend in with the other actors.' If that was the case, why redub her voice with a truly atrocious American accent? One only has to hear her speak in *Curse of the Crimson Altar* (1969) and *Caged Heat* (1976) to know there's nothing wrong with her voice.

'I was very shy during that period,' said Steele. 'I was extremely frightened when I did that film because I was struck by the idea of working in the States. I was frozen in my own particular panic at the time; I was myopic and wasn't sure what was going on around me.' An actor like Price would have put her at ease straight away. It didn't lead to further film roles in Hollywood, so it was back to Italy where she consolidated her position as Queen of Euro Gothic.

Actor and co-star Antony Carbone enjoyed working with Price. 'Vincent had a gift. He was always thinking two or three things at the same time, and that keeps you guessing. He was also one of the most professional people I ever worked with. He knew his lines better than anyone else. Wonderful, just wonderful.'

Price was paid $125,000 on *The Pit and the Pendulum* plus a percentage, so the film's success enabled him to take a lengthy vacation with Mary. With his three-picture AIP deal coming to an end, the couple returned to England in April 1961, and then toured Greece and Egypt. His son Barrett had graduated from high school and offered to house sit while they were away. Also at home was Price's brother, Mortimer, who had been diagnosed with terminal cancer. It was a wonderful opportunity for uncle and nephew to spend time together.

The extended vacation also offered a six month sojourn and some lucrative film work in Italy, courtesy of AIP, who continued Stateside distribution of those low budget musclemen epics starring Steve Reeves or Gordon Scott. With AIP paying expenses, Price, knowing the films were hardly Oscar winners, saw it as a golden opportunity to spend time in Rome, which was at the height of sixties glamour. It also enabled him to pursue his other hobby – buying art.

The first of his two Italian films was *Rage of the Buccaneer* (1963) opposite old friend Ricardo Montalban, who was also doing the film for money. 'Terrible picture!' exclaimed Montalban with good humour. 'Those are the times when work was a little scarce here (USA), and Italy offered all those spaghetti westerns and this kind of adventure story. They were terrible, but I guess they served a purpose; they paid us reasonably well.'

'I made some dreadful pictures in Italy,' said Price. 'They were terrible. But I had the best time, and I bought so much good art. Oh, I had a wonderful time.' Location work in the unspoiled seaside town of Porto added to the good times, and Price's performance as slave trader Romero is played with typically sinister relish.

Rage of the Buccaneer remains one of Price's most obscure films, as was his second costume picture *Queen of the Nile* (1964), which took three years to make and featured fading Hollywood stars Jeannie Crain and Edmund Purdom. It was a far cry from his previous biblical epics but at least he added class to the proceedings.

The downmarket trend continued on his return to the States with a cameo appearance in the real life drama *Convicts 4* (1963). It gave him a rare opportunity to play an art expert, but despite the star cast, the film died at the box office. Worse still was *Confessions of an Opium Eater* (1962), described by critic Leslie Halliwell as 'bad enough to be funny – but not very.' Based on Thomas de Quincey's 1822 novel, Price plays Gilbert de Quincey, an opium-addicted gunrunner turned government agent working undercover in San Francisco's Chinatown where he's out to destroy the local slave trade. This is a terrible film, and for the first time in his career, Price is out of his depth.

While Price enjoyed his paid vacations, Roger Corman had grown tired of the financial arrangements with AIP. The success of his previous films was an effective bargaining tool for a better deal with Arkoff, but when negotiations stalled, he received an offer from Pathe Film Laboratories, who were going into film production, to direct *The Premature Burial* (1962). Since the Poe stories were in public domain and Corman's loyal team of technicians would follow him, he agreed to the offer on condition that Pathe distributed his personally financed pet project *The Intruder* (1962), an intelligent and controversial film about racism, starring William Shatner.

Vincent Price however, was unavailable. His AIP contract was non-exclusive, but Arkoff, with typical foresight, deliberately gave him the Italian films to prevent him from taking part in *The Premature Burial*, forcing Corman to hire horror stalwart Ray Milland. On the first day of shooting Arkoff and Nicholson paid an unexpected visit to the set and promptly informed Corman that they were partners once more. Arkoff had contacted Pathe to remind them that AIP were still their lab customers and that they would consider going elsewhere if the company distributed *The Premature Burial*. Pathe then sold their interest in the film to AIP.

Arkoff and Nicholson went into further negotiations with Corman that lasted two months, but at the end of the day, AIP still honoured the terms of the director's Pathe deal. Although *The Premature Burial* was a moderate box office success, *The Intruder* died a death, making it the only film Corman lost money on.

The Premature Burial suffers from a poor script by Charles Beaumont and Ray Russell and the miscasting of Ray Milland. If the series was to continue it was clear that Corman needed Price.

Price's return to AIP was more than welcome. *Tales of Terror* (1962) is a portmanteau of three Poe stories adapted from four (the middle story combined *The Black Cat* with the *Cask of Amontillado*). By this time both Corman and Richard Matheson had grown tired of the format. After the controversy of *The Premature Burial*, Corman's creative energy started sagging. Matheson was equally fed up with repeating elements from his previous films. To give the formula a fresher approach, both men decided to add comedy to the second tale.

Tales of Terror focuses on Poe's obsession with death. The first tale, *Morella*, is a shorter reworking of *The Fall of the House of Usher*. Price's performance as the alcoholic Locke is Roderick Usher all over again as he yearns for his late wife Morella (Leona Gage), whose corpse remains in the master bedroom. When his dying daughter Lenora (Maggie Pierce) visits the decrepit family home, the spirit of Morella takes possession of her. Morella then kills Locke in the obligatory fire scene (stock footage from *House of Usher*).

Morella is the weakest of the tales. Price is unable to breathe much life into his role while Corman fails to add any enthusiasm to the proceedings. Clearly this segment needed a quick shot in the arm.

The Black Cat is much more fun thanks to Peter Lorre's remarkable performance as alcoholic Montressor Herringbone. Lorre's layabout souse is also a nasty piece of work, especially with his brutal treatment of his long suffering wife Annabel (Joyce Jameson). Stealing her sewing money to blow on booze, he stumbles into a wine merchants' convention where he challenges mincing wine connoisseur Fortunato Lucresi (Price) to a wine tasting duel.

Taking the inebriated Montressor home, Fortunato begins an affair with Annabel, using Montressor's drink problem to their advantage. When Montressor finds out, he kills them both and walls them up in the cellar. But in doing so, he walls up his wife's hated black cat, whose meowing attracts the attention of the police and brings about Montressor's pickled downfall.

The Black Cat is a delightful piece of comic macabre played to perfection by Price and Lorre, in the first of their trio of horror spoofs. Moving away from the tormented souls of his previous films, Price gives a broad comic performance. 'Comedy and terror are very closely allied. We tried to make audiences enjoy themselves, even as they are being scared. My job as an actor was to try to make the unbelievable, believable and the despicable delectable.'

Price also enjoyed working with Lorre; their natural chemistry made them a perfectly dark double act. 'Peter loved to make jokes and adlibs during the filming,' he recalled. 'He didn't always know the lines, but he had a basic idea what they were. He loved to invent; improvisation was part of his training in Germany.' Price may have got top billing in *The Black Cat* but it is Lorre's show all the way. He gives a splendid comic turn that revived his horror career.

The tale's highlight is the memorable wine tasting duel between Montressor and Fortunato. Even in his inebriated state, Montressor matches his challenger by correctly guessing each vintage wine he tries out. With the help of Harry Waugh of John Harvey and Sons, Price uses the correct technique for wine tasting and exaggerates it to comic effect while Lorre consumes bottle after bottle without missing a drunken beat. It's a brilliantly timed sequence with both actors in fine form. 'That scene of wine tasting was really something that has remained in people's minds,' said Price. 'Peter and I play two drunks but before we did it they brought in this very famous wine taster to show how it was done. We enjoyed that enormously; we got very drunk in the afternoons! Roger really allowed us to comedy it up on that scene. I did it exactly the way the wine taster showed us, but added just a little bit more, and Peter was doing it the way they didn't do it, which made for a very funny scene.'

The third tale, *The Facts in the Case of M Valdemar*, reverts back to the serious tone of the first story, and features an excellent performance from Basil Rathbone as Carmichael, a reptilian mesmerist who hypnotises the dying Valdemar (Price) at the point of death. This 'momentous experiment' has less to do with pushing the boundaries of science and more to do with Carmichael getting his hands on the poor man's wife (Debra Paget). Eventually Valdemar awakes from his slumber and attacks Carmichael while melting in the process!

Ever since Rathbone's Richard III drowned Price's Duke of Clarence in a vat of wine, they remained firm friends, but by the time *Tales of Terror* was made, Rathbone had become extremely bitter about the decline of his own career. Ever the professional, he remains a commanding presence, and like Lorre in *The Black Cat*, he walks off with the acting honours.

Shot in 16 days during November 1961, *Tales of Terror* took $1.5 million on its initial release – lower than the earlier films but still decent enough to keep the series going.

Tales of Terror gave Lorre and Rathbone one last burst of horror stardom; Boris Karloff would later join the creepy ensemble. 'Even in their final years,' said writer Bruce Lanier Wright, 'these consummate pros possessed a style and effortless grace not often seen on screen today.'

Reviews for *Tales of Terror* were mixed, but the critics were unanimous in their enjoyment of *The Black Cat* story. That provided Corman and Matheson with the decision to make the next Poe film a full blown comedy.

In the meantime, Corman secured Price's services for another chiller, independent of AIP.

Taking a well-earned break from Poe, and pondering over his career options, Corman received an interesting offer from Edward Small of Admiral Pictures to direct *Tower of London* (1962), a remake of Price's 1939 film with the actor getting promoted to Richard III. Corman's initial enthusiasm quickly gave way to disillusionment. 'I found myself working on a movie with a script that was weak to say the least.'

When production began in February 1962, Corman originally thought *Tower of London*, originally called *A Dream of Kings*, would be shot in colour and on a large budget. 'That damn *Tower!*' he exclaimed, 'I had a feel for it. I'd have liked to have had Basil Rathbone, but Rathbone wasn't to be had you know.'

Instead Corman was lumbered with a $200,000 budget that included black and white film stock. 'To my great surprise, I found that I was supposed to shoot the picture in black and white. Somehow nobody bothered to tell me that! I was just flabbergasted. I shot the movie, but I think it suffered from the lack of colour. The film didn't have the impact it could have had.'

Budget restrictions also meant he had to insert stock footage of battle scenes as well as use the Spanish sets from *The Pit and the Pendulum*, which gives the film a claustrophobic look. The poor supporting cast, with the exception of old hands Michael Pate and Morris Ankrum, all have intrusive American accents, and the script owed even less to the original film, let alone Shakespeare.

And there's Price as King Richard, acting more like a pantomime villain than a Shakespearean one, and giving a hammy performance; an aging Rathbone would have been more interesting. 'Every trick of dastardly I ever learned, was preparation for my role in *Tower of London*.' Sadly, he overdoes the leers and while he dominates every scene (almost entirely from inside the tower) it's a case of less is more. With the addition of some lurid moments and a few ghostly visions, *Tower of London* is not without interest, but it's a misstep for all concerned.

On 27 April 1962 Price became a father, one month short of his 51st birthday, with the arrival of Victoria. 'It was completely unplanned and unexpected – though, paradoxically, very much wanted.' Price also became a grandfather later that year with the birth of Barrett's son Jody.

Shortly after Victoria's birth, department store Sears Roebuck approached Price with a lucrative offer to appoint him art buyer for the company. Despite Mary's initial objection, his connection with Sears helped him establish *The Vincent Price Collection*. 'For 25 years I had been carrying on the battle to bring art to people in their daily living.' That dream became a realisation with his new contract.

Price carefully developed a programme that enabled him to travel for the company and buy art work that would be on sale at the various department stores across America. Armed with a blank chequebook, his film commitments abroad meant he could buy up pretty much anything for Sears. 'It's like being a second hand millionaire; spending other people's money.'

'I have a kind of self-appointed mission to try and interest the public in American art,' he added. 'We're bringing fine art to the people. What matters in art is the beauty, not the money.' The contract had its drawbacks in the fact that Sears, being a business, used Price's name as a merchandising tool. The actor saw things differently, and did his best to maintain a certain amount of influence with regards to quality control. 'I made certain provisions. If I bought from contemporary artists, living artists, I paid them on the spot. Well, that nearly killed Sears. But they gave me a chequebook, which they had never done in the history of Sears.'

The Vincent Price Collection began with 2,700 art works. For the next five years Price bought over 50,000 oil paintings, etchings and canvases for Sears. With a new mouth to feed, the financial benefits were more than welcome.

Price's next film was a step up from *Tower of London*. Produced by Admiral Pictures, *Diary of a Madman* (1962) is an adaptation of two Guy de Maupassant stories: *The Horla* and *Diary of a Madman*. Price plays Simon Cordier, a 19th Century French magistrate driven to kill by a malevolent entity known as the Horla. After hamming it up in *Tower of London*, Price this time opted for a more low key approach.

Directed by Reginald Le Borg, a talented filmmaker reduced to a journeyman career in B movies, production began in June 1962. Both actor and director enjoyed a happy working relationship. 'I found (Price) to be entirely professional and very, very nice,' said Le Borg. 'I enjoyed working with him very much.'

Co-star Nancy Kovack also enjoyed working with Price 'He was very respectful, and I found that unusual. I knew that I wasn't known, and yet he was very respectful, of me and kindly. He didn't have to be. He was professional, and I appreciated that.'

With a dialogue heavy script and a weak supporting cast, it was left to Price to carry the film, and while he does a professional job, it hardly ranks as one of his best performances.

So it was a return once more to Corman and AIP for *The Raven* (1963), which commenced production in September 1962. The screenplay has little to do with Poe's famous poem other than featuring a talking raven (whose vocabulary extends beyond 'Nevermore') and the lost Lenore (played by Hammer veteran Hazel Court). What audiences got was an inspired horror spoof combining the talents of Price, Peter Lorre and Boris Karloff.

'I don't think the picture was really meant to be a comedy,' said Hazel Court. 'It evolved into one on the set. Roger Corman just let the whole thing roll.' '(It was) tongue in cheek from the very beginning,' said Matheson. 'The AIP executives had found out that the middle portion of *Tales of Terror*, which had been done for laughs, was very successful so they decided to do a whole funny picture. I couldn't have done another serious one. It would have been more than I could stand. I had to do them for laughs by then.'

AIP saw the potential of a horror spoof starring the Price/Lorre double act, and Price was equally overjoyed with the news that old friend Boris Karloff was taking part. 'When Boris, Peter and I heard we were going to be in *The Raven* together we were really very excited, and we called each other up and Boris said to me, "Have you read the poem lately?" and I said, "Yes," and he said, "What's the plot?" Of course there is no plot!'

Also involved is a young Jack Nicholson, but judging by his charisma-free performance, one wonders how he managed to become a Hollywood legend. It certainly adds to the film's camp value. Conceived as a comedy, nobody was quite prepared for the end result. 'The picture didn't turn out the way it was meant to turn out at all,' said Arkoff. '*The Raven* was a bastard in its own way, although a successful bastard. I remember going to see the rushes and I thought to myself, "What the devil are we breeding?" But you see, Vincent and Peter did have a sense of humour. Boris Karloff was a typical English well-behaved gentleman. And he just went along reluctantly.'

Set in the Middle Ages, *The Raven* is more fantasy than horror. Dr Craven (Price) is a reclusive sorcerer yearning for his missing wife Lenore. Turning up out the blue is the raven of the story, who is in reality fellow sorcerer Dr Bedlo (Lorre). It transpires that another sorcerer Dr Scarabus (Karloff) not only turned Bedlo into the bird, he also has Lenore as his mistress. When Bedlo is turned back to his old self, the two men journey to Scarabus' castle home.

Forget the plot because there really isn't one! It only serves the purpose of having three horror greats playing off each other with magnificent aplomb, culminating in an impressive magical duel between Scarabus and Craven. It also makes a refreshing change to see Price not ending up dead!

There is an amazing chemistry between the legends, even if their approach to acting often caused difficulty, especially with Karloff, whose classical training went against Lorre's improvisational skills. It was up to Price to provide the all-important link to the contrasting styles. 'Boris frankly didn't like Peter's way of doing things,' said Corman. 'It threw him off his memorised line readings. Vincent was the one who could work both ways. He understood Boris, he understood Peter, and I think that helped bring unity to the film.'

Hazel Court had great fun with her amazing co-stars. 'Here you have three very good minds. Peter was absolutely fascinating, although he was very sick at the time. He was always pinching my behind! Boris had a bad hip. He was a very gentle man. Vinnie was the healthy one although he frequently groaned, "Ohhh, my knees!" He always had a dirty story.'

With a budget of $350,000, *The Raven* was the most expensive of Corman's Poe series. Most of the budget was spent on the cast, giving the production a rather cheap look despite Daniel Haller's good work on the castle interiors of Scarabus' home. The entire film is set inside the castle and apart from the climax there's very little action. Had it not been for the presence of the horror trio, even Matheson's funny script could not save the film from being a bore to those who didn't get the joke.

The Raven took a healthy $1.4 million at the box office so the demand for Poe remained as strong as ever. The film wrapped two days ahead of schedule and with Price departing for a lecture tour, Corman utilised the extra two days by directing *The Terror* (1963), using the same sets and keeping Boris Karloff and Jack Nicholson on the payroll.

Price returned to more serious horror work with *Twice Told Tales* (1963), his third film for Admiral Pictures and another portmanteau consisting of three tales based on the work of Nathaniel Hawthorne. Directed by Sidney Salkow, the film went into production in December 1962 under the title *The Corpse Makers* with Price starring in all three stories.

The first is *Dr Heidegger's Experiment* which features Price as Alex Medbourne, the alcoholic best friend of Dr Carl Heidegger (Sebastian Cabot). The elderly doctor has kept the body of his dead wife Sylvia (Mari Blanchard) in the family crypt (she died suddenly 38 years earlier). Heidegger has discovered an elixir of youth that not only revives his wife, it brings all three back to their youthful selves. It is only then that a dark secret is discovered for Alex also loved Sylvia and poisoned her on their wedding night. Things erupt and Alex ends up killing his friend. The elixir wears off, Sylva crumbles into dust and Alex is an old man once more, and alone – all because of an old grudge.

In *Rappaccini's Daughter*, Price is an obsessive alchemist who has chemically modified his daughter (Joyce Taylor) in order to protect her from the outside world, meaning everything she touches turns purple and dies. When she falls in love with a handsome young man (Brett Halsey), and later infects him with a kiss, she takes her own life, leaving her father alone.

The third tale is a remake of Price's earlier film *The House of Seven Gables*. In this abridged version, the actor plays debt-ridden Gerald Pyncheon, who returns to his ancestral home to seek out a hidden treasure only to stumble on an age old curse that leads to his downfall.

Although not without interest, *Twice Told Tales* did not work as well as *Tales of Terror* and further Hawthorne adaptations fell by the wayside. The presence of Sebastian Cabot, Abraham Sofaer and Beverly Garland made up a stronger than usual cast, but at the end of the day it was Price who was left to carry the weight of the screenplay.

In January 1963, Price returned to Italy to star in an adaptation of Richard Matheson's outstanding novel *I Am Legend*.

Getting *I Am Legend* to the big screen was an unsatisfactory baptism of fire for Matheson. Published in 1954, the novel centres on Robert Neville, the sole survivor of a plague that has turned everyone into vampires. Spending his days hunting them down, he locks himself up in his house at night as they roam outside. It is a perfect Matheson concept of the lone individual coping with the terrifying events around him as his descent to near paranoia is replaced by the quiet dignity of his fate.

I Am Legend cries out for cinematic treatment and who better than Matheson to write the screenplay. It was Hammer who first approached the writer with an offer to adapt it to the big screen. Arriving in England in a wave of publicity, he completed the script within two months under the title *Night Creatures*. Val Guest was scheduled to direct with Peter Cushing, Stanley Baker, Kieran Moore, Paul Massie, Ian Hendry and Laurence Harvey being serious contenders for the role of Neville.

'I wrote the screenplay for Hammer Films but they told me that the English censor wouldn't pass it,' lamented Matheson. John Nicholls, secretary of the British Board of Film Censors, objected to the bad language and profanity in the script (which is extremely mild by today's standards), a feeling that was shared by Geoffrey Shurlock of the Motion Picture Association of America, who wrote to Hammer, refusing the film the Code Seal of Approval.

Hammer sold the script (at a reduced price) to their associate Robert Lippert, an independent producer linked to 20th Century Fox's subsidiary company Associated Producers. Lippert arranged a co-production deal with Italy's Produzioni La Regina. Ugaldo Ragona took up the directorial duties with Sidney Salkow overseeing the American version (to avoid costly dubbing, much of the film is narrated by Price). It finally came to the cinema as *L'ultimo Uomo della Terra* or *The Last Man on Earth* (1964).

'I did the script again,' recalled a frustrated Matheson, 'and made it even better because I was told Fritz Lang was going to direct, but it turned out otherwise.' The writer was far from happy with the end result. 'I thought it was terrible. That's about the only way you can describe it. I had written a good screenplay but they had someone re-write it and made it abysmal.' The script had been re-written by Bill Leicester with Matheson receiving a credit under the name Logan Swanson. He was equally unhappy with Price's performance as Neville (renamed Morgan). 'Price, who I like as an actor, was completely wrong for the part.'

71

Although the bleak landscapes shot around Rome retain the novel's downbeat atmosphere, the production looks shoddy with a miscast Price giving too low key a performance to be effective. The *Monthly Film Bulletin* summed the film up: 'Both the opening, with some extremely effective Antonioni-ish shots of deserted streets and buildings are strikingly bold. But despite Richard Matheson's intriguing story, the production languishes sadly into crude effects, erratic editing and silly dialogue. Vincent Price goes through the motions of a flamboyant performance, but he's not really on top of his game.'

Robert Neville in the book is an ordinary Joe, and Price is far too baroque to be convincing as an everyman character. Critic Jonathan Rigby hit the nail on the head when he felt the part needed to be played by, 'somebody more meat and potatoes (and) a bit less *pate de foie gras.*'

With a great deal of art supplied by the Rome galleries and the coffers, courtesy of Sears, to buy it, Price the actor played second fiddle to Price the art collector. That, and the fact it was a paid vacation, contributed to his lacklustre performance.

Unlike Matheson, Price liked the film, despite the location difficulties. 'I thought it wasn't too bad, (but) the problem was that it was supposed to be set in Los Angeles, and if there was a city in the world that does not look like Los Angeles, it's Rome! We had to get up at 5 o'clock in the morning to beat the police, and try to find something that didn't look like Rome. We had a terrible time! And I was never so cold in my life as I was in that picture! I had a driver, and I used to tip him a big sum to keep the car running so I could change my clothes in the back seat.'

Returning to the States in March 1963, Price made a guest appearance in *Beach Party* (1963), one of AIP's groovy beach movies that showcased the clean cut good looks Frankie Avalon and Annette Funicello. Lots of beautiful teenagers, cool music, surfing, hip dialogue and Robert Cummings as the token 'square' adult, all naïve, dated fun. Price makes the most of his uncredited turn as beach guru Big Daddy. Dressed in a white suit, striped T-shirt and sporting a beard, he spends the entire film slouching barefoot in a large chair, his face covered by a wide-rim straw hat while his followers sit around and wait in anticipation for him to say 'The Word!'

'The Word' finally occurs at the end of the film when he awakes from his sleep (coma might be more apt), lifts his head and utters, 'The Pit! Bring me my pendulum, kiddies, I feel like swingin'!' before returning to his catatonic slumber.

In April 1963, Price received a new contract from Arkoff that would tie him to AIP. The new contract had an exclusivity clause: in addition to regular salary increases and a succession of major projects, Price could not make horror movies for other studios. He could still star in other films but horror was definitely out!

Looking at Price's output between 1960 and 1963, his best work remained with AIP, and while his other movies did well, they lacked the Corman touch. Aware of the financial responsibilities that came with a new daughter, Price signed up without hesitation. He was now Arkoff's public property.

Before Price had a chance to breath, Arkoff lined him up to star in *The Haunted Palace* (1963). Once again he was working with Corman, who was unhappy with AIP's financial arrangements. Corman had decided to film the novella *The Case of Charles Dexter Ward* by reclusive American writer H P Lovecraft and Arkoff had insisted that the new production be called *The Haunted Palace* after a Poe poem, with Price narrating a verse at the beginning of the film. Corman protested but to no avail.

With Richard Matheson out of the picture, the script duties were taken up by American science fiction writer Charles Beaumont. Chicago-born Beaumont had an unusual and unhappy childhood, dogged by poor health and ridicule over his original surname, Nutt. After a variety of jobs, he broke into professional writing in 1950. His science fiction output consisted of grim futuristic worlds: *The Crooked Man* for example shows a homosexual utopia.

Beaumont later contributed to the popular TV anthologies *Alfred Hitchcock Presents* and *The Twilight Zone*, and had worked with Corman on *The Premature Burial* and *The Intruder* (which he adapted from his own novel). By the time he provided the script for *The Haunted Palace*, his TV commitments had become so extensive that he hired ghost writers on several shows for half his fee.

Price assumes the dual roles of wizard Joseph Curwen, whose burning at the stake by the residents of Arkham leads to a curse on the town, and great-great grandson Charles Dexter Ward, who arrives in Arkham with his wife Ann (Debra Paget) to claim his ancestral castle. Also on hand is the castle's 150 year-old butler Simon Orne, played with despatch by Lon Chaney Junior.

Price delivers an agreeable two-sided performance. After the general indifference of his previous outings, working once more with Corman gave him added enthusiasm. There was always genuine chemistry between them; they appreciated each other as professionals and gave each other exactly what they wanted.

Shortly after completing *The Haunted Palace*, Price took a welcome break from film work to develop *The Vincent Price Collection* for Sears Roebuck as well as to sit for the White House Art Committee. By September 1963, he was ready for some more fun and games, and this marked the peak of his American horror career.

Returning to AIP and taking up the position of associate producer, Richard Matheson's next script followed on from *The Raven*. *The Comedy of Terrors* (1963) was the third horror spoof to star Price and Lorre, and by this time they had honed their remarkable double act to macabre perfection. 'Their comic instincts formed an easy compliment,' noted Matheson.

In addition to Price and Lorre at their comical best, Boris Karloff and Basil Rathbone were added to the cast and the film featured the famous tag-line: 'Your Favourite Creeps Together Again.'

The plot revolves around crooked, alcoholic undertaker Waldo Trumbull (Price), who, in the face of bankruptcy and eviction, decides to drum up some illegal business by speeding up the demise of certain people, with the help of put upon assistant Felix Gillie (Lorre). Also on hand is Waldo's equally put upon wife Amerylis (Joyce Jameson), who harbours feelings for the ineffectual Felix, her decrepit father Amos Hinchley (Karloff), and wealthy Shakespeare-spouting landlord John F Black (Rathbone), who happens to be their first victim, but refuses to stay dead, turning up at various inopportune moments. Karloff was going to play the landlord but the physical requirements prompted him to swap roles with Rathbone, who, despite being in his seventies, did his own stunts with the skill of a much younger man.

'Working on *The Comedy of Terrors* was a lot of fun,' said Matheson. '(Price, Lorre, Karloff and Rathbone) were all very charming, marvellous people, and it was really a delightful experience just talking with them on the set. They loved doing the film.' Price also enjoyed working with his co-stars. 'They were divine people, with great senses of humour. We had a wonderful time.'

'The premise for *The Comedy of Terrors* was really very funny,' he added. 'It shows how simple comedy is. It's about a family of out-of-work undertakers. Now what do you do? You kill somebody! So you kill the richest man in town – who is played by Basil – and you have the most expensive funeral. That's all the plot was.'

Despite spirited performances, especially from Lorre, and some inspired comic moments, *The Comedy of Terrors* doesn't quite come off with Matheson's script being far from consistently funny. The main fault is the subtle approach taken by director Jacques Tournier, whom Matheson persuaded AIP to hire instead of Roger Corman. 'I think he's a marvellous director, but with a two-week shooting schedule you can't spend too much time on anything. That's all the time AIP ever spent on any of those pictures. That's how they made their money.'

Matheson's choice of director was ill advised. Unlike Corman, who let his actors do their thing, Tournier's perfectionism was constantly at odds with the broad script and broader performances, especially from Lorre. As with *The Raven*, there was a stark contrast in acting styles between the four stars: Karloff and Rathbone – traditionalists who stuck to the script; Lorre – the improviser; and jack-of-all-trades Price, who worked both ways and provided the all-important link between the two styles.

'*The Comedy of Terrors* was a transition film,' said Tournier. 'It was a parody on Shakespeare, a comedy on horror films, which was not I believe, understood very well.' Sadly, the film bombed at the box office. Released on Christmas Day 1963, a month after the assassination of President John F Kennedy, many Americans were in no mood to laugh at death. The fact that Rathbone's character is called John F Black only added to the audience's indifference.

The Comedy of Terrors is a valuable record for its once-in-a-lifetime cast. Despite the film's failure, AIP were keen to reunite Price and Lorre for an adaptation of Poe's *The Gold Bug* as well as to film another Richard Matheson script that would bring Price, Lorre, Karloff and Rathbone together again.

Sadly all these proposed projects were shelved indefinitely following the death of Peter Lorre on 23 March 1964. 'I was doing *The Red Skelton Show*,' said Price upon hearing the news from his agent Lester Salkow (who also represented

Lorre). 'I wrote the eulogy and I went to Red and said, "Red, you know Peter died yesterday morning. Would you mind if I took an extra hour for lunch, because I'm going to his funeral to read his eulogy." So Red said, "Peter's dead? We'll all go!" So the entire company went to Peter's funeral, which was marvellous.'

Lorre's death marked the end of an era. Price never worked with Karloff or Rathbone again. Rathbone passed away in July 1967 with Karloff dying in January 1969.

Looking at cost cutting and general economics, Sam Arkoff decided that AIP should establish a new base outside of Hollywood. He had filmed in Italy where it was cheaper, but the place he had in mind was England where there was a similar studio system in place. Arkoff could also gain access to high quality British actors and technicians, and with the Poe films doing well in the UK, he decided that the next one should be shot in London.

For Roger Corman, this meant he could take his films in a new direction. For Vincent Price, it was the start of something wonderful.

The Masque of the Red Death

'Horror movies don't date because they were dated to begin with, they were mannered, and consciously so – Gothic tales with an unreality. They have the fun of a fairy tale.' – Vincent Price

Apart from the occasional vacation, Vincent Price hadn't worked in England since his 1936 stage debut at the Gate Theatre. The time was right to return to his beloved Blighty.

Price's theatre background and unique voice made him ideal for British films,

and his status as a horror icon was well known in the UK. 'He welcomed the opportunity to re-establish his professional reputation in England,' said Victoria Price, his daughter. 'In turn the British seemed to appreciate his work, both on screen and off.' When Price arrived in London in November 1963 to start work on his latest Poe film, he was met with a great deal of press attention.

For Roger Corman, the trip to England brought renewed enthusiasm for the Poe series. With access to British actors and technicians, and a five week shooting schedule (instead of his usual three), he could now do something bigger and better. 'English crews work much slower than American ones,' he said. 'So, five weeks in England is the equivalent of four in the United States.'

And there were the financial advantages, something Sam Arkoff was fully aware of. Following the devaluation of the Pound, Harold Wilson's Labour government established facilities for overseas filmmakers to shoot their productions in the UK. By arranging a co-production deal with Anglo-Amalgamated (who distributed the Poe films in Britain), AIP qualified for the Eady Levy: a tax incentive introduced to support the British Film Industry. With a larger than usual budget at his disposal, Corman was able to invest more care into the next project: *The Masque of the Red Death*.

Price also took advantage of the financial rewards of working in England by claiming higher expenses. Having signed his new AIP contract, he wasn't about to be fobbed off with excuses. 'Vincent wanted more money,' said Arkoff. 'We finally agreed that we would give him $1,000 a week, which was a lot of money in England at the time.'

Along with his Sears contract, the actor was on a roll financially. According to Victoria, 'Vincent took advantage of his increased expense allowance to spend more weekends in galleries and on the Portobello Road hunting for art.'

Corman wanted to film *The Masque of the Red Death* as a follow up to *House of Usher*. However, there had been some legal controversy over the project when independent producer Alex Gordon planned to film the story in 1958 as *Mask of the Red Death*. A script had been written and Price was considered to play Prospero with Mary designing the costumes. Gordon was unable to raise the finance and the project fell through.

In the meantime Corman was working on his own script ideas. Deciding against using Richard Matheson following *House of Usher*, he considered several new drafts (including one from talented but unknown screenwriter Robert Towne), none of which he found satisfactory. Finally a script from Charles Beaumont met with his approval. It was Beaumont who made major changes to the main character. Instead of the vain, pompous prince from Poe's original story, Prospero was now an intelligent, debonair Satanist.

Corman felt there were too many similarities to Ingmar Bergman's excellent morality play *The Seventh Seal* (1957), and out of admiration for Bergman, and worried about possible plagiarism, he shelved the project. 'I kept moving *The Masque of the Red Death* back because of the similarities, but it was really an artificial reason in my mind.'

With the project on hold, Alex Gordon resurfaced once more with his version. Production was planned for the summer of 1962 with, ironically, Ingmar Bergman scheduled to direct if it was set in Europe. Once again the proposed film never materialised.

It wasn't until October 1963 that Arkoff finally gave the project a green light. With the co-production deal set up, and filming due to start at Elstree Studios the following month, Corman resurrected Beaumont's dormant script.

Poe's story, which was inspired by the death of his beloved young wife Virginia, is about four pages long. There is little action and character development but it did boast a better than usual plot. Even so, Beaumont's script needed to be fleshed out to a decent running time. Unfortunately Beaumont was unable to come to England because of his health problems, and so Corman hired Robert Wright Campbell who inserted another Poe tale, *Hop-Frog*, into the script.

This particular story is based on a real event that occurred in 1393 when King Charles VI of France threw a masquerade ball and had five of his lords dressed and chained up as 'wild men'. Sadly a stray spark from an open fire quickly engulfed the costumes, killing four of the lords. The incident became known as the *Bal de Ardents* or *Ball of the Burning Men*!

The Masque of the Red Death marked a new journey for Corman as a filmmaker. 'I had a little bit more time, more time to rehearse, more time to go for more takes, to go for more intricate camera angles and go for a bigger look. We were able to raid the scene dock at the studio, where they had these magnificent sets left over from pictures like *Becket* (1964), and, particularly in *The Masque of the Red Death*, we were able to assemble sets that we would never have the money to build in the United States. We wouldn't have the money to build them in England either.'

Apart from the ever-loyal Daniel Haller, Corman relished the opportunity to work with a brand new crew, enabling the fresher feel he wanted for the series. Art director duties were filled by Robert Jones, whose work complimented Haller's outstanding production design. Replacing Floyd Crosby and Les Baxter, Corman opted for the brilliant cinematographer Nicholas Roeg with David Lee stepping into the breach to compose a music score that effectively incorporated mediaeval themes. The magnificent costumes were provided by Laura Nightingale. Their involvement alone gave *The Masque of the Red Death* a more opulent feel that set it apart from the rest of the Poe sequence of films.

Casting too was different. In addition to Price, Hazel Court, recruited from *The Raven*, provided the only other link to Corman's earlier work. Lower down the cast list were two great stalwarts of British cinema: Nigel Green and Patrick Magee. One of the great interpreters of Samuel Beckett on the London stage (Beckett wrote *Krapps' Last Tapes* especially for him), the Irish-born Magee was a British horror regular who previously starred in the Corman-produced, Francis Ford Coppola-directed *Dementia 13* (1963). His creepy turn as Alfredo impressed the director. '(Magee) could find all these strange little quirks which he would bring out during his performance, making it a richer and more rounded characterization.'

One point of interest was the casting of the small but pivotal role of The Red

Death. Although not confirmed, Basil Rathbone was a serious contender. It would have been perfect casting, but Rathbone, a devout Roman Catholic, would not have been comfortable playing a character too closely linked to Satan. The role finally went to British actor John Westbrook.

A familiar face on British TV, Westbrook was also a successful writer and voice over artist. There was a rumour that the actor was dubbed by Christopher Lee. This is not true. Aurally both actors have similar voices, and what is heard in the film belongs to Westbrook.

'Vincent loved London,' said Hazel Court. 'It was wonderful. I was staying with my sister, and Vincent stayed at the Cadogan Hotel. He loved it: he had a particular room he liked on the corner.' In addition to enjoying his time in London, Price monopolised his expenses under Sam Arkoff's nose. As was his usual routine when filming abroad, Price claimed heavy expenses and then lived a more economical lifestyle while he used the expense money to buy art.

Price made the most of his time in London, and not just with his expense money. With funds allocated to him by Sears Roebuck, he purchased around $30,000 worth of art for the company. 'I've bought works worth nearly three-quarters of a million dollars. I guess no one has been buying on this scale since the Medici.'

'When we moved to England,' recalled Arkoff, 'we argued out with Vincent the stipend he would get for his living expenses. We had illusions that Vinnie was living like an Oriental potentate in some deluxe London penthouse. One day I called him up and asked him if he wanted to look at a new script and give us an opinion. He said, "Drop it off and we'll have a cup of coffee."'

Arkoff was in for a shock regarding Price's living quarters. 'Driving into what seemed to me the worst part of London, and I'm looking around and thinking, Jesus Christ, Vincent's getting all this money a week. We come to seediest block of all, and there's a run-down hotel; I can't believe it. I go inside. There's no elevator in the damn place. No room service, no elaborate suite, just one seedy room with no bathroom. I said, "For God's sake, Vincent, why don't you even have a bathroom?" He said, "Well, you really don't use a bathroom too much." I thought he probably peed out the window or something. Anyway, it turns out he was buying art work with the expense money.'

Hazel Court offered a different explanation regarding Price's lifestyle. 'He stayed at the Cadogan on Sloane Street! I suppose to Arkoff, who always stayed at the Ritz, maybe it was a hovel! It's a nice hotel, turn of the century.'

The Bergman influence in *The Masque of the Red Death* is obvious, despite Corman's efforts to distance the film from *The Seventh Seal*. *Masque* is the complete opposite of *House of Usher* and *The Raven*. The bright colours of Floyd Crosby's camerawork were replaced by Nicholas Roeg's dark and subtle use of visuals that creates a striking sense of foreboding, especially in the opening scene. Beaumont and Campbell's literate script couldn't be far removed from the increasingly tongue-in-cheek efforts of Richard Matheson. Utilizing the sets from *Becket*, Daniel Haller captures the atmosphere of Mediaeval Italy. The great hall, complete with a large cast of costumed extras, evokes a sense of gothic splendour that surpasses anything produced by Hammer.

Another Bergman concept that Corman makes good use of is the subject of religion, especially the separate faiths of Prospero and Francesca (Jane Asher), both of whom are pious but misguided in their beliefs. This is all blown wide open during the masked ball when the Red Death casually kills everyone regardless of what they believe. Death has no master and religion has no truth. This makes *The Masque of the Red Death* an interesting and perceptive chiller that questions religion and the corruption surrounding it.

The *Danse Macabre* climax is the highlight of *Masque*, but a disappointed Corman felt it was the film's greatest flaw. 'I still regret my decision not to pay extra mandated union fees for going over a day at Christmas. I still feel that would have made the large-scale ball sequence – with dozens of extras, plenty of fire and lots of action – a true *tour-de-force* instead of merely a good sequence.' Striving to make the ultimate Poe film without going over budget, Corman is a little hard on himself because this sequence ranks as one of the finest moments in horror film history.

Another famous scene, that caused a great deal of uproar, was Hazel Court's nightmarish vision of being attacked by four demons while lying on a slab, and with her amazing cleavage on show – too strong for the censors of the day. 'From the standpoint of nudity, there was nothing,' said Corman. 'I think (Hazel) was nude under a diaphanous gown. She played the consummation with the Devil, but it was essentially on her face; it was a pure acting exercise. Hazel, fully clothed, all by herself, purely by acting, incurred the wrath of the censor. It was a different age; they probably felt that was showing too much. Today you could show it on 6 o'clock television and no one would worry.'

It's too bad because Hazel Court gives her best screen performance. Her tragic Juliana evokes more sadness than hatred when she realises her time as Prospero's mistress was a mistake to begin with, and with the arrival of Francesca, it was only a matter of time before she becomes surplus to requirements. Perhaps the sight of the younger woman is a reflection of her former self (Prospero definitely has a penchant for red heads). Her demise owes less to marrying Satan and more towards an elaborate suicide in a life filled with decadent emptiness. *The Masque of the Red Death* was also her final film. Pregnant at the time, she retired from acting to become a successful sculptor.

But it was Court's magnificent décolletage (enhanced by her pregnancy) that provided what would be the last word on the film when *Time Magazine* famously commented that 'in whose cleavage you could sink the entire works of Edgar Allan Poe and a bottle of his favourite booze at the same time.'

The supporting cast are equally good with juvenile leads Jane Asher and David Weston being a vast improvement on Mark Damon, Myrna Fahy and Jack Nicholson. And while they lack the obvious presence of Peter Lorre and Boris Karloff, Patrick Magee and Nigel Green offer reliable, and very British support.

Despite not being credited, John Westbrook dominates the film with his few scenes. With the hood of his red robes covering his face, Westbrook's impassive manner and deep voice makes him a chilling interpreter of The Red Death. The casual way he eradicates the populace around the countryside and within the castle walls adds to his menace. When he plays cards with the little girl, he shows surprising warmth, compassion and even humour. The Red Death is a fascinating and ambiguous figure, and Westbrook's chilling performance gives the character a real mystique.

But at the end of the day, *The Masque of the Red Death* belongs to Vincent Price. Prospero could not be far removed from the weak willed, doom laden, tormented souls he played in the earlier Poe films. Prospero is a strong, complex individual in charge of his own destiny. He doesn't suffer fools gladly and punishes or kills those who get in his way.

Prospero also cuts a sympathetic figure despite his obvious cruelty to those around him. His devotion to Satan is more from piety than evil. His constant challenges to Francesca regarding God's so-called love are based on his ancestry, education and intelligence. 'A hundred years ago,' he tells Francesca, 'an ancestor of mine was a Christian monk; he was an Examiner of an early inquisition. He tortured 600 men, women and children in order to save their souls for your God of love.' He is equally disgusted at a world that lives, in his words, in 'pain and despair.'

Prospero's interest in Francesca is ambiguous. The first sight of her pleading for her menfolk's lives, he is taken more by her Christian purity than her physical beauty. 'Can such eyes ever have known sin?' asks Alfredo to which Prospero causally replies, 'They will Alfredo, they will.' Yet the Prince is not sexually attracted to the young maiden. 'I'm not corrupting, I'm instructing,' he says with heartfelt honesty that walks hand in hand with his brutality. He does not seduce Francesca but educates her to his philosophical view of the world and its cruelty.

Francesca's final scene with Prospero is equally ambiguous, and one that says a lot about her. When she kisses him prior to leaving the masked ball, Prospero is surprised and touched by the gesture. Did Francesca finally prick the heavy armour of cynicism surrounding the Prince, or did she surrender her faith to make Prospero her new mentor?

Either way it's too late for both: Prospero succumbs to the Red Death, while Francesca, despite being reunited with her boyfriend Gino (David Weston), faces a brutal world ravaged by a deadly plague. Even if they survive, it's unlikely their relationship will last following her time with the Prince.

Price's acting takes a different route following the soliloquizing of Roderick Usher and the comical antics of Dr Craven. While still cutting an overtly flamboyant figure, the actor abandons the camp approach to give a commanding performance, his most serious to date. Thanks to Prospero, Price once again immersed himself into a character instead of allowing his 'Uncle Vinnie' persona to take over.

Hazel Court always enjoyed working with Price and knew how effective he was in such roles. 'I like Vincent as a heavy. He had a sinister quality which he could portray which was quite marvellous and penetrating. He was a very sexy man; he had an aura about him, a sensuality. The other side was fun, the comedies, but the dramatic qualities that he always brought to the movies should have been put to use in pictures that were not horror films.'

The Masque of the Red Death went on general release on 24 June 1964, but prior to that Alex Gordon filed a lawsuit at the Los Angeles Superior Court against Price, AIP and Anglo-Amalgamated asking for an injunction against the film's release. Gordon felt the film plagiarised the script from his abandoned project. The judge denied the application since the Poe stories were in public domain.

Reviews for *The Masque of the Red Death* were positive with *Cinefantastique* saying, 'Had it been shot in a foreign language and subtitled, it would probably still play at art and revival houses.' *Sight and Sound* also said the film was, 'a refreshingly un-British (or at any rate non- Hammer) British horror movie.'

Although successful across the UK and Europe, the film did indifferent business in the States. Arkoff found it 'too arty farty' for the drive-ins. Corman in retrospect felt Arkoff was correct. 'I think that is a legitimate statement. The fault may have been mine. I was becoming more interested in the Poe films as expressions of the unconscious mind, rather than as pure horror.' Despite Arkoff's commercial sensibilities going against Corman's new found artistic integrity, *The Masque of the Red Death* remains the director's favourite Poe film.

The Tomb of Ligeia

'I sometimes feel that I'm impersonating the dark unconscious of the whole human race. I know it sounds sick, but I love it.' – Vincent Price

On 29 June 1964, a few days after the release of *The Masque of the Red Death*, Roger Corman embarked on his final Poe film. This was AIP's second co-production deal with Anglo-Amalgamated, and once again Price, who had just recorded the narration for the short film *Chagall* (1964), returned to Shepperton

83

Studios on 25 June to start work on the new picture.

Under the working titles *The House at the End of the World* and *The Tomb of the Cat*, *The Tomb of Ligeia* returned to the familiar Poe concept of doom-laden obsession. Corman wanted to approach this tired formula from a completely different angle, and even though *The Masque of the Red Death* wasn't performing as well as expected, access to a longer shooting schedule meant he could pursue his artistic freedom to greater effect.

To provide the script, Corman hired Robert Towne, who had been previously linked to *The Masque of the Red Death*. Towne's script provided a fresh psychological angle to the familiar Poe theme.

The story involved an aristocrat, Verden Fell, who becomes reclusive following the death of his wife, the Lady Ligeia, but her spirit seems to have been reincarnated in a cat. Fell remarries a woman called Rowena, but she soon finds out the truth about Fell's obsession with his dead wife.

On Price's recommendation, Corman decided to shoot the film on location.

'*The Tomb of Ligeia* was vaguely based on an idea that Roger and I had once,' Price recalled. 'I had said I had always wanted to do a picture in a ruin, but actually using the ruin around it, with real furniture in it and the ruin around it, which I thought would be very effective.' Location work took place in the village of Swaffham, situated near Norfolk's Deer Leap Woods. The 900 year old Church of St John was used for Fell and Rowena's wedding, and the abbey ruins situated near Fell's manor house were filmed at Castle Acre Priory in Norfolk.

Apart from Daniel Haller, who created the sets within the confines of the abbey (interiors were shot at Shepperton), Corman brought in more new faces, notably Hammer's regular cinematographer Arthur Grant and his camera operator Morey Grant (no relation). This horror cross-over worked in Corman's favour as the photography on *The Tomb of Ligeia* is the finest of the series with Arthur Grant's vivid but economical use of colour surpassing anything he ever did for Hammer.

Casting posed more of a problem. Towne had written the part of Verden Fell for the much younger Richard Chamberlin, who was setting women's hearts racing as television's Dr Kildare. The new casting appealed to Corman, who felt that a change of star might continue the fresh approach he wanted. Towne had specifically asked Corman not to use Price for the film.

But Price was still AIP's top star, and a Poe movie without him would be unthinkable. Price was also an established name and Chamberlin hadn't yet made the cross-over to big screen stardom. Uncomfortable about his matinee idol image, Chamberlin was itching for more serious acting roles, making it highly unlikely that he would have wanted to star in a horror film. Corman's reply to Towne regarding Price's involvement was, 'Don't worry Bob, I've got Marlene Dietrich's make-up man!'

Despite Price's best efforts, Corman felt the actor's casting, 'changed the orientation of the film quite a bit.' Even with a black wig, the clean shaven, heavily made-up Price looks too old, especially when playing opposite 27 year old Elizabeth Shepherd. But setbacks aside, Price gave an excellent performance, utilising the similar characteristics of Roderick Usher and Nicholas Medina, to create the new and fairly low key Verden Fell. Following on from Prince Prospero, he abandoned the camp acting style by getting his teeth into a well-rounded character.

Price's view of Fell's dark side was not without sympathy. 'He is a man who, had he not married an absolutely monstrous woman who would not leave life, even in death, would have been a perfectly normal man and married the other girl. And of course things like this do happen; there are men who are obsessed with their dead wives.' Dressed in black from head to foot, Verden Fell looked like a photographic negative of Roderick Usher.

Despite his reluctance to cast Price, Corman enjoyed their working relationship, and remained impressed by the actor's versatility and professionalism. 'Vincent required very little from the director. He, as all good actors do, researched, prepared, and studied in general, I would talk with Vincent before each picture so that we are in unity on words that most have become clichés – the motivation, the subtext – so that we would evolve and define the character before the picture started. Once having done that, Vincent came to the set prepared and was wonderful to work with. I didn't really have to go for more than two or three or maybe four takes at the most and Vincent understood that and was able to give that performance from the beginning.'

'I would say that Vincent gave full performances,' Corman added. 'He was not afraid to go all the way with an emotion, but I wouldn't call it hammy. He was very flexible. He could modify lines, improvise to a certain extent; come up with bits of business of his own. He was a great gentleman. He was one of the finest actors I've ever worked with.'

Because of the character's change in age, Corman needed to carefully choose a leading lady who had the maturity to compliment the 53 year old actor. Jane Asher was certainly out the question and Hazel Court had retired. He eventually chose Elizabeth Shepherd, a versatile actress with a string of TV credits to play the dual roles of Ligeia and Rowena.

'Having read the original story, I was quite surprised that they were so completely different,' Shepherd said of her characters. 'I went with it because this Rowena, she's a meaty character to play! Really the character of Rowena was quite made up by Robert Towne. We kept to the script. As film scripts go, it was very tight and very playable.'

Shepherd also enjoyed working with her co-star. 'Aside from having the most eloquent voice on earth, he has enormous personal charm and charisma. I loved working with Vincent Price; he made sure everything seemed easy. He is such a superb actor, and extraordinarily generous. He was very open to working on our scenes together, which certainly put me at ease. But I must say, for all the intensity in the film, off screen he had a wickedly witty sense of humour. He kept us laughing.'

The onscreen chemistry between Price and Shepherd does a great deal in removing the age gap between the actors. More importantly it gives their well-rounded performances a degree of edginess. Possibly the most crucial of Poe's anti-heroines, Shepherd is nothing short of excellent, creating two diverse characters. It was enough to fool writer Bruce Lanier Wright, who admitted in his book *Nightwalkers* that, 'the first time I saw *Ligeia*, I didn't realise the two characters were played by the same woman until the (end) credits.'

In addition to being a beautifully mounted production, *The Tomb of Ligeia* also boasts a strong supporting cast. After his memorable turn as the Red Death, John Westbrook plays Rowena's former suitor Christopher Gough. It's a bigger role but Westbrook is less effective. While he gives a decent performance, he lacks the essential glamour to be a convincing romantic lead. Reliable British stalwarts Derek Francis, Richard Vernon, Oliver Johnstone and Frank Thornton add solid gravitas, but at the end of the day it is Price and Shepherd's film.

The production did have one major problem when it came to the climax were Fell dies in a fire that engulfs his home. Because Corman could not obtain permission to film inside the manor house, he got his crew to set up the big fire sequence at Shepperton Studios, only for it all to go up in smoke for real!

'The scariest thing about the horror films were all those fires blazing,' recalled Price. 'I have been singed many times. While making *The Tomb of Ligeia*, in which the whole set was sprayed with liquid rubber, someone lit a cigarette and the whole thing went up. But then Roger's a fire fiend. He's a firebug.' With the fire going out of control, Price rushed to Shepherd's aide and managed to pull her to safety. 'I didn't even get it on film,' Corman lamented. 'I had the whole set I was ready to burn up! I was envisioning a Great Fire!'

The Tomb of Ligeia opened in London in November 1964 with its American premier taking place the following January in Los Angeles. Price took part in a well-staged publicity stunt where he and fellow guests Elsa Lanchester, former TV horror hostess Vampira (AKA Maila Nurmi) and Bela Lugosi's protégé Carroll Borland were chauffeured in a motorcade down Hollywood Boulevard to Tinsel Town's first Ghoul Premiere at the Pix Theatre.

Like *The Masque of the Red Death*, *The Tomb of Ligeia* received positive reviews. Leslie Halliwell described the film as, 'Complex but rather fascinating horror suspensor which re-jogs familiar elements into something new; the best of the Corman Poes.' *The New York Times* was equally enthralled, 'Mr Corman has made stunning ambient use of his authentic setting, an ancient abbey in Norfolk, England, and the lovely countryside. The picture is not nearly as finished as *The Masque of the Red Death*, but the Corman climate of evil is as unhealthy and contagious as ever.'

Price received excellent notices for his performance with *Variety* saying, 'Price is the very essence of evil, albeit charming when he needs to be, and as the film progresses the dark workings of his mind are stressed.' *The Los Angeles Times* hit the nail on the head when they complimented, 'The fluid camerawork, first rate colour, sumptuous period sets and an impassioned performance from Vincent Price blend perfectly to bring a great gothic tale of terror to life on the screen.'

Roger Corman summed up his own feelings about *The Tomb of Ligeia*. 'One of the best Poe pictures and Vincent's performance in the film is very good. It was simply a matter of age.'

Sadly, the American box office takings did not equal the film's brilliant notices, although it continued to do well in Britain and Europe. Sam Arkoff felt the series had become too artistic for the teenage market that AIP relied on. 'All the Poe films made money,' said Corman. 'But *Tomb of Ligeia* made the least amount. I think it was because the series was just running out of steam and also because it was overly complicated.'

The film still made a decent enough profit to continue the series. The next Corman/Price/Poe production was *The Gold Bug*, a project that was under serious consideration while Peter Lorre was still alive. The script was provided by Charles Beaumont, and keeping in tune with the more off-beat premise of *The Raven*, it was written as a comedy horror.

'It was set in the South,' said Corman. 'Vincent was a plantation owner who had convinced his one slave – to be played by Sammy Davis Junior – that the South had won the Civil War. Basil Rathbone was a visiting English carpetbagger who comes upon this deserted plantation. It was really very funny, but it was becoming outrageously distanced from Poe.'

The horror element did not sit well with Price. 'They wanted to turn (*The Gold Bug*) into a horror film. You can't do that without completely perverting the story, because it's a story of detection.'

In any case, Corman was through with the series. 'After *Ligeia*, AIP wanted me to do another Poe picture, and I said "That's it! It's time to move on."'

The time was right for Corman to quit while he was ahead. 'I was repeating myself, taking ideas, images, themes, and techniques from my own earlier work. I just stopped because I didn't want to do it anymore.' Using real locations for *The Tomb of Ligeia* gave the series a new look, but that was as far as Corman was willing go.

The series continued in one form or another but was never the same without Corman. 'I think the series suffered when Roger left,' said Price. 'We were going to do *The Gold Bug* when he decided that he had had enough. I could understand his reasoning, but his absence was certainly felt. Roger had a feel for the subject matter, a point of view that subsequent directors seem to lack.'

Price's association with Corman marked a creative and commercial achievement for both men, and the actor was quick to pay tribute to his friend and colleague. 'My greatest respect for (Corman) was for his wisdom in choosing the best people in various fields of the art to launch his career. We all worked together on all those Poe films and Roger achieved, through his appreciation and use of all their talents, and, I might add, the talents of the actors, young and old, who believed in him, something very similar to the unity and dedication that once existed under the studio system.'

Corman went on to a varied career as an independent filmmaker whereas Price, tied to a long term contract, faced the second half of the decade knowing he would work, but being unsure about the quality of his assignments. *The Masque of the Red Death* and *The Tomb of Ligeia* began his British horror career, but it would be four years before he starred in another UK based chiller. In the meantime, and with several internal changes within AIP, he had to mark time.

The Intervening Years (1965 – 1968): Part One

'Hollywood's worst fault is typecasting. John Wayne, Cary Grant, everyone who has been a success – we all had the same problem. And they tell me I'm too important to play small character roles. You can't win!' – Vincent Price

Price in *City Under The Sea* (1965)

Corman's departure wasn't the only problem that took place within the offices of AIP. The relationship between Samuel Z Arkoff and James H Nicholson also changed drastically. Nicholson had been having an affair with a young actress named Susan Hart. Once it became public, his wife Sylvia sued for divorce and the settlement included half her husband's shares in the company. This reduced Nicholson's status as equal partner with Arkoff, who then promoted himself to Chairman of the Board. Over the next few years the situation between both men became increasingly volatile.

In the meantime Arkoff searched for new assignments to accommodate his contract star. Thanks to his extensive work in other areas, Price remained his own best publicity machine so Arkoff didn't need to spend much when it came to promoting new movies.

Remaining artistic supervisor, Nicholson announced several upcoming film projects. 'The terror and science fiction pictures will be made in Britain. The light entertainment will be produced in Hollywood.' For Vincent Price, it meant further trips to London.

AIP's third and final co-production with Anglo-Amalgamated was *City Under the Sea* (1965), a fantasy adventure which began production in October 1964. In Corman's absence, the directorial chores were taken up by Jacques Tourneur.

The screenplay was provided by Charles Bennett and although AIP wanted him to come to Britain to work on the film, they would not pay for his flight. Instead Arkoff hired Louis M 'Deke' Heyward to do the relevant script revisions. A writer and producer with an extensive track record on American TV, Heywood became AIP's 'Third Man' when Arkoff established a UK base and appointed him head of European film production.

On his arrival in England, Heyward ended up re-writing the entire script as filming progressed. To keep the Poe theme going, he included the opening verse of one of the writer's poems, narrated by Price. Bennett was far from happy with the arrangement, describing the film as, 'The worst thing I was ever involved with.' Price didn't receive the script until six days before shooting.

City Under the Sea is a laboured effort where Tourneur's subtlety didn't suit the film's rip roaring adventure style. He also succeeded in annoying Daniel Haller, who was itching for his own career as a director. Haller was unhappy with Tourneur's approach to the film and made his feelings clear to Heyward, who tried to smooth things over between both men.

City Under the Sea lacks the swashbuckling magic to make it classic entertainment. A director like Don Chaffey or even Roger Corman could have given it that special something. The reason the film was a misfire was due to having the wrong director.

Heyward had no problems working with Price. 'Vincent and I had a community of interests – art and cooking among others – to keep us busy talking between takes. Occasionally he would read a line, then look at me and say, "Deke, you are screwing my career into the ground!" And indeed I may have. But I appreciate his frankness about it. He was a delight to work with.'

After the artistic highs of Prince Prospero and Verden Fell, Price's performance as Sir Hugo Tregathion was lacklustre, his appearance further undermined by the weak casting of Tab Hunter, Nicholson's mistress Susan Hart (they married shortly afterwards), David Tomlinson, and an annoying chicken called Herbert. Only the reliable John Le Mesurier (replacing Boris Karloff) provided much needed dramatic weight.

During the making of *City Under the Sea*, Price spent his time buying $25,000 worth of paintings and fine art for Sears Roebuck. He took in London's noisy nightlife and partied with Ringo Starr before returning to Los Angeles, and to the stage as Captain Hook for a Christmas production of *Peter Pan*. A variety of TV appearances followed, as well as voice-over work on AIP's exploitation 'shockumentary' *Taboos of the World* (1965).

By the mid-sixties Price epitomised the art of high camp. In between writing serious articles on art, he edited two books on the subject and collaborated on *A Treasury of Great American Recipes*. This ran alongside hamming it up on TV in *The Man From U.N.C.L.E.* and *Batman* (a recurring role as supervillain Egghead), which he approached with typical good humour. 'Vincent was never one to look a gift horse in the mouth,' Victoria observed, 'if there was an audience for his movies, he would continue to make them.' Playing starring roles was rare for actors in their fifties, so Price played it to the hilt.

The high camp continued with *Dr Goldfoot and the Bikini Machine* (1965), AIP's attempt to bring the tired beach party series up to date by capitalising on the *James Bond* franchise. Using the name Goldfoot was an obvious reference to Eon Productions' recently released *Goldfinger* (1964).

Price would not be considered as a James Bond type; that was left to over-the-hill beach hunks Frankie Avalon and Dwayne Hickman. As an in-joke, *Beach Party* regulars Annette Funicello and Harvey Lembeck also made guest appearances. With Bond supervillains being equally popular, it was obvious that Price took centre stage as the Blofeld-inspired Dr Goldfoot.

The film was the idea of James H Nicholson, who wanted to showcase Susan Hart. Production began in August 1965 and with a budget of $1million, it was AIP's most expensive film to date.

Price's Goldfoot has built an army of bikini-clad women (including two *Playboy* centrefolds) to prey on several wealthy and influential men. That's about as logical as you can get! It is up to Avalon and Hickman's inept CIA agents to save the day.

Dr Goldfoot had been conceived as a musical comedy. However Robert Kaufman's script did not impress director Norman Taurog, who hired Elwood Ullman to do a complete re-write that included the removal of three musical numbers.

Price was disappointed at not getting the chance to show his fine singing voice on film. 'It could have been fun,' he lamented, 'but they cut all the music out!'

Susan Hart also agreed that the omission of the songs affected the film. 'One of the best scenes I've seen on film was Vincent singing about the bikini machine. It was excellent! And I was told it was taken out because Sam Arkoff thought that Vincent looked too fey. But his character was fey! By taking this particular scene out, I believe they took out the explanation and the meat out of that picture. It was a really unique explanatory scene and Vincent was beautiful in it, right on the money.' At least the half hour TV special called *The Wild World of Dr Goldfoot*, starring Price and Hart, featured the deleted songs.

Resplendent in a black and gold jacket and gold pixie slippers, and sporting a beard, Price (affectionately referred to by Victoria as, 'My hip Daddy-O!') is clearly having a blast even if the film is far too silly for a modern viewer to appreciate. A modest success in the States (it did nothing in the UK), *Dr Goldfoot* was a massive hit in Europe, especially in Italy, taking a box office gross of $2million.

The success of *Dr Goldfoot* started a brief series of *Bikini* movies. It was also enough to warrant a sequel, and with the first movie being a hit in Italy, Arkoff decided that the follow up would be shot in Rome with Mario Bava, the talented director of the influential *Black Sunday* (1960), at the helm.

Le spie vengono dal semifreddo or *Dr Goldfoot and the Girl Bombs* (1966) began production in March 1966 and was basically a repeat of the first film only this time the bikini babes blow up when coming into contact with high ranking NATO officials! The cast featured another singer/actor, Fabian Forte, who replaced Frankie Avalon as the last minute. For the European market the main casting consisted of Franco Franchi and Ciccio Ingrassia, the Abbott and Costello of Italian cinema, although their comic antics ended up baffling English speaking audiences.

This weird casting must have come as a shock to Price, who was obliged to do the film whether he wanted to or not. 'As for *Dr Goldfoot and the Girl Bombs*,' said Arkoff, 'we fed several pictures to Vincent that, if times had been different, if horror pictures had been doing well, we probably wouldn't have made. Since we had him under contract, we had to use him. I don't know if Vincent enjoyed doing all those films; he certainly enjoyed some more than others.'

Price did not enjoy this particular effort! From the onset the shoot proved difficult with Bava dealing with the break-up of his marriage and his father's death. According to Price, Bava made up most of the film as he went along. With the production being so haphazard, Deke Heyward, who acted as co-producer came in to do a few re-writes only to find the language barrier an obstacle. 'We had one person speaking Portuguese, several of them spoke Italian. Vincent would shake his head in disbelief and say, "What is happening to me?" Not only did he not understand the Italians or the Portuguese or the Spanish; he didn't understand Fabian.'

There are two versions of *Dr Goldfoot and the Girl Bombs*, one edited by the Italians to emphasize their comic duo and the stunning brunettes on show, and the other, edited by AIP for American audiences, focusing on Price and the various blondes on display. The latter was completed without Bava's participation – not that he cared; he merely fulfilled a contractual obligation.

In any case, both versions are unwatchable with Price hamming it up to no real effect. It can't have done his long term career any good, nor was dressing up as a nun particularly dignified. It comes as no surprise when *Variety* asked the question, 'Could this be the same actor who once played Prince Albert to Helen Hayes' Victoria on Broadway?'

Dr Goldfoot and the Girl Bombs wasn't a commercial success although it scored a hit in Italy, making it Bava's most successful film. A disgruntled Price regarded it as, 'The most dreadful movie I've ever been in. Just about everything that could go wrong, did!'

For a welcome change of pace, Price turned up in an obscure South African based western called *The Jackals* (1967), an inferior remake of *Yellow Sky* (1948). As the grizzled gold prospector Oupa Decker, he gets top billing despite his role being a cameo, which he plays very well.

The career downturn continued with *House of a Thousand Dolls* (1967). Arkoff had a contract star but didn't know what to do with him, other than put him to work. This sleazy exploitation piece about white slave trafficking in Tangiers was a Spanish/German co-production that Arkoff got involved in via Harry Alan Towers.

Born in London, Towers was a globetrotting independent producer who travelled extensively around Europe producing low budget exploitation flicks while on the run from the law. Arkoff was certainly taken by him. 'He was totally fascinated by Harry Alan Towers,' said Heyward. 'Arkoff always had a penchant for falling in love and getting into bed with rogues and scoundrels.'

Towers was exactly that, but he was also very successful, his most recent efforts being the *Fu Manchu* series starring Christopher Lee. Arkoff negotiated a deal with Towers to loan out Price, who signed on without having any idea what he was supposed to be doing.

While filming *The Jackals* in Johannesburg, Price received a script that he found interesting. The film was supposed to be a Victorian period piece based on Sax Rohmer's *House of Dolls*. Production was due to start in November 1966 with Hammer's in-house director Terence Fisher at the helm. Locations were scheduled around Dublin and the cast included Vic Damone, Klaus Kinski and Rupert Davies.

The wonderful opportunity of Price and Fisher working together never came to fruition. According to actor Herbert Lom, Fisher had become a 'sweet old alcoholic.' The director's penchant for Guinness was allegedly responsible for his stumbling onto a main road and straight into an oncoming car which left him with a broken leg.

With Fisher out of action, the production shifted to Madrid and got underway in March 1967 with Jeremy Summers as director. George Nader replaced Vic Damone and Towers completely re-wrote the script. What Price originally got in the post had nothing to do with the end result.

This dire potboiler has Price playing Felix Manderville, a stage illusionist who uses his act to kidnap young girls for the white slave market; actually he does this for his lover, played by Martha Hyer. Eventually they are thwarted by some one-dimensional heroics from George Nader. Other than it being a paid holiday in the sun, Price goes through the customary ham slicing with a world-weary air about him.

Price remained professional and carried on without a word of complaint. 'I don't remember him ever protesting,' said Arkoff. 'Even in *House of a Thousand*

Dolls. I think there were a couple of times when we had some minor differences. But basically I never had any problems with Vincent, which is more that you can say about the bulk of actors and of course actresses today. He not only had talent, but he was a professional, which is more than I could say for a lot of actors.'

Both Price and the equally professional Martha Hyer shared a love for art; Hyer owned a fine collection of French impressionist paintings. With Price's Sears contract still ongoing, they spent their time off visiting the art galleries around Madrid, unaware that an alternative version of the movie was being made behind their backs. 'What (Martha) and I didn't know was that they were making a dirty version of the film at the same time. Every day we'd have off, they'd make a dirty version.'

The actors found out the hard way as Price continued. 'Martha and I were led off, so we went to visit the set and found that they were remaking all of the scenes we'd been in but a pornographic version of it. I never got the see that version.'

House of a Thousand Dolls didn't advance the careers of anyone involved, nor did it do much at the American box office. Arkoff's association with Towers continued with another interesting project that would have teamed Price up with his British horror contemporary Christopher Lee as well as giving him a second chance to work with Terence Fisher.

This production was to be another screen adaptation of *Dracula* with Lee getting the chance to play the Count as Bram Stoker had written him in the novel – a moustachioed old man who gets younger as the story unfolds. Price was due to play Dracula's nemesis Professor Van Helsing, a rare opportunity to play a famous character from horror literature.

Unfortunately the production went through several problems with Fisher once again being hit by a car, breaking the same leg and on the same stretch of road. He was replaced by Jesus Franco, but by that time Arkoff ended his association with Towers and the part of Van Helsing went to Herbert Lom. Considering how bad the film was, Price was wise to jump ship although his AIP contract had a lot to do with his decision. With hindsight, both Lee and Lom should have done the same!

Price was experiencing a serious downturn in his film career. If there was a time for the actor to jump off the horror bandwagon, this was it. With his other projects, he didn't need to continue the treadmill of starring in one inferior movie after another. He could have focused on resuming his stage career, where respectability was guaranteed. In addition to the theatre, there were plenty of big budget international co-productions that made good use of (mainly British) classical actors of the same calibre.

Ever the globetrotter, Price would have been happy to fly to Europe at a moment's notice to star in a biblical epic. Being a freelance had its risks and the lure of the dollar kept him shackled to AIP, preventing him from doing potentially better assignments.

Despite the downturn, Price remained busy with the visual arts, and being his own best publicist meant his profile and popularity was extremely high. In between film roles and buying art, he took two months off a year to concentrate on the college lecture circuit. He was on committee for the Whitney Museum in New York and the Cleveland Amory, and acted as trustee for the Archives of American Art. These activities helped bolster his sagging confidence with regards to his chequered film career, which was interspersed with camp appearances in *F Troop* and *Voyage to the Bottom of the Sea*.

Price's contract was up for renewal and Arkoff, keen to retain his services, offered him a new seven-year contract with the promise of more money and better acting roles. 'Sam was a genius at being a lawyer,' said Deke Heyward. 'He knew how to make contracts.'

As a man who constantly worried about money, Price signed on the dotted line. He still couldn't do horror films for other studios, and with his screen image overtaking his prominence as a serious actor, he knew Arkoff would lock him away in horror movies for some time to come.

The actor remained philosophical about his decision to stay with AIP. 'I'm sure if I'd done other things in my career, I could be more distinguished. On the other hand, of course, I could be starving.'

Louis Heyward summed it up best, '(Arkoff) tied up Vincent Price.'

There were other changes afoot. Arkoff decided to set up a permanent base in London's Grosvenor Square with Heyward in charge. The producer was more than thrilled at the prospect. 'I was glad to get out the US. I was unhappy with what was going on socially and politically.'

Price had also grown tired of California. 'I never thought it would happen,' he lamented. 'The smog, the city that became physically enormous but never grew with it. You don't feel safe anymore. I was in London when Sharon Tate and the others were murdered. The ideal thing would be to live half the time in London.'

From then on, most of Price's films were made in England under the watchful eye of Deke Heyward. His next venture into horror marked his second definitive performance, and in one of the most controversial films ever made.

Witchfinder General

'Matthew Hopkins was a really evil person, and it was a true story. He wasn't just a sadist! If he were I wouldn't have wanted to play him' – Vincent Price

One of the greatest British films ever made, *Witchfinder General* is a remarkable, controversial and ultimately outstanding piece of cinema that still courts debate, discussion and conjecture 50 years after its initial release. It also provided a tragic swansong for Michael Reeves, a brilliant but erratic director whose promising career had barely got started.

Born in Sutton, Surrey on 17 October 1943, Reeves was cinema-mad from a young age and a millionaire when he turned 16 following the suicide of his wealthy father. Living the typical playboy lifestyle, his other passion was fast cars.

As a teenager he made short films with his boyhood friend Ian Ogilvy. 'We first met when we were both 15 years old,' recalled Ogilvy. 'Michael was at Radley School, I was at Eton, but a mutual friend suggested we meet. "Mike wants to be a director and you want to be an actor," said Paul Vestey, "so why don't you get together?" With Paul's help, we did and we got on wonderfully well, discussing many mutual likes and dislikes and spending hours discussing films, a subject he knew far more about than I did. We quickly became the best of friends.'

Reeves corresponded regularly with Hollywood director Don Siegel. . Upon leaving Radley College, he flew to Hollywood and turned up on Siegel's doorstep. Impressed by this young man's determination, the director hired him as his assistant.

Working up the ranks in various movies, Reeves went to Italy to work as assistant director for Paul Malansky's *Castle of the Living Dead* (1964). Impressed by the young man's enthusiasm, Malansky hired him to direct *Revenge of the Blood Beast* (1966), starring Barbara Steele and Ian Ogilvy. It turned out to be one of the better Italian horror flicks of the sixties and a good start for Reeves. 'We were all inordinately proud,' said Ogilvy, 'if only for the accomplishment of having made a real film.'

Returning to England, Reeves caught the attention of an entrepreneur who had recently ventured into film production – Tony Tenser.

Tenser was born in London on 10 August 1920 to Jewish-Lithuanian immigrant parents. Tenser was an incredibly ambitious and intelligent young man, and after wartime service with the RAF, he pursued his love of movies by becoming a trainee manager for a major cinema chain.

Like James Carreras at Hammer, Tenser was a natural showman and his own best publicist. Becoming head of publicity at Miracle Films, he was responsible for the distribution of imported foreign language movies to the UK, which included the Brigitte Bardot classic *And God Created Woman* (1956). Marketing the film led to Tenser meeting a Soho strip club owner named Michael Klinger.

Like Tenser, Klinger had an Eastern European Jewish background and a love of movies. Together they formed the Compton Cinema Club where they screened nudist movies including George Harrison Marks' infamous and hilariously awful *Naked as Nature Intended* (1961).

Renamed Compton-Cameo following a merger with the Cameo cinema chain, Tenser and Klinger moved into film production with *That Kind of Girl* (1963) and *Saturday Night Out* (1964). Reforming as Compton Films with writers Donald and Derek Ford and director Robert Hartford-Davis, the East End duo went full throttle into horror with *The Black Torment* (1964) and *A Study in Terror* (1965).

It was Compton's association with a young Polish filmmaker named Roman Polanski (who had just arrived in London) that gave the company a degree of respectability. Polanski's first film for Compton was the excellent psychological horror *Repulsion* (1965). He followed it up with the art house thriller *Cul-de-Sac* (1966) before heading off to bigger things in Hollywood. Tenser and Klinger also parted company, with Tenser forming Tigon Films while Klinger continued producing large scale efforts that included the Michael Caine gangster classic *Get Carter* (1971).

By the time the Tenser/Klinger partnership had dissolved, Michael Reeves had been signed up by Compton to direct Peter Cushing in *The Devil's Discord*. When the assignment fell through, Reeves got in touch with Tenser regarding another interesting movie project, and one where the young director hit his stride.

'Mike soon set about getting his next project underway,' said Ogilvy, 'which turned out to be another low budget affair called *The Sorcerers* (1967). Mike had met a young American producer called Patrick Curtis in Rome. Curtis was married to the statuesque Raquel Welch at the time and they were a glamorous and helpful couple to know. Patrick liked the *Sorcerers* project and started shopping it around. He ended up with Tony Tenser's Tigon Productions. Being in the business of making extremely low budget horror films, Tony had heard about Mike and *Revenge of the Blood Beast*. So he was at least aware of this new young film director.'

The Sorcerers was an effective little chiller that gave Boris Karloff one of his best latter day roles. As disgraced hypnotist Professor Monserrat, he invents a device that is designed to experience the sensations of the person under its control. Testing it on a bored young man named Mike Roscoe (Ian Ogilvy), things go wrong when Monserrat's wife Estelle (the excellent Catherine Lacey, who found playing a sexually malevolent old woman distressing) takes it further by driving Mike to kill.

The Sorcerers was a big hit for Tigon thanks to Reeves' good work. 'Michael Reeves knew exactly what he was doing,' said Tenser, 'so there was no need for me to intervene.'

'*The Sorcerers* was exactly the kind of project (Tenser) wanted at the time,' recalled Ogilvy, 'and he agreed to be a partner with Patrick and Raquel, with Mike to direct. For some reason Tony chose not to watch *Revenge of the Blood Beast*. This must have come as a relief to Mike and it certainly did to me!'

'Mike's professional relationship with actors on his film set was a slightly aloof one,' Ogilvy added. 'He was in awe of actors and their processes of producing a performance, and preferred to leave them alone to get on with their jobs. Some actors thought he didn't like them; in fact Mike loved actors and enjoyed their company, but he was nervous about delving deep into what they did and how they did it.'

Despite being seen as unapproachable to his cast (Susan George, who starred in *The Sorcerers*, hated him), Reeves struck up a wonderful rapport with Boris Karloff. 'Boris was old school,' said Tenser. 'Once he agreed he was going to do something he got on with it. He had a lovely nature. Mike seemed to respond to that professionalism. I watched them chatting all the time.'

Pleased with the success of *The Sorcerers*, Tenser's next assignment for Reeves was a novel by historian Ronald Bassett which was in the process of being published. Tenser had already bought the film rights as he felt it, 'had some scope, had some breath; there was canvas for a film.' The novel was called *Witchfinder General* by Ronald Bassett and it was a fictional account of history's most notorious witch hunter Matthew Hopkins.

Little is known about the real life Hopkins. He was originally a failed lawyer from Manningtree, Essex. Finding a profitable income travelling around East Anglia persecuting alleged witches during the English Civil War, his methods of torture brought about 120 executions for witchcraft. Hopkins' reign of terror lasted a short time and he soon stepped down following opposition from the local authorities. He remained in Manningtree where he lived in relative obscurity before dying from tuberculosis at the age of 27.

Tenser had known Bassett's literary agent for over 20 years. The purchase of the film rights came about during a beneficial lunch between both men. 'I had read the galley proof (of the book) and said "I like it, how much do you want?" We agreed a deal and I bought the film rights. I phoned Michael Reeves and said I'd like you to read this book. He read the book and I said I have the rights to make a film. Would you like to do it? He said, "I'd love to," and we went from there.'

'Tony Tenser saw the potential in the story for a lot of blood hurling,' said Ogilvy, 'which made it a perfect fit for Mike Reeves.'

Reeves brought in old school friend Tom Baker, who had previously collaborated on the script for *The Sorcerers* – 'Not the *Doctor Who* actor,' said Ogilvy, 'this Tom Baker was a quiet self-effacing man!' As both men worked on the script, they saw something that was more than just a horror film. Once submitted, Tenser increased the budget to include location shooting around Suffolk. The production was scheduled for September 1967 to avoid the oncoming winter weather.

With the bulk of Tigon's finances invested in the Peter Cushing chiller *The Blood Beast Terror* (1967), Tenser needed to strike up a co-production deal in order to increase the budget further before the film could get off the ground. Like Reeves, he saw something special in this new production. 'I thought it would make a wonderful picture, but a lot more expensive than my other pictures, so I would have to look for a new partner.'

'Tony Tenser started to hunt around for a financial partner to carry half the load,' said Ogilvy. 'He found it in AIP.' 'I spoke to "Deke" Heyward,' said Tenser, 'and we made deal.' Heyward saw Tenser as a man with a 'dodgy reputation' because he wanted to produce a film based on a book that hadn't yet been published.

Heyward agreed to provide £32,000 on top of the £50,000 raised by Tigon and a further £5,000 from associate producer Philip Waddilove. In return, AIP handled the overseas distribution rights that included re-editing the film. It was still a relatively modest budget. The deal was given the go ahead by Sam Arkoff who saw *Witchfinder General* as a tax write-off.

There was one stipulation with the deal – AIP insisted their contract star Vincent Price should play Matthew Hopkins. 'It was my edict to find things for Vincent to do,' said Heyward. 'I was able to make a deal for less than $150,000. The attractive thing about the picture was the price.'

Tenser was happy with the arrangement. 'AIP felt that it would enhance their market if Vincent Price played Matthew Hopkins. I was totally happy with that, because Price would enhance my market as well.' Tenser also felt that, 'Vincent Price was a good choice, I thought, and I knew they needed a name to sell the film in America. I wouldn't have accepted anybody just for the sake of it but Vinnie was ideal.'

Price wasn't too impressed by the script following his last few duds, so Heyward set things right with a £12,000 fee plus expenses. To finally win Price over, Heyward also started playing up Michael Reeves' reputation as the new golden boy of the British cinema.

Heyward wrote a letter to Price explaining that he would be involved in, 'one of the most inspiring things that's happened to you as an actor in a long time … (Reeves) is not only bright and imaginative and well organised, but he has the cujones to force a crew through doing things the way he wants to. He wafted off in a fairy-like cloud when he heard we were casting you in the lead.'

It was enough to convince Price, and of course a few weeks in his beloved England cemented his decision even though he wasn't too keen on the location work. Arriving at Heathrow Airport in September 1967, he enthusiastically told Philip Waddilove, who met him as he got off the plane, to, 'Take me to your goddam boy genius!'

There was one slight problem – Michael Reeves! He was absolutely furious with AIP's decision to use Price. When working on the screenplay, Reeves initially wanted Boris Karloff to play Hopkins, but the horror veteran was approaching 80 and not in good health. Being a physically demanding role that required a lot of horseback riding made it impossible for Karloff to participate, and that meant Reeves had to go elsewhere.

'AIP promised half the budget on one condition,' said Ogilvy, 'Vincent Price was to play the witchfinder. But Mike Reeves and Tom Baker had somebody else in mind. They envisaged the character was a small, flea-bitten man, an unattractive, diminutive clerk with ideas above his station, resentful of the laughter his unprepossessing appearance, engendered and vicious in his revenge on those who dare to snigger. They wrote a weakling, a sickly little man, with bad breath and staring pale blue eyes; a creature who hated the hand the world had dealt him and was prepared to deal with the world accordingly. A cold, quiet, calculating monster, whose power lay not in his physical presence but in the dark recesses of a warped and vicious mind. In Mike and Tom's eyes, there was one actor who could embody all these ideas and that was Donald Pleasence.'

'What they got was Vincent Price,' he added, 'he of the imposing stature and

99

the long handsome face, with its long aristocratic nose leading to the pencil moustache that hovered above a pair of lips designed expressly for the sardonic quip. Vincent Price – famous for his nasal vowels and queenly consonants. Vincent Price – known mostly by contemporary audiences for his roguish, eye-rolling and over-the-top performances in the Edgar Allen Poe films he made for Roger Corman.'

The character of Hopkins in Bassett's novel perfectly matched the description of Pleasence, and Reeves even approached the actor with the role. 'To Mike, the character of Matthew Hopkins was a little ugly, ineffectual little man,' said Ogilvy. 'When Donald was going to do it, Mike was going to have a scene in which he would get up on his horse in front of a group of villagers and fall off the other side, because he couldn't even ride. He was meant to be a pathetic Napoleonic figure, who was bitter about his inadequacies. But all that changed when Vincent came along, since he is rather handsome and virile looking.'

Tenser was a big fan of Pleasence and would have happily approved of Reeves' choice if it wasn't for AIP paying part of the bill. After all, Price was a star and Pleasence was a character actor working mainly in high profile supporting roles.

The real Matthew Hopkins died young so in reality Price, Karloff and Pleasence were all miscast because of their ages with Pleasence being the youngest (he was born in 1919). Age-wise Ian Ogilvy would have been ideally suited, but Hopkins would have needed a far more intense and aggressive young actor to make it work. The perfect choice would have been Oliver Reed. By 1967 Reed had already moved away from Hammer horror and powered his way to international stardom, making him too expensive for a low budget chiller.

With Price on board, Reeves reluctantly re-wrote the script to accommodate the actor. Initially Hopkins was a supporting character used to provide back up to the tragic romance between Richard and Sara. As it was, Price's involvement meant Reeves had to expand the role and make it more central to the story. The 'ineffective and inadequate' authority figure became a more conventional villain, ideally suited for the tall, imposing American.

When the first draft was presented to the British Board of Film Censors (BBFC), the chief examiner, who cruelly referred to Tony Tenser as 'an ape,' regarded the script as 'perfectly beastly and ghoulish,' adding that, 'such a script being a study in sadism in which every detail of cruelty and suffering is lovingly dwelt on. A film which followed the script at all closely would run into endless censorship troubles.' The second draft, submitted 11 days later, met the same outraged response from the same examiner, who provided Tenser with a long list of requirements to reduce the level of sadism.

Reeves and Baker finally presented a toned down third draft, and although this is the script that would be filmed, several sequences were either trimmed down, revised or removed, one of which being the Battle of Naseby. Concerned by budget restrictions and the hiring of hundreds of extras to take part, Tenser ordered the scenes to be removed leaving the meeting between Ogilvy's Richard and Patrick Wymark's Oliver Cromwell taking place after the Roundhead victory over the Royalists.

With the script finally approved, production began on 18 September 1967. Two aircraft hangers near Bury St Edmunds were converted for interior shooting at a cost of £1,500, but because of the echo caused by the tin roofs, much of the dialogue had to be re-recorded after filming. Locations included the Dunwich coastline, Black Park in Buckinghamshire and the main square at Lavenham. The setting for John Lowes' church was St John the Evangelist in Norfolk and the film's climax took place at Orford Castle in East Anglia.

With script, locations, casting and production schedules sorted out, now was the time for the arrival in London of Vincent Price, enthusiastic about working on a brand new film and with a promising young director set for bigger and better things. In his book *Vincent Price: The Art of Fear*, author Denis Meikle wrote, 'If he (Price) had known then how he would feel towards both (film and director) only a few weeks later, he might have had second thoughts about boarding the plane.'

So began a difficult and very intense relationship.

Reeves made his feelings abundantly clear by refusing to meet Price at Heathrow. He also refused to take part in the obligatory photoshoot that was always required between a director and a star. Sam Arkoff was far from happy with Reeves' attitude and regarded it as, 'a deliberate snub to offend both Vincent and me.' When they finally met on the first day of filming, Reeves told Price in no uncertain terms that, 'I didn't want you and I still don't want you, but I'm stuck with you!'

'That's the way to gain confidence!' exclaimed Price. A sensitive individual behind his good humoured exterior, the actor was deeply hurt by Reeves' obvious contempt towards him.

The camp mannerisms that became the trademark of his horror career were unacceptable to Reeves. 'Mike felt that Vincent was having too good a time whatever part he was playing,' said Heyward, 'and however horrible the man he was portraying was, there would be an overtone of "You and I both know we're kidding" which Mike didn't want. Reeves did not feel Vincent could do the acting job necessary.'

Things got worse during the first day of shooting when Price, not the most confident of horseman, was thrown from his mount, sustaining minor injuries but was otherwise unhurt. Rather than pay him a visit at his hotel while he was recovering, Reeves sent Philip Waddilove over to sort out insurance requirements while the director planned the next day's schedule. The actor returned to work the following morning.

History repeated itself when Price, once again on horseback, had to fire his flintlock pistol between his mount's ears. Reeves insisted on a blank charge so the smoke would be visible from the pistol. 'You want the gun to go bang between the ears of this fucking nag?' shouted Price, obviously not keen on the idea. 'How do you think he's going to react?' Reeves wouldn't budge, the gun went off, and once again the actor was thrown from his horse. He wasn't hurt, but was extremely angry towards Reeves about the incident.

Cast as the hero Richard Marshall was Ian Ogilvy. 'Mike and Tom put together a script pencilling me in as the hero, which was flattering for me and comforting for Mike. By now he felt safe with me and would probably have used me in these kind of roles forever, or at least until one of us had got too heartily sick of the other to continue.'

'I (first) met Vincent while I was trying out my film horse for the first time,' he continued. 'The horse they gave me was called Captain, and he was huge and excitable and almost unstoppable. Captain and I were cantering along a gravel lane. In the ditch bordering the lane was what looked, at first glance, to be a pile of old black rags in a top hat but turned out to be Vincent Price in his witchfinder uniform, having a rest by the side of the road. As Captain and I rode nobly by, I heard a famous voice. 'Oh my Ga-a-a-d, would you fucking look at her. She's so pretty and she rides that fucking horse so well. I hate her!'

But as the filming progressed, the actor became increasingly disheartened. When Ogilvy's partner, model Diane Hart, saw him sitting alone and looking dejected, she offered him a lift in her car. 'Are you going past California?' was his reply.

'He hated me,' said Price of Reeves. 'He didn't want me at all for that part. He wanted some other actor, and he got me and that was it. I didn't like him, either, and it was one of the first times in my life that I've been in a picture where really the director and I clashed.' Price had his own ideas regarding Reeves' contempt of him. 'He didn't know how to talk to actors, he hadn't the experience, or talked to enough of them, so all the actors on the picture had a very bad time. I knew though, that in a funny, uneducated sort of way, he was right, in his desire to approach the part in a certain way. He wanted it very serious and very straight, and he was right, but he just didn't know how to communicate with actors. Actors are very sensitive people.'

'For Vincent, it was not a happy shoot,' said Ogilvy. 'There were several reasons: somebody tactlessly let slip that Mike had wanted Donald Pleasence for the role; Vincent missed the comforts of studio filming and found working in draughty old aircraft hangars in the wilds of Norfolk unpleasant; he had to do a lot of riding and he didn't like horses, and worst of all, he didn't get on with Mike. The feeling was mutual and there was friction from the start. The upstart of a young pipsqueak of a young director either ignored Vincent, or told him not to do things – things that Vincent had been doing successfully for many years. But Mike was determined. If he couldn't get the actor he wanted, then at least he would do his damnedest to get something good from the actor he didn't want – and for the first time he actually tried to direct his star's performance. But it was all negative.'

There was no ill feeling between Price and Ogilvy. 'Vincent didn't hate me. He didn't have time to hate me. We have very few scenes in the film because our story lines run parallel and separate through most of the movie and we meet briefly at the beginning and end of the picture. I also didn't give him any particular reason to hate me. Since I only interacted with Vincent in a brief scene at the beginning of the film and couple of scenes at the end, I saw little of the conflict between him and Mike and, for the most of the time, enjoyed myself. I charged about the Norfolk countryside on my enormous horse being impossibly heroic!'

On one of his rare visits to the set, Tony Tenser saw the tension between actor and director as Reeves tried to tone down Price's performance as much as possible. 'There was a scene they were shooting where Vincent wasn't happy with Michael; (Price) felt (Reeves) wasn't saying much to him. We were all set up and Vincent says his lines. Michael stops and says, "Vinnie, please don't shake your head about." Vincent replies, "Don't shake my head about. Thank you young man." They started again and Vincent keeps his head still but he is projecting his voice too much and waving his arms about. "Stop. Vinnie please keep the voice down and don't throw your arms about." "Don't shake my head, don't throw my arms about. Thank you young man." They started a third time and I think he was shuffling his feet. Something like that. Michael stops again and says, "Please Vinnie." Vincent drew to his full height, looked down on Michael and said, "Young man, I have made 92 films. How many have you made?" Michael shouted at him, "Three good ones!"'

Price concurred with the constant head shaking. 'Michael could not communicate with actors. He would stop me and say, "Don't move your head like that." And I would say, "Like what? What do you mean?" He'd say, "There! You're doing it again. Don't do that." So we didn't get along at all.' Such was the tension between both men, Price refused to watch the rushes, preferring to keep to himself or chatting with the cast and crew.

Difficulties aside, Price remained a consummate professional. 'He never complained to me once,' said Tenser. 'We would have a chat in the hotel and he would tell me about his real love, hunting for paintings. Never once did he make any comments about Michael. I think there was also an element of envy. I also think that Vincent had a crush on Mike and when Mike treated him so indifferently he was hurt.' A rumoured bisexual, Price took more than a passing interest in the handsome young director and was upset when the openly heterosexual Reeves gave him the cold shoulder.

On a professional level, Price could see Reeves' potential. He was also sympathetic to the young man's obvious personal problems during filming. 'He showed great promise. He was a wonderful director, but what problems he had. Working with Michael was a very sad experience. He was a boy who had a lot of problems which nobody seemed to know about. He was very unstable. He was very difficult to work with because he didn't know how to tell an actor what he wanted. It was sad. All I can tell you is that he communicated the wrong way, and he rubbed everyone up the wrong way. But we all knew he had tremendous talent, so we tried to overlook it.'

'Mike never directed actors,' said Ogilvy. 'He always said he didn't know anything about acting and preferred to leave it up to us. If it wasn't good he would tell us, but he didn't know how to make it better. The only direction he ever gave was, "A bit quicker" or "A bit slower". If he trusted you, he left you alone.' In Price's case, Reeves didn't trust him an inch and made things extremely hostile.

Hillary Dwyer, who played tragic heroine Sara, found a different Reeves when working on the set. 'Mike was just wonderful. He was really inspiring to work with. And because it was my first film, I didn't know how lucky I was, especially when I had to do lots of torture and rape scenes, which was rather stressful.'

Born in Liverpool, Dwyer had studied ballet and piano before training at the Webber Douglas Drama School. After appearing in several provincial theatre productions, she joined The Bristol Old Vic. Following several TV appearances, she caught the eye of Deke Heyward and Tony Tenser. She was put under contract by Tigon, who later cast her as a scientist in *The Body Stealers* (1968). At 21, *Witchfinder General* was her big screen debut.

'Once I was on board,' said Ogilvy, 'Mike and I had discussions as to who should be the leading lady. I pushed for my old girlfriend Nicola Pagett and we set up a meeting with her, but there was something in the air at this meeting that smelled a little noxious in Nicola's nostrils. Perhaps she took us for a pair of amateurs, or maybe we mentioned the nude love scene once too often, or possibly it seemed unprofessional to be holding the casting meeting in my flat. Mike said he didn't think she wanted to do it. With no help from me, he found a newcomer, Hilary Dwyer, who not only played the part to perfection, but who looked far more like a country parson's niece than Nicola's dark exoticism ever could.'

Price continued like an old trooper without a word of complaint. Aside from Reeves, he got on well with the cast and crew, especially the young actors, who were in awe of him. 'Vincent was a very funny man,' said Ogilvy. 'Vincent would hold court at the Angel Hotel with tales of Hollywood.'

Ogilvy found Price funny, 'in a queeny sort of way. I remember Vincent being a very funny, funny guy, but a lot of it was fairly unprintable, the stuff he came out with.'

Away from filming Price happily partied with his young co-stars. 'In the evening,' said Ogilvy, 'at the Angel Hotel in Bury St Edmunds and away from Mike and the draughty stage hangars, Vincent would relax and have fun. He would sit in the bar, poised and elegant and witty, his wrist jangling with turquoise bracelets; telling stories of Hollywood. Once, Nicky Henson – my old RADA and rock group friend, whom Mike had cast as the hero's best friend – appeared beside him sporting several bits of jewellery of his own. "Don't push it, Alice," drawled Vincent and went upstairs to put on more turquoise.'

Nicky Henson was totally in awe of Price as an actor and as a person. 'Vincent was wonderful with us, we all had an absolute ball. We were young and we were up all night, every night and he would stay up with us, drinking and telling stories right through the night and then he would go to work the next day and be word perfect.'

Price's generosity and kindness extended towards helping out the production when it ran into a tight spot during location filming in Bury St

Edmunds. According to Deke Heyward, 'One day the catering truck didn't show up, so Vincent had his driver take him into town. At his own expense, he bought fresh vegetables, pasta and shrimp and took it back to the kitchen of the hotel, where he whipped up lunch for sixty people.'

Reeves wanted more than just a horror film. With most chillers entrenched in the world of werewolves, vampires and gothic castles, *Witchfinder General* focused on genuine horror and being based on a real life person, Reeves wanted realism at any cost. 'On *Witchfinder*,' added Henson, 'we all knew were onto something special.'

Reeves wanted brutality that reflected the horrors of the English Civil War. 'There wasn't much funny about torture, hangings and burnings at the stake,' said Sam Arkoff, 'but it was effective.' Ogilvy agreed, 'Mike wanted to show rotting corpses lying in ditches and us ride by without noticing them, because that's what the ditches of England were full of at the time.'

Ogilvy further added that, 'Mike didn't believe, as John Wayne believed, that a saloon bar brawl is ok, and everybody can bash each other and hurl each other through windows, and nobody gets seriously hurt. Mike said this philosophy is very wrong. He said, "This will surely teach kids they can go into a place and start hitting people and think they're not actually hurting anyone. I think if you hit someone in a film, you should see the knuckles break and the teeth fly out and the blood spurt and somebody possibly getting a broken jaw before he leaves – just once. This idea of banging away at people's chin for hours is ludicrous. It's inclined to make violence seem rather jolly." Mike always believed violence should be seen to be horrible, and to put people off, not to glorify it.'

'Mike used to walk about with a viewfinder and a blood squirter,' said Henson. 'He'd just come up and squirt it all over you. He had it with him all the time. He'd also come at you with scissors and cut your clothes so that there were proper bullet holes in them.'

'Hopkins was not just a sadist,' said Price, regarding the character's own brutal demeanour. 'He was a human being – not a humane one perhaps – but he had all the usual weaknesses, including a fondness for young women. I saw him as a man who, at first, really believed in the Christian justness of his cause but, when he found he could turn it into a profit, degenerated into an ogre whose lust for power and greed ran away with him. He became a complete hypocrite – cowardly as well as demonic.'

'It was one of those real old hard bitten English units!' exclaimed Nicky Henson about the film crew. Making the most of the wet autumn weather, Dutch cameraman John Coquillon's stunning visuals combines the beauty of the English countryside with the grim atmosphere of a world gone mad. A former documentary cameraman, his effective use of natural life and the ability to work on tight budgets was brought to Reeves attention via writer Alfred Shaughnessy. *Witchfinder General* was his debut as cinematographer. He went on to a very successful Hollywood career.

And it rained! 'Very fine rain,' said Tenser, 'though you hardly saw it on the screen. It did cause concern when we were shooting the witch burning though!

We had the whole Territorial Army dressed in costume, all the houses had been dressed, the cobbles covered in straw, television aerials removed. We had three days to get the shots and of course Vincent was only there for a fixed time, after which he was moving onto the next film. We could not afford to have any hold ups. I called the insurance broker and said we needed something in case it rained. We took the payment and of course after that it didn't rain for those days.'

Lavenham resident Anne Churchill was present at the witch burning scene. 'I remember watching the witch burning scene in the market place. Lorry loads of sand and straw made it look authentic. They lowered the stunt girl into the fire and lifted her up when her eyebrows singed and they put in the dummy. The fire brigade was hiding behind the cross.'

The Lavenham residents also told Ogilvy of the ghostly goings on shortly after filming the scene. 'There was a lot of ghostly banging and crashes. It had caused reactions in the spirit world. Mike thought it was very funny that a film could cause upset among ghosts!'

Actor Bernard Kay, who briefly appears as a boatman, had his own experiences of the weather. 'I remember it was very cold. I was supposed to be there for one day, and I looked at the lines and thought we would get through this in a couple of hours. I think it turned out to be the longest day I ever worked! Michael was adamant that he had to capture the right shot, which would show a dissolve from the waves, into the flame of Lavenham. He insisted on take after take while the crew stood around freezing on the beach.'

Despite the wet weather, Reeves' quest for perfection, and the antagonism he held towards his star, filming went smoothly enough. Money remained tight and the rotting corpses strewn around the English ditches had to be dropped for being too expensive to set up. Interior shooting at Orford Castle posed a few difficulties because it was open to the public during the day, so Reeves had to shoot everything at night, causing lighting issues for John Coquillon. These technical problems put Reeves under more pressure than he could really handle.

'Mike was running over schedule and the budget was a worry,' said Tenser. 'We were still a small company and we had to keep it down. I sat down with Mike and the producers and came to an agreement on the number of rehearsals and the number of retakes. It was very amicable and in the end it came in about £20,000 over, mainly because of the locations and the weather. I didn't ask AIP to pay their half. It wasn't in the contract and I wanted to see that when they do business with an English company we stick to our responsibilities.'

Witchfinder General going over schedule and over budget forced Price to turn down a cameo he'd been committed to in the satirical comedy *The Magic Christian* (1970), depriving him of another chance to appear alongside Christopher Lee, who played a vampire on board a ship.

Arkoff continued to make certain compromises when it came to filming the 'continental' version. According to Ian Ogilvy, 'The American producers sent endless little directives by letter or telegram. In the tavern scenes we had lots of naked girls running around. Mike ignored these messages.' Deke Heyward, on a rare visit to the set, made sure Reeves complied with these requests. This included retakes of the tavern scenes showing plenty of exposed breasts from model, actress and future *Carry On* regular Margaret Nolan.

Reeves was unhappy about the situation insisting that, 'We're making a historical movie here,' and felt the additional scenes meant, 'Some prick of a producer is putting his oar in and messing up what the director had done.' As an act of subtle revenge, Reeves gave Heyward an additional dialogue credit in the film's titles.

There was further controversy when a BBC crew filmed a report for the *Six O'Clock News*. The footage shown on TV featured the witch burning scene, and this prompted several complaints from the public. Ironically the scene was removed from the final print. It eventually resurfaced in the digitally remastered version along with several other deleted scenes.

The problems continued when British technicians called a strike towards the end of filming because the production company did not hire a large enough crew. After Reeves hired a new man, things went back to normal. When he found himself short of actors, Reeves cast Philip Waddilove as a roundhead soldier and his wife Susi as a suspected witch imprisoned in the animal enclosure.

On the final day's filming at Orford Castle, Reeves had planned the death of Matthew Hopkins to be spectacular; falling on a case of burning coals and getting engulfed in flames. Unfortunately time constraints prompted a drastic rethink. 'That whole sequence, the most notorious in the film was made up on the spot,' said Nicky Henson. 'We winged it. We had to shoot the whole of that scene in one day.' Initially Henson was to shoot both Hopkins and Marshall, but as the pistol was a flintlock, it could only fire one shot and needed reloading for a second. Reeves decided that it would more effective to shoot Hopkins and leave Marshall descending into madness.

The climax was a 36-hour marathon session and filming in the cold and damp interiors of Orford Castle, prompted Price to drink a bottle of wine to combat the chills. Turning up worse for wear enraged Reeves. 'He's drunk! How dare he be drunk on my set! I'll kill the bastard!' As an act of revenge for such unprofessionalism, Reeves asked Ogilvy to, 'really lay into Vincent,' with his rubber axe. Ogilvy wasn't faking it at all despite Price wearing foam padding under his costume. 'This was a very violent time in English history,' said Ogilvy. 'The story is set in 17th Century England during the bloody civil war between Oliver Cromwell and King Charles I.'

He further added that, 'One of the last sequences we filmed was in Orford Castle, a well-preserved 12th Century keep near Ipswich in Suffolk. We had the castle for a limited time, one night only, from 6 o'clock until midnight, and Mike had set an almost impossible task for himself, involving at least 35 shots with complex lighting, in many different parts of the ancient building. This was the night Vincent decided to turn up drunk. He was truculent and inclined to be uncooperative – on the very night when Mike needed everybody to pull together. Everybody except Vincent did pull together. We fumbled our way through the multiple set-ups, doing the best we could under the circumstances, and by the time the scene in which I attack the witchfinder with an axe came round it was nearing our filming deadline and Mike was blazing with fury. "I want you to hit that bastard," he hissed in my ear. "I want you to hit him really hard."'

Ogilvy objected. "'I'm not going to do that Mike," I said. "I'll try to make it look real but I'm not going to hurt him."' Reeves however was adamant and told Ogilvy, 'It's just a rubber axe. It won't hurt him. Anyway the bastard's drunk. He won't feel a thing.'

'The rubber axe wasn't sharp,' Ogilvy added, 'but it was hard as wood and weighed as much.'

'Mike and I hissed our arguments at each other in the corner of the dungeon, and Philip Waddilove, our producer, managed to hear just enough of them to get an idea of what Mike was after. He hurriedly gathered a lot of foam rubber padding and stuffed in under Vincent's costume. When Mike called "Action!" – in a tone of unmistakably savage glee – I went after Vincent with my rubber axe just a little harder than I would have normally, and probably bruised his ribs a bit – and it was quite pointless, because most of the blows ended up on the cutting room floor, victims of the censor's disapproval. But as Vincent was fairly drunk at the time, he probably didn't feel as much pain from the blows.'

Witchfinder General was supposed to have a happy ending. 'They ran out of time to film the final three pages of the script,' said Ogilvy, 'a happy mistake!'

When the production wrapped up, Price was more than relieved that it all came to an extremely painful but more than welcome end!

Reeves wasn't quite finished with Price. With the film ready for post-production work in the cutting room, he already felt Robert Russell's soft spoken voice did not suit his brutish appearance as Hopkins' henchman John Stearne, and had his lilting tones redubbed by Bernard Kay. Now it was Price's turn when he got summoned back to London. Reeves felt his voice was still too overtly theatrical for what was supposed to be an exercise in realism and had to be toned down considerably. With Reeves' resentment towards Price still intense, he did not partake in the post synching work.

Although relieved that Reeves wasn't there to supervise, Price's experience on *Witchfinder General* left him deflated. 'Vincent was convinced that (the film) wouldn't be any good because of the relationship he had with Reeves,' said Tenser, who was with him during post-synching. 'I spoke to him when he came back over to redub his dialogue, and he thought it was a waste of time. He thought the film wasn't any good. I'm certainly not a betting man but I made a wager with him that he would like the final print when he saw it. I know it was screened by AIP, but I never found out if he liked it – certainly he never came to me for the money.'

Reeves still had to deal with the director's nightmare of the British censor, who happened to be his distant cousin John Trevelyan. Described by Ogilvy as having, 'A face like a 1933 walnut case radio set,' Trevelyan was good friends with Tenser, who had kept him informed of all script rewrites and the shooting process throughout the production.

'Trevelyan knew his job,' said Tenser, 'he also loved films and he would not cut things for the sake of it. The cuts he asked for were because he genuinely thought that they were needed.' Tenser had high hopes that the film would be passed without any major problems.

They may have been cousins but Trevelyan bestowed no favours towards Reeves, who had to comply no matter how reluctant he felt towards the censor's final decision. 'Michael was very much a director who wanted it to look realistic,' said Tenser. 'During the scene where Ian Ogilvy kicks back with his spurs and catches Robert Russell's eye with one of them, you see blood spurting out the eye. Then there's the vicious fight with an axe.' Reeves wanted to use real pig's guts to give Hopkins a much bloodier death scene. 'I pulled Michael aside and told him he could not do that, the censor would not allow it and he would have shot a whole scene that had to be cut. I knew Trevelyan very well and I knew how his mind worked. If I were him I would ban it too and I suggested he shoot round it. So reluctantly, very reluctantly he did just that.'

Being a reasonable man, Trevelyan accepted Reeves' good intentions and the fact that the director deplored violence; his film was about man's inhumanity towards man and he wanted to make the violence too intense for people to stomach. 'The film gave the impression that it was exploiting violence and in particular sadism for commercial reasons,' argued Trevelyan, who advised that further cuts should be made. Once again the reluctant Reeves had to comply.

According to Ogilvy, 'Mike Reeves liked and respected him; possibly because John Trevelyan seemed to have put Mike into his art film category, or maybe because they were distant cousins – or perhaps it was a combination of both. There were still clashes between them about what should go and what should stay and Mike fought hard against every proposed cut in the film, while Trevelyan bent over backwards to let him keep as much as possible. But in the long run the BBFC had its way and much of the excessive violence was removed.'

It was when Trevelyan saw the final print that he summoned Reeves to his office and provided an extensive list of further changes. Reeves then took no further part in the editing process, disappointed at Trevelyan's interference and Tenser's lack of support.

'When Mike saw the final version of his film,' said Ogilvy, 'with all the offending sections gone, he found himself pleasantly surprised. The overall effect of the cuts hadn't really harmed his movie at all, and even he admitted that leaving more to the imagination and less to the eyes and ears was perhaps no bad thing when it came to manipulating audiences' emotions.'

Cuts, redubbing and everything else in the can, the final print reached the Tigon offices, and Tenser absolutely loved the end result, praising the good work from everyone involved. He started planning the advance publicity, as well as sending the completed film to Deke Heyward for his approval.

Heyward was equally impressed with the film, saying it was, 'one of the best we have gotten from England. It may be one of the better things that Vincent

Price has done.'

Sam Arkoff and James H Nicholson were next the view the film when it reached the States. According to Ogilvy, 'it was reported that one turned to the other and said, "Jesus Christ, we got a fucking art movie on our hands!"'

Any thoughts of *Witchfinder General* being a tax write-off for AIP quickly vanished after watching Price's performance. 'Michael Reeves brought out some elements in Vincent that we hadn't seen in a long time,' commented Arkoff. 'Vincent was more savage in that picture. Michael really brought out the balls in him. I was surprised how terrifying Vincent was in that. I hadn't expected it.' And despite his own misgivings about the film, Price admitted that, 'it's one of the best performances I've ever given.'

Arkoff made further changes for the American release. In addition to adding the bare breasted tavern scenes for the continental version, he replaced Paul Ferris' magnificent music with an inferior synthesiser score by Kendall Schmidt. To satisfy American horror fans, Arkoff renamed it *Edgar Allan Poe's The Conqueror Worm* from an obscure poem about death.

'Sam Arkoff wasn't a gambler,' said Tenser, 'he made sure every step he took had a reason. A very shrewd man and very good at putting a film together. He wanted to make sure it would be a complete success and thought the title *Witchfinder General* wouldn't appeal to the average American. He knew he could sell it if there was a connotation to Edgar Allan Poe.'

'Although the story had a Poe flavour to it,' said Arkoff, 'we had worried that *Witchfinder General* was an English tale that wouldn't have much appeal on this side of the Atlantic. We weren't exactly sure what (*The Conqueror Worm*) meant, but it was pure Poe and seemed to fit with *Witchfinder General's* story line. We felt if we had Vincent recite the poem at the beginning of the film, we could legitimately call the picture a Poe movie.' Deke Heyward apparently suffered a memory lapse when he described *Witchfinder General* as, 'the best production in the Poe series for the past few years!'

Price was recalled by AIP to recite *The Conqueror Worm*. 'They just picked a title that (AIP) thought would sell. I thought *Witchfinder General* was a wonderful title, because that's what Matthew Hopkins was, but *The Conqueror Worm* was the title of a poem by Poe, so they could sell the film as Edgar Allan Poe in America. *The Conqueror Worm* was the most ridiculous title for *Witchfinder General*. It took me six months to find the goddam poem!'

Price wasn't too happy that AIP marketed the film to include Sears Roebuck, who Price was still under contract with. It finally got released in America as *Edgar Allan Poe's The Conqueror Worm* – based on the book *Witchfinder General* by Ronald Bassett and the poem by Edgar Allan Poe. Producer credits for the UK release were also changed with Arnold Miller and Philip Waddilove being replaced by Deke Heyward; Tony Tenser remained executive producer. The AIP press release even stated that it was filmed in Hollywood!

Released in May 1968, *Witchfinder General* received a diverse reception from critics. 'Peculiarly nauseating' was the response from Dylis Powell of the *Sunday Times* while the *Guardian* felt the film was, 'less concerned with narrative than exploiting every opportunity for gratuitous sadism, lingering over hangings, protracted torture sessions, rape and mutilations.' The *Sunday Telegraph* found *Witchfinder General*, 'an exercise in sadistic extravagance all the more repugnant for being ably directed by Michael Reeves.'

There were positive reviews with the *Observer* saying the film was, 'Surprisingly muted in its violence, and superbly shot in Suffolk, the film is not without its longueurs, but it does have real style and presence.' The best review came from *The Times*, especially with regards to the director. 'Mr Reeves is no longer merely promising. He already has real achievements behind him; not merely making good horror films, but good films. Period!'

The Monthly Film Bulletin was equally positive although aware of how negative the violence could be to cinema audiences. 'Not since *Peeping Tom* (1959) has a film aroused such an outcry. Throughout the whole film there is a vivid sense of a time out of joint, which comes as much from the stray group of soldiers who skirmish against unseen attackers in the woods or hang wearily about by the wayside waiting for the next battle to commence, as from the bloody crimes committed in the name of religion by Matthew Hopkins.'

With the good reviews running alongside the bad ones, the tabloids were also filled with letters from angry readers complaining about the level of violence. There was even speculation that many local authorities would not screen the film, which caused concern for Tenser regarding box office takings.

The most vocal critic was playwright Alan Bennett, who found *Witchfinder General* so repulsive, he wrote a letter to *The Listener* describing it as, 'the most persistently sadistic and morally rotten film I have ever seen. It was a degrading experience by which I mean it made me feel dirty.'

It was the violence he was objecting to,' said Ogilvy. 'In 1968, movie violence was nowhere near the pitch that is seen today and the brutality pictured in *Witchfinder General* appears mild by contemporary standards. But in 1968 it was considered by some to be a dangerous and immoral film and questions were asked about it in the Houses of Parliament. All this controversy did wonders for its success at the box office and helped propel to the cult status it still enjoys today.'

Reeves was outraged by Bennett's outburst and his subsequent written reply provided a positive tone regarding the film's violence. 'Surely the most immoral thing in any form of entertainment is the conditioning of the audience to accept and enjoy violence. Violence is horrible, degrading and sordid. Insofar as one is going to show it on the screen at all, it should be presented as such – and the more people it shocks into sickened recognition of these facts the better.'

Reeves had the last laugh on Bennett when he added, 'I wish I could have witnessed Mr Bennett frantically attempting to wash away the "dirty" feeling the film gave him. It would have been proof of the fact *Witchfinder General* works as intended.'

Whatever the reaction of critics, outraged readers – and Alan Bennett, *Witchfinder General* played to packed houses all over the UK, turning in a massive profit for Tigon.

Critical reaction in America was just as vicious with *Hollywood Citizen News* calling the film, 'A disgrace to the producers and scriptors, and a sad commentary to the art of filmmaking. A film with such bestial brutality and orgiastic sadism, one wonders how is ever passed customs to be released in this country.' *Films and Filming* were more positive. '*Witchfinder General* has no explicit message, but it does say something the springs of despair and it says it forcefully. It is a very frightening film … *Witchfinder General* is emphatically not a horror film; it is however, a very horrifying one.'

Films and Filming also added that, 'Matthew Hopkins is the best of Vincent Price's recent performances.'

Despite the title change, and the negative criticisms, the film took a healthy $1.5 million profit at the American box office. Deke Heyward summed it up best by saying, '*The Conqueror Worm* is a good film for that genre and that time.' It even started a new horror trend in Germany with *Mark of The Devil* (1970), *The Bloody Judge* (1970) and *Hexen: Mark of the Devil II* (1973) being in some way inspired by *Witchfinder General*. These brutal movies and other subsequent efforts had what could best be described as 'The Reeves Effect.'

'*Witchfinder General* has been a cult film for over 45 years,' said Ogilvy. 'It's been discussed endlessly, written about voluminously, and nominated by several people who know about these things as one of the greatest films ever made. It has also been vilified in the press, most notably by the playwright Alan Bennett.'

While there is little to shock a modern audience, *Witchfinder General* still packs a solid punch. It's a remarkably well made effort, directed with a real sense of place and period by Michael Reeves. The realism is effectively captured by John Coquillon's outstanding photography and Paul Ferris' haunting score. Locations are put to good use, and despite the budget restrictions, Reeves doesn't waste a single scene.

The scenes of violence and torture are sadistic for its time. For what is classed as a gothic horror, there is no hint of fantasy; the witches being accused of their crimes are real people; no one gets turned into a toad! This is violence put across in an uncompromising manner and Reeves makes no excuses for it. There are times when the pessimistic atmosphere works against the movie, but otherwise *Witchfinder General* is a brilliant piece of cinema.

The acting is uniformly excellent. Ian Ogilvy and Hilary Dwyer make a likeable and attractive couple so their descent into madness is all the more tragic. Hailed by Tony Tenser as, 'a new and stronger Vivien Leigh,' Dwyer is excellent, her acting being all the more remarkable considering her young years. Ogilvy also shows great promise with an intense, multi layered performance.

Of the veteran cast, Patrick Wymark makes the most of his guest appearance; the *Morning Star* stating that his performance as Cromwell was one of, 'the only things which stand out in this crude and savage bit of non-history.' Rupert Davies is equally excellent as John Lowes. 'As the priest he is terrific,' said Tenser. 'Full of life and bonhomie at the beginning and completely spent, haggard and injured after all that he's been through at the end.' His descent from affable father figure to broken man still makes uncomfortable viewing.

From Price's first appearance on horseback as he arrives in Brandeston, the actor cuts his usual impressive figure in period costume, but there's no easy-going air about him, and when he speaks, the voice is unmistakable, but the melodramatic overtones reminiscent of previous performances are conspicuously absent.

The sartorial flamboyance is also missing. No camping it up here. What we see is an acting performance, and an excellent one to boot. Despite their antagonism, Reeves brought out qualities never seen from Price in a long time. Hopkins is a truly frightening figure, but not without sympathy: he is an intelligent individual corrupted by the financial rewards of his position.

According to writer John Brosnan, Price's performance, 'was a masterly portrayal of evil that serves to remind one that when he wants to, Price really can act – a fact often forgotten when one observes him doing his familiar mugging routine film after film.' *Witchfinder General* may have been an uncomfortable experience for Price, but his performance remains a fantastic career defining moment.

Any doubts Price had about working with Michael Reeves were soon dispelled after watching *Witchfinder General*. 'I realised what he wanted was a low key, very laid back, menacing performance. He did get it but I was fighting almost every step of the way. Had I known what he wanted, I would have co-operated.'

Price wrote a letter of praise to Reeves, describing *Witchfinder General* as, 'a very impressive, moving and exciting picture. Congratulations! I'm sure you have a big success and a long feather in your cap. So my dear Michael, in spite of the fact we did not get along too well – mostly my fault, as I was physically and mentally indisposed at that particular moment of my life (both public and private) – I do think you made a very fine picture, and what's more, I liked what you gave me to do!'

Reeves responded to Price's 24-page letter with, 'I knew you would think so.'

With *Witchfinder General* on major release on both sides of the Atlantic, to commercial success, mixed reviews, different titles, outraged critics, and a brilliant central performance, all interested parties went their separate ways, but for one of the principle figures, he would never return.

Tony Tenser continued producing a variety of movies. After an abortive attempt to buy Hammer, he sold Tigon to the Laurie Marsh Group and the company ceased production altogether. Now a wealthy man, he eventually retired to the life of a country gentleman. Tony Tenser died on 5 December 2007.

On his return to the States, Price began rehearsals for an ambitious Broadway production of *Married Alive*, a comedy-musical adaptation of Arnold Bennett's play *The Great Adventure* (adapted from his novel *Buried Alive*). Directed by Irish actor Noel Willman, music and lyrics were written by Jule Styne and E Y Harburg with Lee Theodore providing the choreography, Price headed up a strong cast that included British actors Patricia Routledge and Peter Woodthorpe.

It was Price's first Broadway play since 1954 and the first time he would sing on stage. Following his creative high in *Witchfinder General*, the actor was grateful for landing a role that had little to do with his screen image. 'For the first time in ages,' said Victoria Price, 'he was hired not for his horror persona, but for the cultivated and artistic image that had been his earliest drawing card.'

Renamed *Darling of the Day*, the plot centres on disillusioned landscape painter Priam Farll (Price – retaining the beard he grew for *Witchfinder*), who assumes the identity of his late butler and takes up employment with kindly widow Alice Challis (Routledge), who soon discovers who he really is.

Budgeted at $50,000 and heavily promoted on TV, the play was fraught with problems. The original director Steven Vinayer was fired before rehearsals started. Albert Marre took over, only to replaced, once more, by Vinayer! Eventually Noel Willman was brought in. After a poor try-out in Toronto in December 1967, the play went to Boston's Schubert Theatre where it met with the same negative response.

The play finally limped into the George Abbott Theatre on Broadway, and despite Patricia Routledge winning a Tony award, reviews were mixed and the play closed after 31 performances. Losing $3 million at the box office, *Darling of the Day* became one of Broadway's costliest failures.

'I guess it ain't my year,' lamented Price, obviously hurt by the play's failure. His feelings ranged from philosophical – 'It got good notices, but it was at a time when *Grease* and *Hair* were popular and this was just a nice old fashioned musical, and the public didn't go for it.' – to anger – 'The next person who says "That's show biz" is going to get my fist in some highly uncomfortable place.' – and finally, to relief – 'it was a sixteen week mess and I'm delighted it's over.'

Price remained optimistic about returning permanently to the stage. 'One day I'll probably stop these horror films and sit back and wait for the right part to turn up. I always felt my greatest success would come at the end of my career.'

But in reality he was deeply saddened by the experience, which was a crush to his professional self-esteem. 'Vincent was extremely upset by the failure of *Darling of the Day*,' said Victoria, 'because to him and to everyone else, its demise was totally unnecessary. It was devastating to Vincent. It was a very sad time.'

Price went on to star opposite Clint Walker in the western *More Dead Than Alive* (1968) as carnival showman Dan Ruffalo; it also gave him a bloody death scene when he's filled full of lead by an outlaw. He followed it up with a guest appearance as Mr Morality in the Elvis Presley comedy *The Trouble with Girls* (1969). He shares no scenes with Presley.

For Michael Reeves, tragedy was just around the corner. *Witchfinder General* proved a hard act to follow, and despite being touted by Hollywood, he was uncomfortable with being pigeonholed as a horror director, a situation not helped by AIP's decision to hire him for further exploitation movies.

Among the interesting efforts at the time were *Easy Rider* (1969), *Bloody Mama* (1970) and Tigon's unfilmed IRA thriller *O'Hooligan's Mob*. AIP also lined Reeves up to direct the ambitious biopic *De Sade* (1969), but his unstable behaviour got him removed from the production and replaced by Cy Enfield. *De Sade* was a commercial disaster that prevented AIP breaking into mainstream cinema.

A manic depressive all his life, Reeves' mood swings became so volatile, his Harley Street doctor prescribed him more pills than his system could manage. Even his girlfriend Annabelle Webb couldn't take it anymore and walked out. For days on end he would sit in the corner of Deke Heyward's office and not say a word to anyone.

'After *Witchfinder General*, Mike seemed to lose his way,' recalled Ogilvy. 'Annabelle had moved on, her own career offering her opportunities she didn't want to resist. Her departure had nothing to do with Mike's subsequent problems. He was always prone to mood swings but now he sometimes plunged into a black depression, drank heavily and swallowed lots of sleeping pills. He worked in a desultory fashion on a number of projects but they came to nothing. He became reclusive. His friends saw less of him. I went on to other projects in film and television and theatre – some of them abroad – and didn't notice this decline as much as others who stayed closer to Mike.'

Already a victim of private hospitals and money grabbing doctors, the drug taking got worse. Some months earlier Reeves collapsed at his home following an overdose of Nembutal washed down with alcohol, but he soon recovered. 'These gestures were made to draw attention to himself because he felt he was unable to cope,' said Tenser of the situation.

On 11 February 1969, Michael Reeves was found dead in his London flat by his housekeeper, the cause of death being an overdose of barbiturates. His death, though unsurprising given his nature, was a shock to those who knew him. It also sparked a mystery as to whether his death was accidental or suicidal. 'Mike was taking a lot of pills,' said Nicky Henson, who disputes the suicide angle. 'He had pills to get up, pills to go to bed, pills for everything. The night he died he went to bed, took his pills, woke up with a headache and took some more. Simple as that – a terrible accident.'

'Michael wouldn't go deliberately,' said Tenser. 'He had a nice girlfriend, he came from a wealthy family, and he had money of his own. He had been depressed and had various prescriptions, but he had his whole future ahead of him and he knew that. He wouldn't have killed himself.'

'It was a shame,' lamented Price. 'He couldn't control himself, and he was on the flip, and then his girlfriend ditched him, because she couldn't put up with him. He was just completely determined to destroy himself.'

'He was just 25,' said a devastated Ogilvy. 'I was numb with grief, not only at the loss of my close friend, but at the waste of a life that held such promise.'

Following a post mortem, the Westminster Coroner recorded an open verdict of accidental death.

'There's a lot to be said about dying young,' said Ian Ogilvy, 'other than the obvious and cynical observation that it's one way of becoming legendary, particularly if the deceased was working, with moderate success, in the arts when he died. Had Michael Reeves survived his accident, I don't think he would have achieved the status he now enjoys in death. But I do believe he would have gone on to make bigger and better films, that he would have enjoyed a long and prosperous career – and that he would have ended his life a famous and respected and prolific film director. I also like to think I would have been in some of those movies, and that we remained close friends until the end.'

The Oblong Box

'Gothic is just a work recalling a multitude of sins.' – Vincent Price

Bolstered by the artistic high of *Witchfinder General*, yet wounded by the failure of *Darling of the Day*, Price filled the void with various TV appearances, mostly on *The Red Skelton Show*.

Had *Darling of the Day* been a hit, he could have re-established his reputation as a serious stage actor. Instead it was back to AIP and his continuing horror image. As reluctant as he was to be at the beck and call of Sam Arkoff, he was glad to be working once more in England. 'Vincent was now in the uncomfortable position of having to act in films he did not choose,' said Victoria. 'His only consolation seemed to be the fact that most of them were shot in England. Whatever the quality of the film, Vincent found continual pleasure in exploring London's art galleries and flea markets on weekends, even as he enjoyed working with British actors and film crews during the week.'

AIP's next effort returned to Poe territory with *The Oblong Box*. Deke Heyward told Price that scriptwriter Lawrence Huntingdon was scheduled to direct. 'I am certain,' said Heyward, 'that you will get along with him quite well. All of us are looking forward to the light and joy that accompanies your visits and hope we have another *Conqueror Worm* on our hands. I'm keeping the brandy warm and the birds cold until your arrival.'

By the time Price arrived in London on 12 November 1968, Huntingdon had been replaced by Michael Reeves. Reeves' involvement with *The Oblong Box* did much to lift Price's enthusiasm, especially when Huntingdon's original script marked him down for the dual role of Julian and Edward Markham and that production would commence in Dublin.

'(Reeves) showed great promise,' said Price. 'He was a wonderful director, but these problems he had. He called me after *Witchfinder General* was released in England, and it got good notices. It was really a hit for him. He said, "There, you see I told you so." It was a mad kind of thing to do. Then we got together on *The Oblong Box*, I said, "Well, I think you were wonderful, you made a marvellous picture. Now let's get along on this one."'

Once production commenced att Shepperton Studios, Reeves, disappointed that the film would not be shot in Ireland, was far from happy with Huntington's script and started doing several extensive re-writes. Eventually he brought in Christopher Wicking to provide additional dialogue and uncredited rewrites.

Born in London in 1943 and a movie fan since childhood, Wicking was studying at St Martin's School of Art when he decided to work in films as a booking clerk for Anglo-Amalgamated and then as a documentary film editor. Now a film critic of some distinction, he alternated from the French magazines *Cashies du Cinema, Positif* and *Midi Minuit Fantastique* to the British publications *Time Out* and *The Monthly Film Bulletin*.

'Michael wanted some changes made to the script," said Wicking, "and it was his responsibility to find someone to do the work. Since we were with the same agent and because I actually liked horror films – and was cheap – he asked if I would do some pages. So I met with Michael, and we found we had some things in common.'

Wicking soon became aware of Reeves' destructive mental state. '(AIP) were trying to rush something into production to take advantage of Michael's talents. But as it got closer and closer to shooting, he became more frightened of it, and apparently he had all sort of problems with doctors. He was on uppers and downers and XYZ and shock treatment, which was all pretty awful.'

On his arrival in London, Price also noticed Reeves' emotional collapse. 'He had this terrible problem of suicide. He tried about four times, and finally they thought they had him cured, but when we started to do the costume tests and all the preparation for *The Oblong Box*, he tried it again, and they just said, "he's too unstable".'

To make matters worse, their old feud, which had never really been resolved, erupted again to the point that Price and Reeves communicated to each other by letter or from a third party. Not surprisingly, Deke Heyward removed Reeves from the film. Any thoughts about bringing Huntington back as director came to a tragic end when he died eleven days into production.

Drafted in as Reeves replacement was documentary filmmaker and TV producer Gordon Hessler. Born in Germany in 1925, Hessler attended Reading University before moving to America. After working on several documentaries, he was placed under contract by Alfred Hitchcock for his shows *Alfred Hitchcock Presents* and *The Alfred Hitchcock Hour*. Starting out as story editor, Hessler climbed up the ranks to producer and director on the latter show.

Hessler's unpublished novel became the subject of his directorial debut. *Catacombs* (1964) is an odd little thriller inspired by *Les Diaboliques* (1955). He followed it up with another thriller, *The Last Shot You Hear* (1969) and some uncredited work on *De Sade*.

It was enough for Deke Heyward to hire him as director and producer on *The Oblong Box*. According to Christopher Wicking, 'Gordon had directed in America and had done small pictures in England, he just instantly stepped in.'

Hessler wasn't happy with Huntington's script and being old friends with Wicking, he gave the writer a free hand in reinventing the whole project. 'Gordon and I were both aware of the need for horror to be made new,' said Wicking. 'We wanted to reflect that by being more realist and more radical.'

Abandoning Poe's original story, Wicking opted for another Poe inspired theme of premature burial, and added the idea of African tribal rights. 'I made the theme of imperial exploitation of the natives the subtext, the cause of the curse.'

Wicking's revised script still suffered from a weak story. 'The (original) script was by Lawrence Huntington, and it wasn't very good. So it was a question of finding scenes to add that wouldn't be padding; that would develop character and add to the narrative. Yet they were padding really. I got a call from Gordon on a Monday asking for more scenes for Vincent Price. They also needed scenes with more production values, scenes of extras in taverns.'

With the troubled production thrown into turmoil by Michael Reeves' departure, Hessler did his best with the abysmal script and the extensive re-writes. 'We made it as imaginative as we could, given the material we had, given the three weeks we had to shoot it in.'

The script's biggest fault provided the film's most disappointing moment. Arriving at Shepperton Studios in November 1968 was Christopher Lee, who had previously worked with Reeves on *Il Castello dei morti vivi* (1965). Of course

Reeves was well and truly out of the picture by the time Lee began filming his scenes on *The Oblong Box*.

Price and Lee were originally linked to an unfilmed project called *Something Evil* in 1967. Later they were to star in *El Conde Dracula* (1969), but Price dropped out. *The Oblong Box* finally marked their first horror teaming.

The best that Wicking could do was provide them with ONE scene together towards the end of the film. 'It was not until I was dying,' said Lee, 'with my throat cut, that my story intersected with Vincent's, so that it was hail and farewell meeting, as I lay expiring in his arms, with him asking me, "Which way did he go?" and I gurgled in answer through a severed artery. He was swathed in a cloak like tent, and by mistake rolled me on to it so that the camera could relish my death agony to the full, and kept hissing, "You're lying on my train!" as I gurgled.'

Price and Lee became lifelong friends, strengthened by the fact they shared the same birthday. 'Everybody told me he was rather stiff, unbending and not very funny,' said Price, who was forewarned by others about Lee's stern persona. 'Well, we screamed with laughter from the minute we shook hands until now. We get along like mad, write each other rude notes and funny letters and telegrams and postcards and, you know, anything we can find that we know will tickle one another. He's one of the few actors in my life that I have stayed in touch with, strangely enough. If you get on a subject that he likes, he's very warm and vibrant. I think he's got a wonderful sense of humour, but I don't think everybody knows how to get at it. For some reason or another we strike each other as funny, and its wonderful fun to be with him.'

Lee also had fond memories of meeting his future friend. 'I remember very clearly when I first met Vincent. It was at Shepperton Studios. I was walking toward the restaurant to have lunch: obviously I'd been doing something on the film before he arrived. A car drew up, Vincent got out. He came over with a great big smile on his face, and we shock hands, and he said, "Oh, I'm so happy that we're doing this picture together." It wasn't until years later that I heard Vincent had been told I was very remote and very reserved and very difficult to talk to and had no sense of humour, all that sort of thing. So Vincent was obvious prepared for the worst, and I like to think he was agreeably surprised.'

Lee further added was Price was, 'an extremely funny man. Indeed he was a dazzling all-rounder. As a professional lecturer he toured in painting, sculpture and cookery, and bought art for Sears and Roebuck. He was as much at ease in the theatre as in the cinema. A model of versatility. He could be acid and devastating, but he was never otherwise than sweet to me.'

Billed as a special guest star, Lee's part as Dr Newhartt was an extended cameo intersected as part of a sub plot. While the main story concerned itself with African curses, Lee's segment focussed on the premature burial side of things. Fitted with a silly blond wig, Lee doesn't have much to do except play reluctant host for the velvet masked Sir Edward Markham (Alister Williamson), who is blackmailing him for his body snatching activities.

Reeves's influence remained long after the director had bowed out. John

Coquillon returned as cinematographer with Rupert Davies making a cameo appearance. On AIP's insistence, Hilary Dwyer also returned, which left Gordon Hessler somewhat perplexed. 'I don't know what the situation was,' he said of Dwyer's casting, 'but they like her and (AIP) kept pushing you to use certain actors. I guess the management must have thought she was star material or something like that.'

For Vincent Price, *The Oblong Box* was a slightly happier experience than *Witchfinder General*, especially when there was little location work to deal with. 'I think I much prefer the control of the studio. Certainly for any kind of intimate scene. And besides you can usually work much faster, and so it is easier to preserve a continuity of emotion. The main problem with location work, particularly in England, is that nobody is equipped for it. I think that when you're trying to make people believe, then it's terribly important for these films to have an element of make-believe about them, and you can only get that inside the studio.'

And after being at constant loggerheads with Michael Reeves, Price enjoyed working with Gordon Hessler, who understood what the actor was going through professionally. 'Vincent often felt, like Christopher Lee in the *Dracula* pictures, that he was just being used as a name, and wasn't being given enough to do.'

Price was equally impressed by Hessler's work on *The Oblong Box*. 'Gordon did a very good job with it, because he only took on the film a couple of days before we started shooting.'

Away from work, Hessler found Price an incredible man to know. On one occasion they invited out to dinner a Nigerian prince who was involved in the dance company that appears in the film. 'Instead of pouring out about all the films he had done,' said Hessler, 'Vincent never talked once about himself. He only talked about African art and parts of Africa he'd been to. Amazing; it was a revelation. I was staggered. That's the kind of person he was.'

The Oblong Box hardly ranks as an all-time classic and suffers in comparison to *Witchfinder General*. That said, Hessler does a superior job even if he cannot quite overcome the poor script. John Coquillon's camerawork is superb, and this being another battle hard film crew with a solid cast to match, the technical aspects are impeccable and most of the performances professional.

Robbed of his chance to play the dual role of the Markham brothers (which might have been more fun), Price's performance is low key. With the failure of *Darling of the Day* still ringing in his ears, the actor looks jaded. And while he remains typically professional, the spark is lacking. He even suffers in comparison to Christopher Lee, who not only has the better part, he actually invests some ghoulish aplomb into his dodgy dialogue.

Price is equally ill at ease alongside Hilary Dwyer as Julian's wife Elizabeth. Instead of looking like a married couple, they look like father and daughter – not compatible at all. Dwyer remains as appealing as ever and the other actors are solid with the stand-out performance coming from Peter Arne as the double crossing lawyer Samuel Trench.

With production of *The Oblong Box* wrapping up at the end of November, Price returned to America to spend Christmas with his family. In the meantime he returned to AIP to provide another Poe voice-over for *Spirits of the Dead* (1969) a Euro gothic portmanteau consisting of three tales, each one directed by luminaries of the European art-house cinema, Frederico Fellini, Louis Malle and Roger Vadim. The continental cast included Brigitte Bardot, Alain Delon, Jane Fonda, Peter Fonda and Terence Stamp.

The Oblong Box made it in the cinemas on 18 June 1969 as a co-feature with AIP's *The Dunwich Horror* (1969). Critical reaction was mixed with the *New York Times* summing it up best – 'The British and American producers, who have been mining Edgar Allan Poe's seemingly inexhaustible literary lode, have now unearthed *The Oblong Box* to illustrate once again that horror can be quaintly laughable and unconvincing at modest prices. All things considered, *The Oblong Box* (coffin in this cheerless charade) might have been better left interred.'

And with *Witchfinder General* turning the gothic horror tradition on its head, even Deke Heyward saw how times were changing after seeing *The Oblong Box*. 'I wanted so much to break away from the Poe nonsense: that day was over. Horror had gotten too old fashioned and so had we.' Heyward's prophetic words gave an indication that all was not well at AIP.

The Oblong Box took over $1million at the box office – enough to keep AIP and the Poe series going for a while yet. 'Because of its financial success,' said Hessler, 'AIP gave me a contract for four pictures.' It even got into some controversy, to the amusement of Christopher Wicking. 'The film was banned in Texas for being too pro-negro at the time, a minor joy I didn't expect from a horror movie.'

Between the making and the release of *The Oblong Box* there were two deaths closely associated with Price, and both within days of each other! The first was his old friend Boris Karloff, who passed away on 2 February 1969 at the age of 81. Considering his age and poor health, it was inevitable. However, Michael Reeves' death on 11 February was a massive shock to everyone. 'That poor boy!' Price exclaimed sadly. 'He was so talented and had such a bright future, but he was a deeply troubled young man. I realised only after I saw *Witchfinder General* how talented he was. It was a great loss to the cinema. Had he been disciplined, he could have become a very good director. Believe me this profession takes enormous discipline. You're out there at six in the morning, and you're up until midnight and back at six in the morning. There's no fooling around if you want to last.'

Although continuing strength at the box office kept the wolf at bay, the British horror market was showing signs of decline; even Hammer's best work was behind them, despite winning the coveted Queen's Award for Industry. With the financial situation in mind Hammer and AIP went into a co-production deal. Instead of constructing a possible star vehicle for Price, Peter Cushing and Christopher Lee, the companies produced *The Vampire Lovers* (1970). Filled with female nudity and lesbian loves scenes, it was a box office winner that made a horror star out of Ingrid Pit.

Internal problems within Hammer's inner circle meant *The Vampire Lovers* was their only co-production deal with AIP, although Price had been considered for a leading role opposite Lee in Hammer's *Taste the Blood of Dracula* (1969).

AIP's next step was co-production deal with Hammer's horror rivals Amicus. Founded by Americans Milton Subotsky and Max J Rosenberg, Amicus carved out their own niche with the portmanteaus *Dr Terror's House of Horrors* (1964) and *Torture Garden* (1967). With Amicus well established, AIP decided to join forces for a new film.

The film that AIP and Amicus finally produced made horror history, and for the wrong reasons.

Scream and Scream Again

'To me, the films that deal with drug addiction, crime and war are the real horrors films. In a world where slaughter and vicious crime are daily occurrences, a good ghoulish movie is comic relief.' – Vincent Price

'I really didn't know what *Scream and Scream Again* was about,' recalled Vincent Price, 'which scream was I playing?' His first contemporary horror film since his work for William Castle, the origins of *Scream and Scream Again* came from a pulp science fiction novel called *The Disorientated Man* by Peter Saxon, a pseudonym for the Irish writer W Howard Baker, who wrote several *Sexton Blake* stories for Amalgamated Press.

First published in the UK in 1966 (and in America the following year) *The Disorientated Man* was a collaboration between Baker, Martin Thomas and Stephen Frances; Frances wrote the bulk of it while Baker and Thomas carried out extensive revisions. The book has a fair share of plots holes, so it's not so much *The Disorientated Man* as *The Disjointed Novel*!

Despite the obvious faults, *The Disorientated Man* proved popular with science fiction fans because of the hodgepodge of contemporary themes inspired by *Invasion of the Body Snatchers* (1955) and *Quatermass II* (1956). It's all there on the printed page; alien invasions, the political climate of the sixties, the Cold War, vampires, the creation of super men, and a British crime thriller all rolled into one!

The Disorientated Man was brought to the attention of an erudite, exceptionally intelligent and enormously well-read writer and film producer named Milton Subotsky.

Even though Subotsky removed most of the aliens from outer space references, the script was still too ambitious to finance. He showed it to Max Rosenberg, who then presented it to Sam Arkoff. Arkoff liked the idea and sent Rosenberg to Deke Heyward in London.

Heyward also liked the idea and provided a $350,000 budget on condition that Subotsky used AIP's production team. Heyward then made an announcement in the trade magazines, confirming that AIP and Amicus were producing a super suspense mystery feature. Shooting was to begin at Shepperton Studios in May 1969.

With the co-production set up, the time was now right to bring Vincent Price, Peter Cushing and Christopher Lee together for the first time. 'We wanted the three top horror stars in one film,' enthused Subotsky. By arranging a deal with AIP, he could now have access to Price.

'I didn't get a very good budget for *Scream and Scream Again*,' he added. 'Vincent Price was under contract with AIP for £75,000 a picture, so I negotiated a deal to use Vincent for £40,000, which meant I could pay Christopher and Peter a lot of money for relatively small roles. Christopher was on the film for three days and Peter was on for one day I think … I'm glad that Cushing and Lee accepted the small roles they had. Perhaps it was a bit of a cheat to advertise them as stars rather than guest stars.'

Subotsky's memory must be playing tricks on him as the film was never constructed to showcase the three Titans of Terror. Price and Lee were already contracted to appear, but only days before shooting began, Deke Heyward made a last minute decision to add Cushing to the cast for one day's shooting. And ever the working actor, he accepted without hesitation. 'I will accept any part, big or small, if I feel my contribution will mean something. Naturally I prefer a large role, because I love to work and need to, for many personal reasons apart from the obvious.'

Years later, Cushing admitted that, 'I can't remember much about that picture. Can you recall it? Which part did I play in it?' Not only did Cushing have no recollection of the film, he did not meet Price or Lee during his time on the set.

Heyward's decision to cast Cushing in a small role was intended to recharge Subotsky's now flagging project as well as keep the increasingly reluctant Lee on board. With AIP footing the bill, Subotsky's role as hands-on producer would be shunted aside as Heyward took control of the production and assembled his team.

Heyward's first choice director during pre-production was Michael Reeves, despite his deteriorating health. By the time *Scream and Scream Again* went into production, Reeves had been dead three months, so the assignment went to Gordon Hessler, who had just signed a contract with AIP following the success of *The Oblong Box*.

Heyward felt Hessler was an excellent choice. 'There's a certain goofy integrity inherent in everything Gordon does, regardless of budget He will fight to do the best job that he can. And I don't know too many people who, without money, can make films better than Gordon.'

Hessler had nothing but admiration for Milton Subotsky as a filmmaker and a person. 'He was an enormous enthusiast for science fiction and horror films, tremendously enthusiastic, almost a naiveté about him.'

Hessler almost quit the project after reading the script, which he considered 'unplayable'. 'I hated Milton Subotsky's script. I like him personally, but it was just an awful script. Chris Wicking, who was introduced to me by Michael Reeves, rewrote the script entirely fresh.' Even Deke Heyward felt that the original was, 'too difficult to do within budget'. After a lengthy discussion with Heyward, Hessler threw it out altogether and hired Wicking to start all over again.

Hessler described *The Disorientated Man* as, 'a throwaway book that you can read on a train. There was nothing in it, just empty pieces of action. But it was Chris who gave it a whole new level by using it as a political process of what might happen in the future. That is what made the picture, he's the one that came up with all those ideas, yet he still managed to keep the nuances of the sort of pulp fiction novel.'

'Gordon didn't like the (original) screenplay,' said Christopher Wicking. 'He didn't feel Milton could deliver what (AIP) wanted. I got a call from Gordon requesting I read the book and then read Milton's screenplay.'

'The book gave me goosebumps,' he added. 'Then I read Milton's screenplay, which was totally flat; it was like watching a soufflé dying, it just caved in after a while. Gordon and I discussed it at length. He saw the police material as *Coogan's Bluff* (1968) country. The one radical thing we did, which changed what Milton had done and came directly from the book, was take out the blobs from space. We wanted to do a Don Siegel style horror – *Coogan's Bluff* meets *Invasion of the Body Snatchers*, and we needed something stronger than lumps from another planet. So we took the aliens away and implied that Vincent Price's mad doctor character was responsible for the super-human creatures. We wanted to investigate science and politics. So we used a lot of material from news headlines, material about transplants and genetic experiments.'

Aliens aside, Wicking's revised script sticks to the novel. With Hessler's decision to take a grittier approach to the material, the new script met with Heyward's unanimous support. '(Heyward) gave us complete control of whatever we wanted to do,' said Hessler. 'Consequently our script was approved, and we went ahead.'

With everything set to go, Vincent Price finally joined the cast on the strength of the new script. This further contradicts Subotsky's statement that the film was constructed as a vehicle for the three top horror stars.

Subotsky wasn't happy with the situation and his continued presence on the set quickly soured his relationship with Hessler. As soon as production began, Subotsky started debating and arguing with Hessler about possible script changes while the director was sorting out the day's shooting schedule. 'It was very tedious,' said Hessler. 'But he was childlike, an infant of the cinema, and he loved movies. On that point, as a filmmaker, you have to respect him.'

Hessler soon grew tired of Subotsky's constant interference. 'I asked Deke to put a stop to that, because obviously we had a completely different concept from Milton Subotsky's. Now he might have thought he had a better script, but we didn't think so. We thought his was very old fashioned and had nothing to do with what we were trying to tell. So he never had any creative say. AIP was paying the bill, so they called the shots.'

Heyward agreed. 'Gordon knows scripts better than most directors. He is one of the most underestimated directors in the business. We were doing things on spit and a shoestring. To have someone like Gordon was like having a minor saviour working with you. He never went over budget to my knowledge, but he will always preserve the integrity of the project. He knew what he wanted, and if I could, I would give it to him.'

Heyward had his own problems with Subotsky, and his partner Max Rosenberg. 'They were difficult for me to work with, too. They tried to take control, and remember this was an AIP picture, not an Amicus picture.'

The combined efforts of Hessler and Heyward successfully barred Subotsky and Rosenberg from the set. Subotsky had no further input into the film, and that included his obsession with editing. 'He loved editing,' said Hessler, 'but we didn't permit him to edit the picture. We put in a freelance editor on it because Subotsky would argue for frame upon frame upon frame.'

At least Subotsky and Rosenberg could take consolation that they retained their producer credits. But from this point on, *Scream and Scream Again* remained in the capable hands of Hessler and AIP, with only minimal input from Amicus.

Scream and Scream Again was shot entirely on location in London, an ideal setting for John Coquillon's superb cinematography. The tight budget and the four week shooting schedule worked in Hessler's favour as he gave the film a real sense of urgency. 'When you have a little film, sometimes there is a spirit of movement and momentum that starts going, and you're into the story the whole time. But when you have a big budget, you may forget where you are in the picture. You shoot a minute a day. You never have any real sense of the whole unit. You might get a better job on a low budget film sometimes.'

And those moments worked brilliantly, especially the scenes in the police station, where Len Harris' hand-held camerawork creates a shambolic, documentary feel as he moves from one busy room to another without any cuts. The well-staged car chase between Keith in his jag and the police in their big humbers is tightly edited and builds up to a satisfactory climax that confirmed Heyward's absolute trust in Hessler's work.

But these scenes would never have been as memorable if it wasn't for the presence of Alfred Marks as the stern but likable Superintendant Bellaver. It is Marks who gives *Scream and Scream Again* real heart, and that makes his unexpected death by the neck pinching composite Konrad all the more shocking and sad for the viewer.

Marks was able to improvise his lines to startling comic effect ('That bloody chicken wasn't killed, it died of old age!' his reaction to some stale sandwiches that were, 'curling up like Charlie Chaplin's boots!'). Hessler admired Marks' work on the film. 'He played millions of police parts, and played them very well. Also, he had a great sense of humour and was a professional comedian. He threw in a lot of lines in, which were very good. I was very lucky to have him as an actor.'

Marks may have been the unintentional star, but there were two other actors who made an equal impression. The first is Marshall Jones as the impassive but deadly Konrad. Robotic in speech and movement, Jones presents a sinister, emotionless and sadistic figure, whether he casually tortures Yutte Stensgaard's Erika or kills off Captain Sollis (Peter Sallis) and Major Benedek (Peter Cushing), while rising up the ranks of power in the unknown fascist state where he works as an enforcer. Jones' calm authority makes him frightening, so much so, it's all the more surprising the actor wasn't used in further horror films.

Jones featured in Hessler's *Cry of the Banshee* (1970) and *Murders in the Rue Morgue* (1971) before disappearing altogether. He resurfaced a few years later as the head of a stereotypical Welsh family in the TV soap opera *Crossroads*.

Of point of interest, Jones is mistakenly billed as Peter Cushing on the trailer for *Scream and Scream Again*: perhaps this also had something to do with the horror star's 11th hour casting.

The other memorable performance comes from Michael Gothard as the vampire Keith. With his Mick Jagger looks, long hair and frilly purple shirt, Gothard is a strong, intense actor who oozes the right kind of charisma to attract his female victims. Seeing the potential of the all-important youth market, Heyward signed up The Amen Corner to perform a couple of songs at the nightclub where Keith is stalking his prey.

Gothard features in the film's most disturbing scene when Keith picks up and kills 'guest star' Judy Huxtable. Her brutal sexual assault and subsequent murder at the hands of Keith is uncomfortable to watch and echoes the sadism of *Witchfinder General*. Being a defective composite, Keith is driven by an unknown force to commit these dreadful acts of violence – the Age of Aquarius going completely wrong!

Gothard had the star quality to become a massive success. 'I felt Michael was going to be the biggest thing that ever happened,' said Heyward. 'He had an insane look and that drive, and he was wonderful. Here is a kid who threw himself into the picture wholeheartedly. Do you remember that scene where he appears to walk up a cliff? That's a stunt. But the kid agreed to do it without a double. He was that driven. He had a lot of class and a lot of style. We felt he was going to be the next big star of either the English cinema or the international cinema: there was a madness to him.'

Gothard proved his worth during the quarry scene. Being superhuman, Keith was able to run up the clifftop without missing a beat. This was achieved by Hessler by attaching a steel cable to Gothard. According to Heyward, 'Gordon came up with the idea of using an overhead cable to give the illusion of his walking up the cliff. This is the only way the stunts could have been included on a low budget.'

Despite sterling performances in Ken Russell's *The Devils* (1971), Curtis Harrington's *Whoever Slew Auntie Roo?* (1972) and the James Bond movie *For Your Eyes Only* (1981), Gothard never achieved the stardom he deserved. Described by Curtis Harrington as, 'the most neurotic actor I have ever worked with,' Gothard, who had never married, battled serious clinical depression for several years. On 2 December 1992 he hung himself at his Hampstead home. The coroner recorded a verdict of suicide.

With the best performances coming from three lesser known actors, how did the horror stars fair in their nominal roles? Who gave the best performance?

Of the three, it is Peter Cushing who walks away with the acting honours. The actor invests Major Benedek with a steely resolve when he tries to demote Konrad for his acts of torture. It's a typically forceful Cushing performance where he turns a throwaway role into a well-rounded character. A dedicated party member, Benedek is also a diplomatic and sympathetic human being, outraged by Konrad's cruel activities. He even gets a memorable death scene, courtesy of Konrad's neck-pinch. It's a small role, but beautifully marked by Cushing.

Christopher Lee, on the other hand, gives the least interesting performance. A fine actor who excelled himself as *Dracula* (1958), Lee was always effective when playing off-beat character roles: anything straight forward and his acting is either inflexible or boring, a situation made worse by his increasing and vocal disenchantment with the genre.

Policemen, civil servants, government officials and academics (unless they deal with the supernatural) are boring roles for Lee, and the character of Fremont, head of British Intelligence is boring, so the bored looking actor gives a boring performance. He has one good scene, effectively shot in Trafalgar Square, where he makes an espionage deal with Konrad, but his lack of interest is obvious from the start.

Like Price and Cushing, Lee was equally confused by the film's premise. 'We were all aliens, if I remember rightly. I couldn't work it out at all.'

At least Vincent Price displays a lot more emotion than Lee does. Whereas Lee looks bored, Price looks baffled! He is urban and affable in his two decently acted scenes with Alfred Marks, but once Konrad murders Bellaver, and Dr Browning takes centre stage, Price is unable to do much with the role.

Lacking the ruthless intensity that Peter Cushing brought to Frankenstein, Price shows off his scientific research to David Sorel (Christopher Matthews) as if it was one of his latest art purchases. Never comfortable with the physical aspects of filmmaking, his lacklustre fight scene with Konrad lacks sufficient impact. 'In horror films the odds are always heavily against me. I'm always evil and in a keen, clean way.' Sadly, in *Scream and Scream Again*, Price may have been clean, but his character didn't come across as evil and his acting isn't all that keen!

'I don't think Vincent really liked the films I made,' said Hessler. 'Vincent liked the more traditional horror film, gothic, classical. But it never affected his performance; he was into it, whatever he was doing. He was wonderful to work with. The shame is that Vincent wasn't put in the right parts; that's the thing. If he hadn't been in horror pictures, he'd be a fantastic actor; playing character parts, where he could really get into the depth of the role.'

For all the disappointments of not seeing the horror stars together, *Scream and Scream Again* is a good movie. It has its faults, mainly because of the low budget. It's fast moving, skilfully directed by Hessler, and of course there's Alfred Marks' career best performance. Sadly once Marks is despatched, the tension tales off considerably.

The film's biggest fault is the climax. After Browning disposes of Konrad in an acid bath, Fremont turns up unexpectedly, and in an odd twist, also happens to be a superhuman composite, with the added advantage of using telepathy to force Browning into the acid bath as well. According to Christopher Lee, they were going to be revealed as aliens but this was dropped prior to the film's completion, leaving the backgrounds of Browning, Fremont and Konrad unexplained.

At least the climax gave Price and Lee a chance to go head to head, or rather face to face. The acid tank which Fremont forces Browning into, is comprised of a yellow concoction, but Hessler had no idea what this awful stuff was. The actors also had a fun time together. 'The first take was completely ruined by our both laughing as we fought to the death,' said Lee.

Lee further added that, 'I suddenly appear in the operating theatre and force Vincent backwards into that noisome vat, which certainly wasn't anything to do with bodily fluids, I can tell you that! And Vincent walked back with immense dignity, stepped into the tank and lowered himself right under the surface. I thought at the time, My God, that must have been a horrible thing to have to do; I'm glad it wasn't me! But he did it, of course, being the great professional that he was.'

But on a more unpleasant note, Price's decision not to use nose plugs when he submerged under that stuff brought about serious respiratory problems years later.

Scream and Scream Again wrapped in June 1969. During post production, Deke Heyward brought in his friend, animator and future member of *Monty Python's Flying Circus* Terry Gilliam to provide animated title sequences. However Gilliam's anarchic style did not blend with the movie's violent content, so James H Nicholson replaced it with a more traditional title design. Also deleted from the film was actor David Lodge as Inspector Philip Strickland, although his name remains in the end credits.

Reviews, as usual, were mixed when *Scream and Scream Again* went on general release on 8 February 1970. *Today's Cinema* described it as, 'A first rate horror thriller with shock piling on shock in rapid succession and adroitly punctuated with humour. A real treat for horror fans.' *Film and Filming* praised, 'The clever and amusing performance from Alfred Marks,' but added that, 'the lack of credibility in the material generally, ultimately defeats the considerable abilities of the rest of the cast.'

The best reviews came from the filmmakers themselves. On his arrival in London prior to the movie premier, Sam Arkoff and his fellow marketing executives were totally baffled by it. 'They just thought we were all mad or something,' said Hessler. 'Since they had liked my previous film, *The Oblong Box*, they wrapped up *Scream and Scream Again* and shipped it out exactly as it was.'

'(Vincent) didn't understand *Scream and Scream Again*,' he added. 'He didn't know what he was doing in the picture; he thought it was all weird and strange. Nobody understood it. Deke Heyward didn't understand it. But it took off with young people and was an enormous success.'

Price remained baffled to the end regarding the film's appeal. 'I know that the film was a favourite of Fritz Lang. I never knew what it was all about, but Fritz really loved it.'

Milton Subotsky added his own thoughts, although his comments were more out of bitterness for his lack of input. '*Scream and Scream Again* made a lot of money and that was different from any other film we've ever done. I don't know why, it wasn't all that good. It might be because we used three top horror stars, and it had a very good title.'

Christopher Lee summed up his own disappointment in the film. 'It would have seemed to me that "Look, if we've got these three people who are so known in this particular area of film, for heaven's sake let's get them all together" – and they didn't.'

Scream and Scream Again did well at the box office; the combined mishmash of horror themes and the excessive violence striking a chord with young audiences. The audience's appetite for horror was changing, however, due in part to films like George Romero's recently released *Night of the Living Dead* (1968), which turned the genre totally on its head. The traditional gothic horror started to look old fashioned thanks to an increasing number of violent chillers being churned out; even Peter Cushing lent his presence to the sadistic *Corruption* (1968) and Boris Karloff did the same in *Targets* (1968).

131

Cry of the Banshee

'I don't believe in the occult, but I do believe there is a power of evil,' – Vincent Price

Maintaining the 'play you rather than pay you' principle, Arkoff was determined to make full use of Gordon Hessler's four film contract. Also keeping Price on a tight leash at all times, the poor actor was barely in the States a few months, during which he recorded an album of American poetry called

Witchcraft and Mystery, when Arkoff summoned him back to the UK for AIP's latest horror picture.

Following the turbulent co-productions with Hammer and Amicus, Arkoff decided to go it alone with *Cry of the Banshee.* This coincided with Price being offered the role of horror star Paul Henderson in the Amicus portmanteau *The House That Dripped Blood* (1970). This indicated a second co-production deal between AIP and Amicus, but with the companies going their separate ways after *Scream and Scream Again,* Price was unable to accept because his contract prevented him from doing horror films for other studios; he was also forced to turn down another interesting role as The Judge in Tigon's *Blood on Satan's Claw* (1971).

Tim Kelly's original script called *Cry of the Banshees* (changed to the singular on release) appeared on Deke Heyward's desk in January 1969. With *The Oblong Box* in the can and *Scream and Scream Again* in production, the script remained dormant until the beginning of October 1969.

Heyward didn't think much of it, and asked Gordon Hessler and Christopher Wicking to have a look at it. 'The script was awful, and Gordon and Chris wanted to do a complete rewrite.'

Hessler and Wicking decided to take a trip to Scotland (on company expenses) to look further into Celtic myths, folklore and legends. Their research found that paganism practised by the druids of old had nothing to do with Satanism, although the Church outlawed it as such. A banshee is a sort of ghost from Celtic mythology whose cry is a signal of impending death. For sheer sensationalism, Hessler and Wicking abandoned this interesting concept to make Oona and her coven devil worshippers.

Another interesting idea from Kelly's script was the inclusion of a character from folklore called a sidhe, a clawed demon who rampaged across the countryside. Kelly originally depicted Roderick (Patrick Mower) as a foundling who was raised in the woods and placed under an enchantment spell that turns him into this creature.

Sam Arkoff wasn't in the least bit amused about footing the bill for this paid vacation. According to Heyward, 'The script was awful so Gordon and Chris went up to Scotland to do research on witches and whatnot. When Arkoff found out what they were doing, he told me, "Look, they've got ten days to finish this script and get on with it," which I relayed to Gordon and Chris.'

'I think he'd had some testy consultation with Arkoff,' Hessler said of Heyward who he knew, 'could also be a very difficult customer.' Wicking wanted to improve the witch characters but was overruled by Heyward in order to get the production off the ground. Wicking had high hopes the film would be shot in Scotland, but the tight schedule made it a non-starter.

Location shooting began in October 1969 around Hertfordshire and Harrow Weald in North London, and once again John Coquillon's cinematography beautifully captures the English countryside. The setting of the Whitman's home was Grim's Dyke House (now a hotel, and also a location for *Curse of the Crimson Altar* among many other film and television projects), the former country estate of Sir W S Gilbert. Costumes were brought in from *Anne of a Thousand Days* (1969). After having his animated credits removed from *Scream and Scream Again*, Terry Gilliam was recalled by Heyward to provide some imaginative title designs – the timing was perfect as *Monty Python's Flying Circus* had just been screened on BBC television.

Casting went ahead, and supporting Price (playing sadistic magistrate Lord Edmund Whitman) once more was Hilary Dwyer. After appearing in AIP's *Wuthering Heights* (1970) as Isabelle Linton, she cut ties with the studio and returned to British television. She retired from acting to run the talent agency Duncan Heath and Associates (now ICM UK). In the eighties she became a successful film and TV producer.

Lower down the cast list in a cameo role was Robert Hutton, an American actor once tipped to be a big star in the forties. When that didn't happen he moved to England where he established himself as a character actor. Another cameo was provided by the electrifying Welshman Hugh Griffith, who had won an Oscar and a BAFTA for his performance as Sheikh Ilderim in *Ben-Hur* (1960).

A lifelong drinking buddy of poet and fellow Welshman Dylan Thomas, Griffith's career was blighted by alcohol, so much so, he became unemployable. Thanks to the lack of acting opportunities, AIP made good use of him in several movies. 'Hugh was a terrific guy,' said Hessler, 'and he was in a number of big pictures, like *Tom Jones* (1963). But at the time of filming he was an alcoholic, and a person would have to assist him on the set and make sure that he didn't receive any alcohol, otherwise he'd be drinking the whole time. A great shame.'

To add a continental flavour to the production, AIP hired Swedish actress Essy Persson as Lord Edmund's mentally unbalanced wife Lady Patricia. Persson had already achieved notoriety in the Danish erotica *I, A Woman* (1965). But the biggest casting coup was respected German actress Elisabeth Bergner, as the Oona the witch. After fleeing Nazi Germany in the thirties, Bergner established herself as a leading actress in British films. She later worked mainly in the theatre on both sides of the Atlantic. *Cry of the Banshee* was her first film for 20 years.

Failing to live up to Gilliam's excellent animation, *Cry of the Banshee* is a botched job that defeats the efforts of everyone involved. 'It was the most appalling script!' exclaimed Hessler. 'It was the worst script I ever worked on. Everybody realised it was disastrous. All we could do with that film was try to make it cinematically interesting: strange angles, moving camera, that sort of thing.' Hessler's feeling towards the screenplay was in no way directed towards Christopher Wicking, who had to knock something together in a short space of time. 'If we had another year,' said Heyward, 'we probably could've done the film they wanted to do.'

AIP made matters worse by shameless studio interference. The opening scene where an accused witch is dragged down the streets, flogged and whipped was replaced by the massacre of Oona's coven. This was supposed to happen later in the movie, and that takes away most of the tension: we know the fate of Lord Edmund and his family as soon as the film starts.

The film's haphazard nature is made all the more obvious by the silly climax. 'We didn't have an ending,' said Price. Initially Lord Edmund was supposed to be sitting alone in his home awaiting his eventual doom. Hessler thought it anti-climactic, and filmed Lord Edmund, trapped in his carriage with his dead children, being driven away by Roderick. The revised ending is even more of an anti-climax because Lord Edmund could have easily jumped out of the carriage! It wasn't going that fast!

Even the title is a joke. The story owes more to the werewolf legend and makes no reference to any banshee, none of which appears in the finished movie!

Cry of the Banshee is repulsive stuff. Hessler, in an attempt to make the film interesting includes plenty of naked breasts and brutal acts of violence. The influence of *Witchfinder General* remains an important factor, but now the level of sadism has gone too far.

The film's greatest fault is the characters, none of whom are remotely likeable. Oona and her coven are a sadistic lot, but Lord Edmund, who is supposed to represent good, is even worse; his constant use of violence towards anyone who gets in his way makes Matthew Hopkins look pious in comparison. On a good day he abuses and humiliates a young woman just because he wants to and his rank of magistrate enables him to do just that.

The rest of Lord Edmund's family aren't much better. Sean (Stephen Chase) is every inch his father's son, and Lady Patricia is a pathetic woman who had long sold her soul to the devil in exchange for wealth and rank. His other kids, Harry (Carl Rigg) and Maureen (Hilary Dwyer) have some redeeming features, but not many, and they both seem a little too friendly towards one another. Although not inferred, incest seems to be a family trait. The suggestion of it in *The House of Usher* works because of its subtlety. Here it's just plain creepy.

'Vincent Price stalks through it all looking vaguely cheesed off.' Jonathan Rigby's comment in his book *English Gothic* accurately sums up Price's performance and the feelings he had towards the genre. With a good supporting cast totally off form, it's left to Price to carry the weight of the film, but he puts no effort into his acting. Even in his lesser movies, he could always be relied upon on to ham it up with good humour. Here he just walks through the film with no conviction whatsoever. Any eye rolling on his part was just his way of saying. 'Get on with it!'

'*Cry of the Banshee* was the final straw for Vincent, who had had enough of unsatisfactory parts in worse than awful movies,' said Victoria. 'His contract with AIP had expired, and though Arkoff wished to renew, Vincent, feeling frustrated and impotent, refused to negotiate. Though he later acknowledged that the scripts offered to Vincent were inferior, at the time Sam Arkoff wasn't pleased.'

The situation was probably heightened by the fact Price could not take part in *The House That Dripped Blood*. His reluctance to negotiate a new contract prevented him from appearing in *Murders in the Rue Morgue* (1971), which was Hessler and Wicking's AIP swansong. Replacing Price in *Murders in the Rue Morgue* was Jason Robards.

Cry of the Banshee wrapped in November 1969 and for publicity purposes, AIP promoted it as Price's 100th horror film (it wasn't even his 100th film). The wrap party was a fancy dress affair with 200 guests in attendance including some of the cast from *Scream and Scream Again*. 'We had a special cake made and a nude girl was going to jump out of it,' said Hessler. 'We had music, dancing, the whole works.'

However, the guest of honour changed his mind, an hour before the festivities. According to Hessler, 'That afternoon, Vincent called and said, "Look, I'm not coming." He was stone drunk and said, "If Arkoff's there, I'm not coming!" So I said, "Vincent you've got to come. You're the guest of honour."'

'He did finally arrive that evening but he was sloshed and in a bad mood. I'd asked Arkoff to make a speech then cut the cake but Vincent said, "If Arkoff makes a speech, I'll disappear." There was obviously serious animosity between them so I told Arkoff not to make a speech and to just cut the cake instead. So we started the ceremony for cutting the cake; we're looking for the knife; I said, "Where's the knife?" and Vincent said, "Take the knife that's in my back."'

When the naked girl finally jumped out of the cake, Price simply looked embarrassed by it all. 'It just wasn't Vincent's thing,' said party guest Robert Hutton.

'There was some kind of bad blood between Vincent and Sam,' observed Deke Heyward. 'I think Vincent resented the fact that he was taking Sam's money for doing things he disliked. Sam tried to make believe that he was a friend of Vincent's but Vincent didn't reciprocate. I think sending Vincent to England was probably the least line of resistance for Sam, plus the fact that Vincent enjoyed having a *per diem*, which he would use to buy works of art.'

Such was his disenchantment with his career direction, in March 1970 Price wrote a letter to his agent saying, 'I'm sure when you made the original contract you never thought of the very serious consequences that the all-exclusivity clause could cause. I hope you can make Arkoff see how it keeps me from doing anything for the next three years in that line. I like the English script *The House That Dripped Blood*. I'd like to do it. It certainly can't hurt to be in a good film; it might even carry me over the next lousy one AIP might make me do.' According to biographer Lucy Chase Williams, 'Price's decade long association with AIP, at first a guarantee of steady employment, was now a double-edged sword.' Even Denis Meikle admitted that America's King of Horror was, 'in danger of becoming a jester.'

The financial side proved strong enough for Price to settle his differences with Arkoff and extend his contract for another three years. He still had his deal with Sears Roebuck, but by this time the company had given up on their art programme, preferring to use the actor's name to sell their goods.

Forever the busy man, Price made a welcome return to the stage as Fagin in *Oliver!* Numerous TV appearances followed that included his one-man performance in *An Evening of Edgar Allan Poe*. Set on a single sound stage, Price, sporting a variety of costumes designed by his wife, recited four Poe tales in his usual customary style, even if it had all been done so many times before.

Poe surfaced once more when *Cry of the Banshee* got its official release in July 1970. Once again AIP tagged one of the writer's poems to the film with Price doing the narration. 'It had nothing to do with Poe,' he laughed. 'You remember when they did a version of *Anna Karenina* (1935), with Greta Garbo, they re-titled it *Love*. It was Hollywood at their worst. They re-titled everything to what they thought would sell.'

AIP made further changes to the American release. In addition to the editing work already done, Wilfred Josephs' original music was replaced by a modern score from Les Baxter. Terry Gilliam's titles were also replaced by still ones and the level of nudity and violence was toned down.

Reviews for *Cry of the Banshee* were mixed with Leslie Halliwell calling it a, 'Modest horror film that fails to do justice to its interesting plot.' *The Hollywood Reporter* described it as, 'the weakest of the AIP horror features.' The film turned in a decent profit, and although Hessler thought it was the least interesting of his AIP chillers, he could feel some consolation about the uncut version that is currently out on DVD.

Hessler and Wicking went from *Cry of the Banshee* to *Murders in the Rue Morgue*, and this marked the jaded end of the Poe series. After leaving AIP, Hessler and Wicking parted company with Hessler enjoying a varied career in film and television, while Wicking briefly joined Hammer as in-house writer.

British horror enjoyed a brilliant run in the sixties. The new decade, however, brought about unwelcome changes that heralded the decline of Hammer, Amicus and Tigon. The increasing animosity between Arkoff, Nicholson and Heyward would eventually destroy AIP.

For Vincent Price, the seventies marked the beginning of the end of his horror career. The new decade also provided him with two more career defining performances.

The Abominable Dr Phibes

'These macabre exercises are pure escapism, and to claim they harm children is the veriest nonsense. For them they are simply fairy tales no grimmer than the Grimm their grandmothers used to read at bedtime.' – Vincent Price

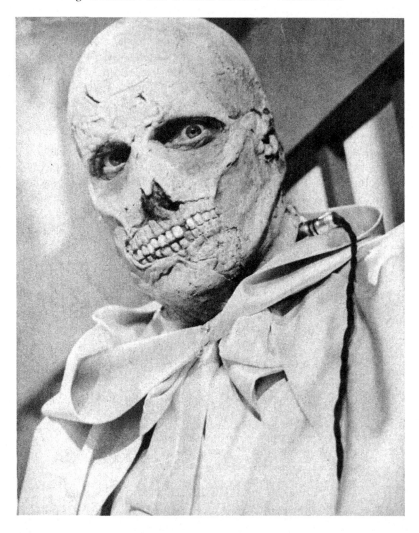

The start of the seventies was a time of reflection for Vincent Price. He kept working, was on good money and still maintained star billing. The financial rewards and his high profile meant he could pursue his serious artistic interests. But his unhappy experience on *Cry of the Banshee* made him re-evaluate his position, both personally and professionally. Now approaching 60, he knew his good fortune wouldn't last forever.

Despite settling his differences with Sam Arkoff, Price remained unhappy at the way he was being treated. It was only because of the regular money and the perks that came with his contract which kept that him in check at AIP. Future contract star Robert Quarry described Arkoff as, 'a gross pig' during his own tumultuous time with the studio. 'Unfortunately, there really isn't anything good I can say about him,' he added. 'He was even terrible to Vincent. But Vincent knew how to screw him up one side and down the other. Vincent used to lie about his *per diem* in London just to steal money from Sam. Trust me, Sam is not the nicest man in the world. Rude, vulgar, crude, and he did absolutely nothing.'

There were external factors to consider. The sixties was a beneficial period for the British film industry thanks to American finance and the overseas tax codes that allowed Hollywood studios to make pictures in the UK. By 1968 the tax incentives were abolished to finance the escalating costs of the Vietnam War, a situation not helped by many British movies doing poorly at the American box office. It wouldn't be long before the Hollywood majors began closing down their London operations.

British horror films seemed immune to these changes. Hammer, Amicus, Tigon and AIP were still going strong, but even they were slowly on the wane. The added bonus of violence, gore and nudity kept things ticking over at the box office, but within the next few years the genre would be completely overhauled.

Arkoff did himself no favours when, undeterred by the financial disaster of *De Sade*, attempted to go up market again with an intense version of *Wuthering Heights* (1970) starring Anna Calder-Marshall and Timothy Dalton as Cathy and Heathcliff. There was further friction within AIP when Deke Heyward threatened to resign if *Wuthering Heights* didn't get a royal premier. Relations between Arkoff and James H Nicholson were also at an all-time low.

Price had his own problems with Sears Roebuck. Despite his $90,000 endorsement, the company suspended their art programme, leaving the actor with little to do except promote furniture and electricals. 'They started using him for every darn thing in the world,' said old friend Wawona Hartwig. 'They were just using him. It was awful. And I think that Mrs Price was getting pretty upset over that, but just went along with it.'

Price remained committed to Sears and even suggested ideas to promote art via books and soft furnishings. Nothing came from it and eventually they terminated their contract, to the actor's lasting bitterness. 'I'll never forget them saying, "We really don't need you anymore, because we can make just as much money selling schlock," as they call it. Or shit as I call it. So it ended unhappily.'

At least there were other projects on the go including Mary and Vincent Price's *Come into the Kitchen Cookbook* and *The Vincent Price Treasury of American Art* (edited by his son Barrett), plus numerous TV appearances. By November 1970, he was back in Britain at the behest of Sam Arkoff.

Heyward received a script from producer Ronald S Dunas written by first timers James Whiton and William Goldstein entitled *The Fingers of Dr Phibes*. A title like that hardly inspires confidence, and the overlong script, contained too many ponderous references to mystical Hebrew customs and biblical stories. The central theme of a madman killing the surgical team he holds responsible for his wife's death held some interest because the madman uses the Ten Plagues to achieve his gruesome task – a perfect horror subject.

'The idea came to me in a dream,' said William Goldstein. 'I began a collaboration with (James) Whiton, a high school chum from New York on *The Fingers of Dr Phibes*. It caught on very quickly at AIP, and within six months after the first look, they were in pre-production.'

Now retitled *The Curse of Dr Phibes*, Heyward envisaged something far more than just another horror film. '(AIP) picked it up with the idea that there would be a series,' said Goldstein. 'We were told in the beginning perhaps five pictures.' By the spring of 1970, pre-production plans and cast and crew announcements had already been made.

With Gordon Hessler ending his association with AIP, Heyward turned to Robert Fuest, who had just completed work on *Wuthering Heights*.

Born in 1943, Fuest was an exceptionally talented artist who attended the Hornsby School of Art following national service with the Royal Air Force. In addition to art, Fuest was a jazz enthusiast who played drums for Chris Barber and George Melly.

In the early sixties, Fuest moved into television as a set designer for ABC-TV. His visual flare proved useful, especially on the popular series *The Avengers*. Working closely with the show's equally visual director Peter Hammond, Fuest was bitten by the directing bug, and with his time on *The Avengers* well spent, he decided to focus on serious film work.

Although his debut feature *Just Like a Woman* (1967) didn't gain an audience, it attracted the attention of *Avengers* producers Albert Fennell and Brian Clemens, who assigned him the directing job on several episodes. When Fennell and Clemens went into film production they hired Fuest to direct *And Soon the Darkness* (1970) an efficient but not too successful little thriller that was good enough for AIP to assign Fuest *Wuthering Heights*.

Fuest wasn't impressed with the original *Phibes* script, but was intrigued by the Ten Plagues being used as murder weapons. Given the go-ahead by Heyward, he re-wrote the script and incorporated his love of art and music. Since the script did not depict a place and time, he decided to set the film in the thirties and made Phibes a doctor of music as well as theology, the latter is never really explained because Phibes doesn't appear to be Jewish. 'It never occurred to me,' said Fuest. 'Then or now!'

The musical theme continued with Fuest creating Phibes' clockwork musicians. Vulnavia, Phibes' female companion and accomplice, was also written as a clockwork model (complete with wind-up key in the neck), but feeling that Phibes needed a human assistant, he changed the character, although Vulnavia retains a blank facial expression throughout.

The relationship between Phibes and Vulnavia also changed. In the original,

Phibes is abusive to his assistant but Fuest wanted to make him more sympathetic. Also removed was the climax where Phibes, after stabbing Vulnavia, escapes in a hot air balloon which catches fire. One of the few things retained from the script was the scene where the Rabbi (Hugh Griffith) explains the plagues to Inspector Trout (Peter Jeffrey) – for visual reasons, the plagues of flies and gnats were replaced by bats and rats, with the doctor's death by rats taking place inside a plane instead of on a boat as the means of escape would be impossible.

Also retained was Phibes' love and devotion towards his wife and his quest for vengeance. 'Phibes is a love story,' said Goldstein. 'That's the great strength. Orpheus; love beyond the grave. Phibes is not a common murderer. He considers himself the Death Geometer to the Universe. He wishes to return to the Eden that he knew with his wife. When that's thwarted, there is a price to pay, a price which is commensurate, but always in his inimitable style.'

Goldstein's concept of Phibes is almost as ponderous as the overkill of Hebrew mysticism he wrote in his script, and in Fuest's capable hands, the character is re-written as a man out for revenge by the unorthodox means at his disposal.

By September 1970, AIP assembled their team with Fuest bringing in Brian Eatwell as set designer. With John Coquillon moving on to other assignments, Arkoff hired veteran cameraman Norman Warwick, who had previously photographed Hammer's Dr Jekyll and Sister Hyde (1971).

Price had already been signed up to play Phibes, not that he had much choice in the matter, but at least it was another trip to London, and with increased expense money to buy art. Small roles were taken by Hugh Griffith and the popular comic actor Terry-Thomas. Heyward was instrumental in their casting. 'It is a wonderful pleasure to hire such wonderful performers such as Hugh Griffith and Terry-Thomas because you know they will be brilliant.'

One piece of casting that didn't materialise was that of Peter Cushing as Phibes' protagonist Dr Vesalius (taken from Dr Andrea Vesalius, the Flemish scientist famous for dissecting corpses to understand the inner workings of the human body). Since Scream and Scream Again could hardly be described as a proper collaboration, this was a golden opportunity for the long awaited teaming of the horror legends; a poster was even designed showing the names of both men. Sadly, Cushing was unable to take part due to his wife Helen's poor health.

The role finally went Price's old Mercury Theatre colleague Joseph Cotton. With his own film career in decline, Cotton had recently starred in Mario Bava's Baron Blood (1970), a film Price had been considered for. Another top star experiencing a career decline was Maurice Kaufman, who played one of Phibes' victims. Other familiar faces down the cast list were Dad's Army legend John Laurie, Carry On regular Peter Gilmore and Price's Oblong Box co-star Alister Williamson, who briefly appears as a policeman.

For the pivotal role of the beautiful but impassive Vulnavia, AIP hired Anglo-American model Virginia North. Already one of Britain's top fashion models, she previously played a Bond girl in *On Her Majesty's Secret Service* (1969). North had been acting on the London stage in *Council of Love* where she attracted the attention of Heyward. 'I played the daughter of the devil,' she said. 'I'd go around and do terrible things. The people who made the movie saw me in the play and decided I was what they wanted. You might say I was ready made for the movie part.'

'I don't know why they didn't let me speak,' she said of Vulnavia's mute status. 'Not speaking is more sinister I suppose. The reasoning behind it is obvious. It's nice to see a pretty girl in the movie.'

Another top model, hired to play the late Victoria Regina Phibes (a reference to Price's early stage success), was Caroline Munro. As the famous *Navy Rum Girl* on London billboards, Munro had been put under a Hammer contract by James Carreras on the strength of those advertisements. Despite the pivotal nature of her role, she appears (uncredited) as a corpse at the end of the film; her remaining appearances consisting of photographs taken from her modelling portfolio around that time – which look somewhat out of place in a 1930s setting.

With Fuest completing the extensive re-writes, *The Curse of Dr Phibes* began production on 9 November 1970 with interiors shot at Elstree Studios. Location work remained in London with the outside of Phibes' mansion home being Caldecote Towers at Immanuel College in Elstree, and the graveyard scenes taking place at Highgate Cemetery. Filming at the Victoria and Albert Museum had to be abandoned.

Production started without too many problems, although Ronald S Dumas, who came in as (uncredited) producer as part of the deal with Goldstein and Whiton, started to make a nuisance of himself. According to Heyward, 'Dumas gave us so many problems that I requested him to leave the set.' On Fuest's recommendation, Albert Fennell was brought in as producer; he too went uncredited.

Although Phibes was an easy enough role to play, Price encountered a few discomforts caused by the heavy make-up. To avoid too much time in the chair, veteran make-up artist Trevor Crole-Rees applied a rubber mask. 'It was just agony for me,' recalled the actor, 'because my face was covered with plastic, and I giggled and laughed the whole time, day and night, and (Crole-Rees) and I were practically married because the make-up kept dissolving and he had to patch me up every five minutes.'

Caroline Munro had her own problems during filming. 'The most challenging scenes involved lying in a coffin with Vincent. You see I'm allergic to feathers and I was attired in this beautiful negligee, but it was covered in feathers! It took a great deal of willpower not to sneeze or sniffle. On one occasion, I would simply have to sneeze and this would result in having to do another take.' Who said playing dead was easy?

'The great thing Vincent had was his voice,' said Fuest. 'So what do we do? Make a film where he doesn't use it!' Phibes is portrayed as a mute, with his few lines of dialogue spoken through a Victrola. In fact he doesn't speak until a good half hour into the movie.

To prevent Price from speaking, Crole-Rees applied a substance called collodion which immobilized his mouth. 'I had to do a lot with my eyes and hands,' said Price, 'Phibes was something I had to take very seriously when I was doing it so that it would come out funny.'

Ever the professional, Price learnt his lines, but that didn't stop him giving Joseph Cotton a hard time. During their scenes together, Price continuously put his co-star off by pulling funny faces. 'I learned the lines but never had to speak them, which made Joe very angry. He used to come up at me and say, "It's not fair. You're not speaking the lines, and I'm having to remember all mine and say them." I said, "Well I remember them, Joe."' As well as knowing his own lines, Price was equally famous for memorising everyone else's too. To make things a little easier for Cotton, a crew member read aloud Price's dialogue.

Of course Price wasn't the only one who had problems being mute; Virginia North vented her own hang-ups. 'It's a bit frustrating, since everyone else is out there doing their bit and you have to depend mostly on your face, especially your eyes, to get your bit across. But then, not speaking is far easier than having to speak since you don't get nervous about your lines and how to remember them. In one way it was good, I guess. In another, bad.'

Make-up aside, *The Abominable Dr Phibes*, as the film was renamed for release, was a happy shoot both for Price and everyone else involved. 'The creativity was flowing like crazy,' observed Heyward. 'Everybody contributed, because Fuest encouraged that. You'd do a funny little shtick during the walkthrough, and he'd say, "Keep that in!"'

After the lacklustre *Cry of the Banshee*, Price returned to winning form in a film that brought out the best in him. 'I had the feeling that the first *Phibes* was going to be a marvellous film. Brian Eatwell had designed some wonderful sets which turned the movie into a small visual masterpiece. Also our director, Robert Fuest, used to be a set designer himself, so he knows how to make every object in the background work for him. He has a painter's eye.'

'Bob Fuest was one of the best directors I ever worked with!' Price exclaimed. 'He was making mad films because he was a mad man!' Fuest also enjoyed working with Price but pointed out that, 'The only problem we had on *Phibes* was that we couldn't stop laughing. Vincent loved all that preening around, playing the organ and conducting the clockwork band.'

'People used to call him Vincent Half-Price,' joked Fuest! 'The first time I met him it was at a hotel, and in spite of him being such a bon vivant, he had shepherd's pie! He was a wonderful man, though; he was very good in the role and I know he enjoyed it.'

Fuest noticed, towards the end of filming, that Price let his personal feelings interfere with his work. Production wrapped just before Christmas, and Fuest arranged an extra hour to shoot the scene of Phibes' unmasking so Price could finish work and return home to spend the festive season with his family. He completed the scene in a single take and walked off the set without acknowledging the crew. 'He left without saying anything,' said a shocked Fuest. 'I was quite hurt because I'd done it for his sake. Then somebody said,

"He's not looking forward to Christmas.'"

With his Sears contract coming to an acrimonious end, Price had sold his home in North Beverly Glen and moved into a smaller house at Coldwater Canyon. The positivity of *The Abominable Dr Phibes* did not hide the fact he was doing yet another horror film and that he would remain chained to Sam Arkoff for his next effort. The New Year did not look promising for an actor approaching 60. Away from the genre, his career options were very slim.

Price's future at AIP looked uncertain, and with further budget cuts facing British film production, Arkoff reduced considerable overheads by moving AIP's London base in Upper Grosvenor Street to more economical offices in Berkeley Square. The tensions between Arkoff and Nicholson came to the surface once more, and even Heyward grew disenchanted when his proposed film version of *The House of Seven Gables* got the short shrift following the failure of *Wuthering Heights*. 'It was a very fragile empire,' observed Fuest.

With preparations under way for the release of *The Abominable Dr Phibes*, Price busied himself in two episodes of Rod Serling's horror anthology series *Night Gallery*. He resumed his usual speaking engagements, which included a performance of four poems recited to music composed by Bernard Slatkin and performed by the St Louis Symphony Orchestra.

The Abominable Dr Phibes received its British release in April 1971. The US premiere took place the following month at the Pacific Pantages Theatre on Hollywood Boulevard. The American premier opted for a 1930s style Hollywood gala with over 100 guests in attendance including James H Nicholson (happy to be away from Arkoff, who stayed in London) and Virginia North, who had flown in from the UK. The event was broadcast live with Los Angeles Mayor Samuel Yorty making the declaration that, 'Hollywood Salutes Vincent Price.' Like *Cry of the Banshee*, *The Abominable Dr Phibes* was promoted as Price's 100th feature, which of course it wasn't!

The Abominable Dr Phibes did well at the box office, although it could have done a lot more if AIP hadn't botched up the advertising campaign by marketing the film as a spoof using the tag line 'Love means never having to say your ugly', a reference to the hit movie *Love Story* (1970); the famous poster of Vulnavia about to kiss the unmasked Phibes was also used for the campaign. Thanks to the poor box office showing during the first week, Arkoff revised the advertising to make it into a horror film with the new slogan, 'There are two sides to Dr Phibes – both of them evil!' With many of the newspapers already promoting it as a chiller, the film became a hit.

Critical evaluation was, as usual, mixed. While praising the set design, Leslie Halliwell described the film as a, 'brisk but uninspired treatment of a promising theme, with more unintended nastiness than intended laughs.' *The Motion Picture Guide* provided a sort of back handed compliment by saying, 'the sets are awful, the plot ludicrous and the dialogue inane – what more could a horror freak desire?'

Village Voice had its own negative feelings about the film. 'Vincent Price has moved up from Daniel Haller's moody Poe landscapes to this tribute to the 1925 style, which seeks to bring in the nostalgia craze as the newest element in the AIP horror film. The general effect is uncomfortably lightweight and unsatisfactory, especially because of the opulent overkill of the art department.'

Price, as always, gets singled out for his performance. 'Price has never been better,' wrote *Chicago Today*. 'His performance is actually touching at times.'

From the moment we see the dark figure of the musical genius in the cavernous hall/studio of his sprawling mansion playing Felix Mendelsohn's 'War March of the Priest' on the Wurlitzer organ, *The Abominable Dr Phibes* has 'camp classic' written all over it. Thanks to Brain Eatwell's magnificent low budget sets, and Norman Warwick's exemplary photography, the film has a lavish period feel, complimented by Fuest's strong visual eye.

The gruesomeness which permeated films like *Witchfinder General* remains, but without the nastiness of AIP's previous efforts. And with camp humour being the order of the day, there is a sense of fun from start to finish.

But of course, like many low budget chillers, the film has its faults. The inventive murders are at times a little too gruesome, and this swamps the camp element. This isn't helped by the fact that the audience knows nothing about the surgeons Phibes kills off. They are simply there to be ... killed!

The only exception is that of Dr Longstreet, expertly played by Terry-Thomas, whose performance is made all the more effective by his confused reactions to Phibes' draining him of his blood (laced with cheap brandy!). His demise evokes comedy and tragedy in equal measures because Terry-Thomas is the only victim who is a well-rounded character.

Memorable cameos from Hugh Griffith, Aubrey Woods (in fine form as an effete goldsmith) and Jon Cater (as the misinformed Superintnedent Waverley) are an asset, but on the whole the film is thin on characterisation.

Another glaring point is the relationship between Phibes and Vulnavia. Both Vulnavia and Victoria are about the same age ruling out the possibility that Vulnavia may be their daughter (perhaps Phibes was married before). She could be either Phibes' mistress or Victoria's sister. Judging by how badly she played the violin, she definitely isn't one of his music students! The relationship is never explained although Virginia North is breathtakingly beautiful and the outfits she wears are magnificent. Plus her performance has an eerie air about it.

Another weak link is the casting of Joseph Cotton, who looks bored. He doesn't invest any emotion into his role, and the scene where he tries to save his son has no impact, making one wish that Peter Cushing had been available.

Of the supporting cast, there is a stand-out performance from Peter Jeffrey as Inspector Trout. A familiar face on British television, Jeffrey invokes Trout with real heartfelt emotion. Policemen in horror movies are either Holmesian or comic relief, and Jeffrey succeeds in combining both stereotypes to create an amusing and memorable everyman character.

But at the end of the day this is Price's show. Playing one of his most memorable roles, he combines camp humour and creepy menace with total aplomb. What makes his performance incredible is the fact he does not use his famous voice directly (it is heard throughout though, coming from the gramophone device). Even though his face lacks emotion, his eye rolling gestures and exaggerated movements gives Phibes real depth. One only has to look at his reaction to Dr Longstreet's dodgy artwork so see how versatile he is facially. It is a true masterclass of horror acting.

The box office success of *The Abominable Dr Phibes* meant a sequel was inevitable. For Price, it was back to Blighty once more.

Dr Phibes Rises Again

'If you look at the history of fright, it is partly a catharsis of a kind. The fairy tales that Grimm wrote and are the first thing we read to our children, are much more frightening than anything I ever made, or that anybody has ever made!' – Vincent Price

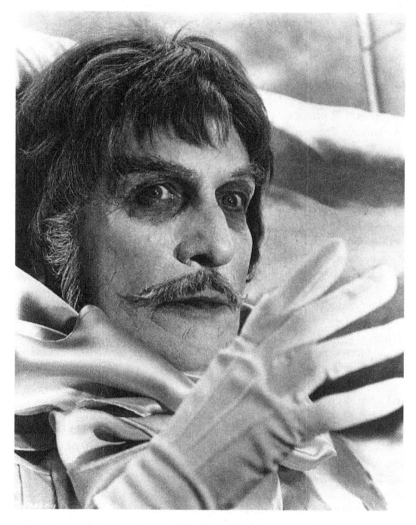

With *The Abominable Dr Phibes* doing great business, Sam Arkoff quickly hired William Goldstein and James Whiton to write a sequel. AIP had just signed a multipicture deal with MGM-EMI, so the possibility of utilising a larger budget brought renewed enthusiasm to the project. And with the positive feedback

Price received from the last film, Arkoff had no trouble persuading the actor to return to London.

To Arkoff, Price was the only man capable of playing Phibes. 'Vincent was the only one we felt had the strength. Physically he's a dominating man. He also has a dominating voice. He could play Shakespeare. There was a magic to Vincent's name. Of all the horror kings, he was the grandest. He played it that way; Vincent liked playing it bigger than life. That's the quality of a real horror star. When you were with Vincent Price, you knew you were with someone who was important.'

Robert Fuest also returned as director, and this time he had more control over the assignment, and that meant working on his own script. 'We were hired to do the sequel,' said Goldstein, 'but the AIP story editor was working on a parallel script with the director, and that was the script that they used. It was bad luck.'

By the time Arkoff commissioned Goldstein and Whiton to write their treatment, entitled *Phibes II*, Fuest had already approached Deke Heyward with his version. With the British Museum's forthcoming exhibition of Tutankhamen's Treasure, Fuest decided to incorporate Egyptian elements to the sequel and dreamt up his own story about Phibes seeking out the River of Eternal Life.

Word was sent to Arkoff about the new treatment, and fearing the worst, he hired veteran story editor and script doctor Robert Blees to collaborate with Fuest. According to Blees, 'The boys who'd written the first one turned in something that just didn't work. AIP had a commitment with Vincent for $75,000 to do the sequel and, to Sam, that was an awful lot of money.' Arkoff's brief to Blees was, 'Give us eight reels, and every reel has a guest star and a horror/comedy payoff.'

Checking into the Hilton Hotel in London, Blees worked on the main story. He also expanded it to include a rival archaeologist also seeking the River of Eternal Life. This new character was originally conceived as a vampire – more of that later!

While Blees was working on the story, Fuest separately worked on his side of the script from home, adding the various eccentric and comedic elements that worked in the first film. They seldom met during their writing sessions, which caused a slight problem because their ideas differed greatly.

'I brought out from LA a writer named Bob Blees, 'said Heyward, 'a dear friend. And he also had a sly sense of humour which I felt would fit into *Phibes*. Now Bob Fuest wanted to write this second film, and the two of them did not see eye to eye on anything. The visions that Fuest enjoyed were in his head; the visions Blees had were on paper, and easier to handle.'

Blees finally completed his side of the script and returned to the States. When Fuest put their separate efforts together, he thought the end result was 'schizophrenic' so he made re-writes, much to his colleague's chagrin, 'While Fuest was a competent director,' observed Blees, 'he wasn't a very good writer.'

With obvious clashes between the writers, Heyward acted as mediator. 'Suddenly you were the referee, placed in a position you did not want to be in because they were both right. It's a question of allowing them to go as far as they could, and then saying to yourself, "Don't worry, there'll be a rewrite at the end and we'll straighten out whatever doesn't seem to work."'

Blees' style of humour was completely at odds with Fuest's off-the-wall approach. In the end, Heyward made the final script decision. 'There was a steadiness to it that I liked. Because after all the fighting was done, it turned out to be a very good script, one that I think could be used in writing classes. Indeed if I ever get around to teaching again, I will use that one.'

Once again Heyward concentrated on the casting with several actors returning from the first film. Peter Jeffrey and Jon Cater repeated their roles as bumbling coppers, and Caroline Munro got more screen time as Victoria, but still remained dead and uncredited. Heyward's favourite actors Hugh Griffith and Terry-Thomas (replacing original choice Frankie Howard) returned in different roles, with Peter Cushing and Beryl Reid making up the solid roster of guest stars.

Around this time, Terry-Thomas was diagnosed with Parkinson's disease, and was going through the usual shock of coming to terms with the illness. Griffith on the other hand had completely succumbed to the bottle. 'Hugh could not be employed,' said Heyward, 'he had a reputation for being an alcoholic. But I desperately wanted to use him, and I knew he could use the work. I told him, "I will accept the fact that you are uninsurable. You've got to accord me the same respect I give you. The respect I want is a promise. From the moment you come on the set, you don't touch a drop. When we yell cut and it's a wrap for the day, do whatever you want, I don't care. But give me your hand-to-god promise that you're not going to touch a drop while we're shooting." He held out his hand and said, "Lad, you've got it." Well, I did six pictures with him and he adhered to that promise.'

While Griffith and Terry-Thomas making logic-defying cameos, further sense went out of the window with the return of Vulnavia. Initially Fuest wanted a new character since she had met a nasty end under a vat of acid, but AIP insisted on Vulnavia returning because they wanted 'name continuity'. 'Plot continuity,' said Fuest, 'apparently, was unimportant.'

Not only would Vulnavia be unscathed from her acid shower, she also looked completely different (perhaps Phibes designed a new mask for her!). Virginia North was pregnant and unable to take part And so replacing her was Anglo-Australian actress Valli Kemp. A former Australian Miss World contestant, the Kenyan-born Kemp was a successful model before she got into acting through the eminent actor-director Sir Robert Helpmann. 'I was given a 10 year contract, as the producers were hoping to develop a *Dr Phibes* franchise with at least four subsequent films being proposed,' she said in interviews.

For the pivotal role of Phibes' nemesis Darius Biederbeck, AIP had an ace up their sleeve in the shape of a new contract star. His name was Robert Quarry, and his subsequent fractured relationship with Price has become part of horror folklore.

Born in Fresno, California on 3 November 1925, Quarry had been an actor since his teens. After grafting away in film and TV throughout the fifties, he established himself as a highly respected Shakespearean actor with other theatre credits including *The Lion in Winter* and *Whose Afraid of Virginia Woolf*.

Quarry made his name as the titular star of *Count Yorga, Vampire* (1970). With his towering presence, dark good looks, well-modulated speaking voice, and sophisticated manner, Quarry's strikingly menacing performance as the modern day vampire sealed his status as a new horror icon.

Independently produced by actor Michael Macready and directed by Robert Keljan, *Count Yorga, Vampire* grossed $8 million on its initial release before AIP released it worldwide, making it the horror hit of 1970. James H Nicholson then put Quarry under contract and the studio quickly produced *The Return of Count Yorga* (1971).

Bringing in a new contract player had a lot to do with Price's disillusionment at AIP. According to Quarry, 'Vincent didn't care to work any more at AIP. His contract was up; they were not going to re-option it. They wanted rid of him, because his salary was going up and up and up, and his last two pictures hadn't done that well. They didn't know where the horror thing was going, and I was being brought it. In me, they thought they had somebody new that they could build into the horror thing.'

Considering Price's popularity, Quarry admitted that it would not be an easy task. 'I was told that I was going to be set up to take Vincent's place at AIP, but that was going to be between me [and the studio]. And it was not as if I was ever gonna be as big a star as Vincent – it would have taken seven more years of good horror films to have gotten me up to that position where I might have been an established name as a horror star.' It was a daunting challenge, but one Quarry was ready to take on.

Price and Quarry had many similarities – excellent actors, highly intelligent individuals and brilliant gourmets. 'Bob and Vincent Price had so many things in common,' observed Quarry's old friend David Del Valle, 'and yet they never connected. They never traded recipes!'

Initially Quarry was to play Count Yorga in the second *Phibes* film so the film was set several decades earlier than the *Yorga* films. However Quarry's involvement in the vampire flick *The Deathmaster* (1972) had so incensed Michael Macready that he refused to work with the actor again, thus ending the *Yorga* series. Macready also refused permission for the name of Count Yorga to be used in *Dr Phibes Rises Again*, and so the character's name changed to Darius Biederbeck and made him a slightly less immortal, though still 150 year old Egyptologist.

Quarry was in awe of Price as an actor and a person. 'He's a funny man; he's also a hard worker. People think it isn't tough to act in horror films. It's the toughest acting in the world. That's why I have nothing but admiration for all those years Vincent played those horror films. They're all peak emotions: they're all phony. And you have to create a characterisation out of something that doesn't exist. There's a great difference between that and being able to play scenes with real situations where emotion comes honestly.'

Dr Phibes Rises Again began production at Elstree Studios in November 1971 with location work planned for the following month in Ibiza, Spain, where the desert terrain doubled up for Egypt. Confidence in the new film was at an all-time high – to begin with!

And it was all down to Robert Fuest. 'Bob has a great sense of style and flare,' said Heyward. 'He struck up a very good rapport with all the actors. He conceptualised a lot, and he also had a very sly sense of humour. He was a working director, and was very conscious of budget.'

Heyward felt that it was Fuest who really added weight to the film. 'Bob knew design, and I'd say (production designer) Brian Eatwell was very important. You need people like Bob and Brian, who have lovely pictures in their head and understand the beauty of what they construct. And you need someone like myself, who controls the dollars with compassion, with not a bread knife but a scalpel, to say, "Hey, it's great, but for the dollars we have to do this; without emasculating, let's take it here and save."'

As in the previous film, Price responded well to Fuest. 'He's genuine registered nut! He even looks like a madman. He's all over the place, like an unmade bed. What an imagination he has! They were all his ideas.'

Quarry also felt the same towards Fuest. 'He never went berserk. He had a lot of that hyper energy that Quentin Tarantino has. A lot of kinky grey hair that was all over the place, just mad as a hatter! But he knew how to put a movie together.'

'We had a difficult time keeping a straight face through some of the scenes,' said Valli Kemp, 'because just before a shot Vincent is likely to pat me on the bottom and joke with me when I'm supposed to go on and be serious. I did one scene with him where I was playing the violin and he took a grape from the fruit bowl and shoved it in my mouth. Then he took another grape and shoved that in my mouth so I had two grapes in my mouth and daren't swallow them because if I did I would have burst out laughing. Then he picked up a pineapple and went to put that in my mouth as well, but then shook his head when he realised it was too big. This has been left in the film and it's hysterical because it was completely improvised and I didn't know anything about it.'

Caroline Munro had her fair share of funny behind-the-scenes problems with Price, especially when she had to play dead throughout the film. 'Vincent always brought his homemade pate on the set. It was lovely pate but it also gave me indigestion so when I was playing my scenes in the coffin, my stomach started rumbling and we all started laughing.'

The fun continued off the set according to TV chat show host Michael Parkinson. 'When (Vincent) was making *Dr Phibes* at Elstree Studios, he would take his lunch alone, sitting by the River Thames wearing his hideous make-up. When passing pleasure boats full of eager tourists were informed by their guide that these were the studios where many horror movies were made, Vincent would appear on the bank and, taking a sandwich from his picnic box, would shove it slowly into the hole at the side of his throat.'

Robert Quarry enjoyed working with Price, but had a few problems playing opposite his mute co-star. 'I can't tell you what it is like to work with Vincent. I mean Phibes is a silly role. How do you know how good an actor you worked with? God knows you couldn't tell anything from the silent facial expressions. The hardest acting I ever did in my life were in those scenes – keeping a straight face and playing it with anger while Vincent was mugging.'

Thanks to Price's mischievous behaviour, Quarry blew his takes during their scenes together. 'He had to learn the scenes so that his expression matched the dialogue. That isn't easy to do either; it looks easy but trust me it is not. He said, "Just wait until you do this scene. Joe Cotton could not stand it." Vincent was enjoying every minute of it, because he knew what he was doing to me.'

Quarry tried out a different approach that helped him get through this difficult situation. 'I thought I'd just relate to someone I really hate in real life, and just look at his ear.' The plan worked, and Price told him once their scenes were finished, 'You did a better job than Joe Cotton did!'

Despite being in awe of Price as an actor and as a person, Quarry felt his co-star 'over egged the pudding when it came to playing villains. Vincent was always playing the bogeyman thing, overdoing stuff, and I was like, "Vincent, for once just play it straight." But Vincent mannerisms took him over. As an actor, you should never allow that to happen.'

Unfortunately, as filming progressed, Quarry found that, 'the atmosphere was decidedly Macbethian' between him and Price. 'We were put at odds by the bastard Sam Arkoff and his slimy errand boy Deke Heyward.'

A week into the production, Heyward threw a big cocktail reception. According to Quarry, 'An English publicist came up to Vincent and asked, "How do you feel about Mr Quarry coming in as your replacement at AIP?" He wasn't happy about it. He was hurt. It was if I was a "threat" to Vincent's career – to this man with this long, distinguished career that nobody could replace. It was the wrong thing for that man to say. That man should have been fired.'

'Vincent was never the same,' Quarry added. 'That made a rift between us. I went to [Heyward] and told him what happened. Well, it was too late. The damage was done. The publicist made it sound as if I was about to dethrone the king. That made the rift between us. I never saw Vincent socially after that. Not ever.'

Quarry became further incensed when Heyward told his London friends about the incident. Not only did it break the confidentiality agreement Quarry had with AIP, it destroyed any good will he had with Heyward, and with Sam Arkoff. 'Sam had little enthusiasm for me. Sam always dismissed me and (Count) Yorga.'

'Vincent tried to pretend we were friendly,' Quarry continued, 'but he wasn't ever that nice again. And he was very funny, you know, like when the press came over to interview me in London; he'd try to take over. And when they came over to see Vincent, I wasn't allowed to even come near him.'

Robert Fuest recalled a famous incident that summed up the ill feeling between the actors. 'In make-up, Robert Quarry used to sing Gershwin, and Vincent Price looked around the corner, and Quarry said, "Didn't know I was a singer, did you Vincent?", and Vincent said. "Well I knew you weren't a fucking actor!"'

Deke Heyward on the other hand saw nothing unusual. 'I wasn't aware of any tension between the actors on-set.' Despite the animosity, Price and Quarry remained professional throughout filming. 'As far as our working together, it was extremely pleasant,' said Quarry, 'Our sense of humour was the one bond that made working with him a pleasure.'

For a man known for his warm, generous and fun loving affability, Price's attitude towards Quarry is surprisingly out of character. A sensitive man behind his casual exterior, the failure of *Darling of the Day*, his departure from Sears Roebuck and the frosty relationship with Arkoff made Price a deeply unhappy man, and the arrival of Quarry undermined his position at AIP, where he could at least pull some weight. Having a younger man assuming his role as king of horror, even if it was a title he resented, had a negative effect on his mindset.

Unfortunately, production of *Dr Phibes Rises Again* was undermined by studio interference from Sam Arkoff, and it pretty much ended his tumultuous partnership with James H Nicholson. 'They dumbed it down,' observed Fuest, angry at internal friction at AIP. 'If they could have made money making hubcaps, they would have made hubcaps.'

Phibes had changed considerably during his three year slumber. The first film showed him maintaining one facial expression (bar the eyes) with his dialogue kept to a minimum; when he did speak, his fractured voice came through a Victrola. In the sequel Phibes never stops talking, and sometimes without the aid of his Victrola, which gives the impression he is now running on batteries! Also the broken English from the original is replaced by his familiar mellifluous tones.

Phibes' immobile facial expression had also expanded into several exaggerated ones that allowed Price to eye-roll to his heart's content, and at times he overdid it. 'Bob didn't know how to control Vincent,' observed Quarry, 'so he let the farce thing in the *Phibes* sequel go a bit far. I think the first one was actually better. There was too much of the "big joke" in *Rises Again*.'

Initially Price wasn't supposed to have that much dialogue, due to Fuest cutting certain scenes for budget reasons, but by the time the film wrapped in January 1972, Arkoff and Nicholson demanded to see the negative, and clashed almost immediately. According to Fuest, 'There were wonderful scenes with Beryl Reid and Terry-Thomas which were cut out by Jim and Sam.' These scenes were removed for being too light hearted, along with a further ten minutes of footage, and that left gaping holes in an already muddled script.

'When we got the film back,' recalled an angry Fuest, 'I played it and, I mean, they brutalised it.'

This was one argument too many for Nicholson, who had had enough of Arkoff's treatment of him. 'It was not a happy marriage,' observed Fuest. When Nicholson received an offer from 20th Century Fox to produce *The Legend of Hell House* (1973), it was a golden opportunity to permanently distance himself from his partner. Signing a five picture deal with Fox, he resigned from AIP in January

1972.

With Arkoff in sole charge, he now had the final say on the film and decided to give Price more dialogue, which was added during post-production. Price arrived at Hollywood's Ryder Sound Studios in April 1972 to do his post-synching work.

Dr Phibes Rises Again got its big screen release in July 1972, and as usual, the critical reaction varied. '*Dr Phibes Rises Again*,' said the *Los Angeles Times*, 'but only to be shot down by a lousy script. Those who enjoyed the campy horror of *The Abominable Dr Phibes* are in for a disappointment.' The *New York Daily News* was equally negative: 'We can only wish that *Dr Phibes* had instead sailed away on the river of no return.'

'It's refreshing to find a sequel which is better than its prototype,' said Philip Strick of the *Monthly Film Bulletin*. The same upbeat feeling was shared by the *Hollywood Reporter*; 'Overall this sequel is even better than the original and should meet with a good reception. Vincent Price brings to Dr Phibes what is one of his most perfect horror villains in his long list of evil doers.'

Although it lacks the charm of the original, *Dr Phibes Rises Again* is an enjoyable effort. Robert Fuest's visual style is well utilised by Brian Eatwell's production design that once again gives the film a lavish splendour far exceeding the low budget. The comical elements occasionally swamp the material, but they do not detract from the overall enjoyment. There's a lot less gore this time around and the murders are well staged.

Fuest's love of jazz is reflected by the number of character names – (Bix) Biederbeck(e), (Bobby) Hackett, (Shorty) Baker, (Charley) Shavers and (Guy) Lombardo. It's a great in-joke for jazz aficionados. Keeping with the film's musical influence, there's an appearance by the Bach Singers, who donated their fee to charity.

Dr Phibes Rises Again is by no means perfect. Thanks to the gaping holes in the script, several moments remain unexplained, including Vulnavia's return and Phibes' new found ability to speak. Valli Kemp is a pretty lady, but her expressionless, doll like features and dodgy dance routines are no comparison to the sinister presence of Virginia North; she looks like she's in a daze for most of the time.

Fiona Lewis fairs even worse, but this had a lot to do with Fuest making cuts to Blees' part of the script that focused on the romantic relationship between Biederbeck and Diana. Blees wasn't happy with the outcome. 'Fuest made changes to my script and took out a lot of subtleties of the Noel Coward-Gertie Lawrence repartee between Quarry and Fiona Lewis.' Stunningly dressed in thirties fashions, Lewis has little to do except pout and look bored.

Of the female leads, Caroline Munro comes off best, simply by playing dead!

The script changes also make Biederbeck a much blander character and Robert Quarry's decision to play it straight works against the film's tongue-in-cheek nature. Nor did it impress Deke Heyward. 'Robert was the weakest link in the film. He didn't integrate, and he didn't have the fun that such a picture demands.'

Despite Heyward's observation, it remains Quarry's finest horror performance. 'It was really the only expensive film I ever did. It was also the best film I ever did. Simple as that.' In fact Quarry almost comes close to acting Price off the screen – a difficult thing to do at the best of times.

The solid supporting cast all give credible performances. Hugh Griffith, vindicating Heyward's trust as far as the booze goes, is in fine fettle Biederbeck's associate Harry Ambrose, as is Gerald Sim as chief archaeologist Hackett. It's also fun seeing future acting legend John Thaw being torn to bits by an eagle!

The guest stars fair less well. Peter Cushing is his usual professional self in a wasted cameo while Beryl Reid appears for a mere cough and a spit. Only Terry-Thomas has a substantial part, but he's surprisingly subdued.

And of course Price himself, who gives his customary high camp performance, complete with over the top facial expressions, which he plays with perfectly timed relish. Once again he proves himself the ultimate craftsman of true horror acting.

However, Price *is* acted off the screen by the brilliant Peter Jeffrey as Inspector Trout, a character that remains an important part of the Phibes universe. Playing effectively opposite Jon Cater (in fine pompous form as his superior, Waverley), Jeffrey's comic turn is a constant delight.

Jeffrey also gets some of the funniest lines. When Trout and Waverley are lost in the desert, Trout asks his superior if he has any idea where they are. 'I don't think, I know,' replies Waverley to which Trout, not missing a beat, responds by saying, 'I don't think you know either sir.' When one of the archaeologists is crushed to death in his own bed, Trout says with deadpan seriousness 'I'm afraid he had a bad night.' From his experiences in the previous film, Trout has a lot of respect for Phibes' genius. 'Every time we build a better mousetrap sir, Phibes just builds a better mouse.'

In fact it is Trout who has the last word as Phibes sails into darkness at the film's conclusion. 'Maybe he won't come back,' says Waverley, to which Trout replies, 'Its Phibes alright. And he always comes back.'

As it happened Phibes would not return.

Dr Phibes Rises Again did not repeat the success of its predecessor, but it made a decent enough profit to warrant the development of further adventures of the mad musical genius. Already several titles were in the pipeline including *The Brides of Dr Phibes*, *Phibes Resurrectus* and *The Seven Fates of Dr Phibes*, but Heyward admitted he couldn't find a suitable script to work on.

Eventually a script was provided under the working title of *Dr Phibes and the Holy Land*, which had Phibes up against Adolf Hitler. Robert Quarry was rumoured to be returning as an elderly Biederbeck along with another AIP discovery: William Marshall, a respected Shakespearean actor who scored a hit as vampire Prince Manuwalde in the blacksploitation chiller *Blacula* (1972).

The script also offered a very interesting premise. 'There was talk,' observed Caroline Munro, 'and the talk I heard, that seemed quite fascinating to me was that (Victoria) would actually come back, and she'd be far worse than (Phibes) was.'

'It's a marvellous script,' said Price. 'A very funny script. I wanted Bob Fuest to direct it. He's the only person in the world who is man enough to direct the *Dr Phibes* films.'

With James H Nicholson and his business manager Paul Zimmerman departing, things didn't look promising for the second sequel. As Nicholson was busying himself with *The Legend of Hell House*, AIP's UK branch was falling apart as key members of the company began to quit.

Robert Fuest was next to go after turning down the sequel. He also turned down *Theatre of Blood* (1973) and *Madhouse* (1974) to avoid being too closely associated with Price, as well as *The Legend of Hell House* because he didn't want to be pigeonholed as a horror director. 'They're all frightened that they were going to get stuck in the horror genre,' Price said of Fuest's decision.

Instead Fuest opted for his pet project *The Final Programme* (1974), an adaptation of Michael Moorcock's science fiction novel. In addition to directing, Fuest wrote the screenplay and designed the sets. After directing *The Devil's Rain* (1976) in America, Fuest was relegated to television work on both sides of the Atlantic before retiring to devote his time to painting.

'Bob has never done anything as good as *Dr Phibes*,' said Price, a feeling shared by Robert Quarry. 'I never understood Bob Fuest's career going downhill like that. He's a brilliant, wonderfully eccentric man. Bob was under contract with AIP and did a couple of things after *Phibes*. A very good director, very imaginative, very crazy. Likeable crazy though.'

Now it was time for Deke Heyward to jump ship. After one clash too many with Arkoff, he felt the time was right to go. 'Things fell apart after Jim left. I told Sam, "I don't want to do any more horror films; I don't want to do any more sex movies."' With his options severely curtailed, Heyward finally resigned his position in September 1972, leaving AIP's UK office in disarray, and effectively ending the *Phibes* franchise. 'Sam didn't know what to do,' said Quarry, 'He knew how to buy movies, but that was it.'

Quarry had the last word regarding the turmoil at AIP, 'It was like everybody pulled the plug and the ark sank – or the Arkoff sank!'

Arkoff still had two contract stars on his books, and with no projects lined up, he had no choice but to loan them out to other studios. While Quarry had to contend himself with TV guest spots in popular American crime shows, Price got loaned out to United Artists for another horror film.

It could not have come at a worse time. In April 1972, the Missouri Repertory Theatre were planning a summer season and offered Price the roles of James Tyrone in Eugene O'Neill's *Long Day's Journey into Night* and Thomas Beckett in T S Elliot's *Murder in the Cathedral*. The plays appealed to Price, who desperately wanted to return to the theatre so it's easy to see his anger when he had to turn them down as both productions clashed with this new horror picture, which was to be filmed in London. Even England began to lose its lustre in view of his situation.

Price vented his anger in a letter to his agent. 'I have been on the road for almost ten years. Obviously I have not been able to save enough to retire if I wanted to. But the question before me at 61 is not the money but peace of mind, some family life and dignity to my profession. I have managed to survive all the crap at AIP, of Sears' destruction of my art image, but the wear and tear has me down at long last, and now I want to settle things before I find myself permanently unsettled by the dissonances of my life.'

Professionally Price was at an all-time low, and the thought of doing another horror film only served to make him more disillusioned than before.

However this next picture gave him the horror role of his career – Edward Sheridan Kendal Lionheart. The film: *Theatre of Blood*.

Theatre of Blood

'I'd like to do Prospero, Shylock and King Lear. I'm old enough to do Lear. You know, I don't think we do Shakespeare as well as the English do. We just don't. It's their language.' – Vincent Price

Price with Diana Rigg in *Theatre of Blood*

Price may have felt disappointed at not being able to take on the theatre roles in Missouri, but he had plenty of reasons to be grateful for *Theatre of Blood*. The role of Edward Lionheart came to him via his old friend Sam Jaffe, who produced the film. It was a golden opportunity to make a horror film while playing

Shakespeare and also a chance to briefly break away from the shackles of Sam Arkoff.

'I got to play eight Shakespearean parts in one picture,' he noted with great enthusiasm, 'which very few actors get to do in their whole life time if they're American. It's one of my favourite pictures for a lot of reasons, one being the premise of it, which is hysterically funny. I'm a Shakespearean actor who thinks he should be given the critics' award, and instead they give it to someone who mumbles like Marlon Brando. So I set out to kill all the critics, and all the murders are done according to a Shakespearean play.'

From an original story by Stanley Mann and John Kohn, the screenplay, under the wittier title of *Much Ado About Murder*, was completed by Anthony Greville-Bell, an Australian born World War II hero who served in the SAS, and later swapped the stiff upper lip existence of an officer and gentleman for the flamboyant bohemian lifestyle of the sixties that included his childhood passion for sculpture. Greville-Bell's first cinematic credit as screenwriter was the comedy crime thriller *Perfect Friday* (1970).

Production began on 10 July 1972, entirely on location in London, with all the interiors filmed inside actual buildings, most notably the Putney Hippodrome, which doubled up as the Burbage Theatre. Built in 1906, the theatre had been vacant for over ten years prior to being used on *Theatre of Blood* (it was finally demolished in 1975 to make way for a housing complex). The dark, dilapidated interiors give the theatre a real gothic splendour; a perfect headquarters for Lionheart to carry out his overtly theatrical activities.

'All the sets in it were sort of wonderful real places,' said Price. 'The theatre where I have my company, and where I lure all the critics to come and then murder them, was the Putney Hippodrome. It was a great place that was going to be torn down. It had really fallen into decay, and was a very dangerous place to work. We really shouldn't have been there!'

'There was another scene which had probably the most spectacular set I've seen,' he added. 'When I'm doing *Richard III*, I'm about to drown Bobby Coote in a vat of wine. We shot it in a place that is now a wax museum in London, but it was a wine warehouse, almost under the Thames River. It had been abandoned for a long time, and had great drips of water that made these stalactites, and it was pitch black. They lit a thousand candles, which made it a very spectacular scene. You could never build a set to look that way in a hundred years!'

Other location work took place at Kensal Green Cemetery in London (where George Maxwell's funeral takes place). Lionheart's monumental tomb situated in the chapel belonged to the Sievier family and shows a stone sculpture of a seated man, one hand placed on an adoring woman kneeling by his side and the other holding the *Book of Luke*. The monument was altered by replacing the man's face with a plaster cast mask of Price with the *Book of Luke* becoming a volume of Shakespeare and Lionheart's name engraved on the tomb.

The interior of Peregrine Devlin's ultra-bright home (a perfect contrast to the grime of the Burbage Theatre) was a modern penthouse apartment at Alembic House (now known as Peninsula Heights), situated at the Albert Embankment of the River Thames. Price's death scene (courtesy of a weighted dummy) took place on the balcony of the apartment: the filmmakers needed permission from the Port of London to carry the scene out. The apartment later became the home of novelist Jeffrey Archer.

Other London-based interiors included the gymnasium at the American School, used for the fencing scene between Lionheart and Devlin, and Robert Fielding's trendy hairdressing salon in Brompton Road, Knightsbridge where Coral Browne met her grisly fate!

With director Robert Fuest turning down the assignment, Jaffe approached Douglas Hickox. Born in London in 1929 and educated at Emanuel School, Hickox worked as an assistant director or second unit director from the early fifties; horror credits included *Grip of the Strangler* (1958) and *The Fiend Without the Face* (1958). He directed numerous shorts and TV commercials before moving into features with *Entertaining Mr Sloan* (1969), an adaptation of Joe Orton's celebrated play, and the thriller *Sitting Target* (1972).

In Jaffe's eyes, Hickox seemed a perfect choice; the vicious black humour of *Entertaining Mr Sloan* and the no-nonsense violence of *Sitting Target* were the right for what the producer had in mind. *Theatre of Blood* was Hickox's horror debut.

Next came the casting. 'The cast was so good,' said Hickox, 'that all I had to do as director was open the dressing room door and let the camera roll.'

Price was equally enthusiastic. 'When I first heard the big names that they had assembled for this picture, I just couldn't believe it!'

'The cast of critics were really extraordinary,' he added. 'They were all the major actors in England! Jack Hawkins, Robert Morley, Arthur Lowe, who was a great comedian, the late Ian Hendry. God, a lot of them are late now. If we go on long enough we'll get rid of them all! It's getting so this is the way I explain most of the pictures I'm in, "so-and-so passed away a few years ago," and it won't be long until I can say that about myself.'

As production progressed, Price found himself completely in awe of his distinguished co-stars. 'It's great that every three or four I would be acting with is another great actor, like Harry Andrews, Coral Browne, Diana Rigg, Arthur Lowe. I just went on and on; Robert Morley, Denis Price, and it was terribly exciting because I was playing eight Shakespearean parts, and all of them were about the best Shakespearean actors in the world, and I was this poor amateur I'm afraid, but I had a great time doing it anyway!'

'It was kind of embarrassing,' he continued, 'because between them all, they had done every single play of Shakespeare's on the stage. Harry Andrews, for instance, is probably the greatest supporting actor of Shakespearean plays. I've known Harry for a long time, ever since he played Laertes to John Gielgud's Hamlet, years and years ago.'

Price's enthusiasm was unprecedented! According to his London agent, 'When Vincent was doing that picture, he came here for dinner one night and I said, "How's the filming going?" He said, "Oh you don't know what it's like! Years ago I had the position, especially at Fox, of working with the finest and the best. Since the horror films stopped being with Peter Lorre and Boris Karloff, since that time, I haven't had really great performers to work with. And now I here I am working with these ladies and gentlemen of the English stage – it's wonderful!" He went into paroxysms and honorifics about it.'

Price is being a little unfair towards the actors he had previously worked with in England prior to *Theatre of Blood*. Christopher Lee, Patrick Magee, Rupert Davies, Alfred Marks, Elizabeth Shepherd, Nigel Green, Elisabeth Bergner, Hugh Griffith and Terry-Thomas could hardly be called lesser talents, after all Patrick Magee was a favourite of Harold Pinter and Samuel Beckett, while Elisabeth Bergner was one of the finest actresses of the English and American theatre.

Douglas Hickox also noticed Price's enthusiasm towards his co-stars. 'He was very happy, because he was surrounded by first class actors who gave him the respect he deserved.'

Among those great talents were the two leading ladies of the English theatre, both of whom had a profound effect on Price's personal life – but for very different reasons.

Playing Lionheart's demented daughter Edwina was Diana Rigg. Best known as Emma Peel in *The Avengers*, she was making inroads into films when she landed the role in *Theatre of Blood*.

Rigg was also enthusiastic about the movie. 'I got cast in this horror movie and it was a very good script. At the time I was working at the National Theatre doing a couple of classics, and it struck me as witty and wonderful and funny to be doing the classics on one hand and a spoof on the classics on the other hand.'

Rigg enjoyed working with her 'father' for the first time. 'We hit it off immediately. His manners were impeccable, and his enthusiasm for the part and the project was very great, and he obviously loved doing it. Frankly I can't find a bad word to say about Vincent. First of all he's a wonderful actor. What people don't know unless they have seen the film, and tend to forget because of his horror movies, is what a great classical actor he could have been. Listening to him deliver some of those Shakespearean speeches, I remember thinking "God, what a missed opportunity!" He was wonderfully humble, sort of deeply impressed that I was at the National and doing these things, and I found it so sweet in a way, because he was a very eminent man in his own right. And it was only later that I discovered that he was, of course, a very great art expert, because he was so modest he'd never talk about it. He'd convey his enthusiasm and he'd convey his scholarship, but he'd never talk down to you, so it as only later that I began to understand what an important part he'd play in this vein.'

The other lady was someone Price desperately wanted to meet for many years, and it was Diana Rigg who was instrumental in bringing them together – for the rest of their lives! 'I was having dinner with Diana Rigg, who I happen to adore,' he recalled. 'I had never met Diana, but I had seen *The Avengers* and loved her in it. So she said, "I hear you're going to meet Coral Browne tomorrow." And I said, "Yes I am, and I'm quite anxious about it, because I hear she's a woman with a tongue like a lash!" So Diana said, "Well you be sure to say hello for me, and take down everything see says because she's supposed to be funny." The next day when I was introduced to her I said, "Hello Miss Browne, Diana Rigg told me to take down everything you say, because you're so witty," whereupon she shut her mouth and never opened it again!'

That would be the beginning of a brand new relationship for Vincent Price.

Coral Edith Brown(e) was born in Melbourne, Australia on 23 July 1913. The daughter of a restaurant owner, she attended Claremont Ladies College and studied art at the National Gallery Art School. Seeing acting as a way to get out of Australia, she made her stage debut in George Bernard Shaw's *You Never Can Tell*. She moved into professional acting for Gregan McMahon at the Melbourne Repertory Company. 'He taught me everything I knew about acting,' she said of McMahon, 'and a great deal about fucking.'

An incredibly mature woman for her young years, Victoria Price once said of her, 'what Coral wanted, Coral got.' Browne was determined to make it as an actress on her own terms. Gregan McMahon provided her with a letter of introduction to stage actress Marie Tempest and her father gave her £50 for her trip to London under the condition that she returned home once the money had gone. She never went back to Australia.

Browne initially struggled to make a stage career in England. Working as an understudy and bit player in several small scale productions, she appeared in *Basalik* opposite Price's old friend Paul Robeson.

Browne and Robeson became lovers, and it was Robeson who prevented her from returning to Australia when things got tough. Thanks to his influence, she established herself as a leading actress in London's West End, and was happy to sleep with anyone to get there. Much of her success was attributed to her personal and professional association with theatre impresario Frith Shepherd.

Shepherd's death left Browne wealthy enough to pursue a more distinguished theatre career. In 1950 she married actor/agent Philip Pearman, a known homosexual (Browne was bisexual and enjoyed the company of young women). No matter how odd the relationship must have been to some people, they were devoted to one another and Pearman's death in 1964 left the actress devastated.

Following her husband's death, Browne reinvented herself as a modern lady about town. As part of the acting world's prominent gay scene in London, her best friend and regular drinking partner was fellow actor Charles Gray. She worked with Gray in *The Night of the Generals* (1967) and gained critical acclaim for her performance as bitchy TV producer Mercy Croft in *The Killing of Sister George* (1968). By the time she took part in *Theatre of Blood*, she was one of the leading figures in the British theatre.

'And then,' according to friend and fellow actress Adrienne Corri, 'she met Vinnie and that was a sort of magic time. She was like a 12-year old, absolutely hook, line and sinker. I honestly think they fell in love like a couple of teenagers.'

Ironically, Browne turned her role down twice! 'No, no,' she said on her initial reaction, 'I can't be doing one of those scary pictures with Vincent Price – don't be ridiculous! And then Bob Morley phoned up and said, "We haven't been together since *The Man Who Came to Dinner* (on stage back in 1944). I'll do *Theatre of Blood* if you'll be in *Theatre of Blood*." And then Jack Hawkins phoned up and said, "If you and Bob are going to be in it, I'll be in it, too." Then Michael Hordern did exactly the same thing, and before you knew it, we had a good cast.'

Browne insisted that her first meeting with Price took place at the cemetery during Michael Hordern's character's funeral. Price was disguised as a grotty looking gravedigger – battered hat, dirty wellington boots – and Browne took one look at him and thought, 'Oh, this man, oh, this dirty looking old creature.' She took no notice of him until she found who this dirty looking old creature was.

According to Sam Jaffe, the couple quickly became, 'very friendly,' and it was Diana Rigg who inadvertently acted as Cupid. 'I was instrumental in bringing Coral and Vincent together insomuch as I think Vincent would not have made the first move. And I must say in hindsight that he had not spoken about a wife and daughter, so I had absolutely no idea that there were other people involved. As far as I knew they were separated. And so, in the light of that, my action appears something less than laudable. But I had absolutely no idea. Here is an absolutely adorable man who seemed quite lonely.'

Things continued that way when Price took Rigg out to a charity event shortly after work had finished for the day. 'My god, this man's got stamina!' she exclaimed. 'After all, he was working from six in the morning. I suppose, in a way, he demonstrated his enormous relish for life. And I went with him to do this and Coral was there. In the interval, she and I both went to the lavatory and she said, "It's a long time since I fancied a man my own age, and I fancy Vincent Price." Well in the car home, Vincent volunteered that it was Coral's birthday the following week and he didn't know what to do about it. So, I think they must have eyed each other. And I said, "Well, I think you can take her out to dinner. If you proffer an invitation, I think it would be looked kindly upon."'

Price's infatuation intensified, regarding Coral as, 'the Great Barrier Reef – beautiful, exotic and dangerous. I was like a bird dog!' 'I remember he electrocuted me on my birthday,' Browne recalled when she performed her death scene with Price. Ironically her acting isn't very good in this scene because she doesn't look remotely terrified of her murderer. Instead, she prefers to gaze into his eyes instead of screaming with fear.

After the day's filming, Price once again approached Diana Rigg for advice. 'I said to Diana, "I understand its Ms Browne's birthday. What could I get her?" And Diana said, "Well, I know what she wants. You!"'

'And from then on,' added Rigg, 'they never looked back. I think they fell into bed and I think it was a wildly sexual relationship. Incredible sexual. I remember Coral saying that they worked out their combined ages were 120-something, and when you saw these absolutely shagged out people on the set, it was really quite funny. And that was the start of it.'

'There were many accounts of Coral and Vincent's courtship,' said Victoria. 'Coral herself told me that my father brought Champagne on her birthday, when they were filming in a graveyard. Others seemed to think that she had her eye on him from the start. Both were certainly willing participants. To my father, Coral seemed the way out of the underlying depression some might call a midlife crisis. Here was a woman who seemed to love the limelight as much as he did. They made a striking couple and they knew it. The both approached life with panache and a great deal of humour.'

Less amusing was the fact that Price had a wife and daughter back in the States, and during the summer they both came to visit him at his rented London flat, which wasn't far from Browne's home. 'It was a difficult summer,' recalled Victoria, 'and my mother thought my dad seemed peculiar and distracted.'

Price promised his family a trip to the South Wales coast where Mary was born, but things remained difficult. 'Throughout the trip,' observed Victoria, 'he was irritable and not at all himself. Back in London, my parents' friends hinted that my mother should watch out for Coral; that the actress had her sights set on my father. But my mother chose to trust her husband, as she had for the past 23 years.'

In between the emotional trauma, high testosterone levels and family betrayal, there was a movie to be made, and almost everyone involved was having a great time, including Jack Hawkins and Dennis Price, both of whom were clearly ill (Both actors died in 1973). 'I did it for fun,' said Diana Rigg, 'because it appealed to my sense of humour; I had no idea it was going to be so enormously enjoyable, which was, mainly because of Vincent, who is heaven.'

'Vincent was often in costume,' she added, 'appropriate for delivering a lot of very Shakespearean soliloquies. He would always find out if the next shot was a long shot or close-up. If it was a medium or close up, he'd clamber into the oldest pair of slippers I have ever seen. My problem was to keep a straight face looking at Vincent delivering these soliloquies sublimely in costume with his feet in those carpet slippers.'

Of Price's own time acting in his carpet slippers, he added 'You had to play a scene of each Shakespearean character and fit it into the scene of the murder because we had to fit the murder in contemporary parlance, so you change how you speak the lines, which is difficult to do.'

Also relishing the opportunity to work with Price was Ian Hendry. 'I have no particular liking for this kind of picture, but the script was good and the cast so marvellous that I couldn't really say no. I think this could become a cult film, a classic of its type. Also, acting with a true pro like Vincent has been marvellous.'

Hendry was the only actor on the set who didn't have a fun time of it, and it shows in his inherently aggressive performance. A notorious heavy drinker, Hendry had a turbulent marriage to former child star Janet Munro, who was also an alcoholic. During the making of *Theatre of Blood* the couple were going through an acrimonious divorce. Shortly after the marriage ended, Janet Munro choked to death after drinking a cup of tea.

Hendry's booze-fuelled behaviour upset an otherwise happy shoot and annoyed the rest of the cast. It was the usually affable Michael Hordern who gave Hendry a dressing down for his unprofessionalism on the set. Ironically, Hendry received a BAFTA nomination for his performance.

Theatre of Blood is similar to *The Abominable Dr Phibes*. We have a long believed dead but very much larger-than-life villain, helped by a beautiful assistant, and out for revenge on those that wronged him. His main protagonist works with the usual bumbling Scotland Yard coppers and the inventive murders are rooted in literature.

The similarities end there as *Theatre of Blood* is the vastly superior movie. While *The Abominable Dr Phibes* is firmly rooted in period gothic, *Theatre of Blood* has a modern and much looser feel. The violence is extremely gruesome, but the humour makes it less offensive. And with producers abandoning the studios for location work, there is added realism. Lionheart couldn't be further removed from Dr Phibes, however, because the former is a real person, not a mysterious bogeyman figure. Nor is he evil like Matthew Hopkins or Prince Prospero. Lionheart is a genuine human being with heartfelt emotions and it shows in Price's committed performance.

Theatre of Blood is anything but a traditional horror flick. 'It's a black comedy,' said Price, 'and of course, you try to play things for comedy, and with a bit of good taste. But it's awfully hard to saw off somebody's head if it's in the best of taste. I have taken carving lessons! I'm very good on mutton or roast!'

One fascinating aspect of the film that is often overlooked is Lionheart's followers, the Meths Drinkers. This grimy and inebriated lot appear to inhabit their own little fantasy world. Their unique ballet like movements and reactions were choreographed by Norwegian actor/dancer Tutte Lemkow. After playing double agents, shifty foreigners and Cossack dancers in several British films of the sixties, Lemkow is best known as the mysterious *Fiddler on the Roof* (1971). He also choreographed the impressive dance sequence in Roman Polanski's *The Fearless Vampire Killers* (1967).

Mixing comedy and horror is like mixing oil with water – not compatible at all, but *Theatre of Blood* is an exception. And because Douglas Hickox wasn't a horror director, he could inject a different approach to the material.

The film is not without its faults, but they are tiny quibbles that don't detract from the overall enjoyment. For example, how did Horace Sprout's head end up on a milk bottle outside Devlin's flat after it was originally discovered in his bedroom by the maid? And did Lionheart really think Solomon Psaltery would kill his wife in a jealous rage? That scene doesn't work well although there is the joy of hearing Price's misbegotten Scottish accent!

Another quibble is Trevor Dickman's demise. While Price delights the audience with his remarkable performance as Shylock, the build up to Dickman's death is a little slow. It also makes the mistake of revealing Edwina's identity too soon. Hiding behind a curly wig and Dave Crosby moustache during her earlier appearances, we kind of guess this 'young man' is really Edwina in disguise, but showing up to seduce Dickman, all mini skirt and fluttering eyelashes, you know it's her, and that makes the scene, where she finally reveals her true identity, a bit of an anti-climax. It might have worked better if Dickman had been gay so he could be seduced by Rigg's hippy instead!

Aside from those scenes, the overlong fencing sequence, and the conventional ending that doesn't quite hit the mark, *Theatre of Blood* is a delightful chiller with splendid murders and first rate performances from an incredible cast of thespians.

And there is, of course, Vincent Price. Whilst everyone was in good form, none of them could come close to Price, who gives the performance of his horror career. It is impossible to imagine anyone but Price as Lionheart. He is simply magnificent, playing it to the hilt and beyond. This is the film he will always be remembered for.

In addition to his excellent rendition of Shylock, Price's Richard III is outstanding, far more convincing than his last attempt in 1962. The contemporary disguises are also a delight. His Swedish accent as the mysterious fencer is almost as misbegotten as his Scottish masseuse, and the French TV chef from *This Is Your Dish* has hilarity stamped all over it.

The one disguise that's worth the price of admission alone is his totally outrageous turn as Butch the hairdresser. It's a classic moment worthy of a *Carry On* film, and features Price at his most camp. Its over-the-top stuff, but who cares? Price certainly didn't!

Price regards *Theatre of Blood* as one of his favourite movies. 'I think that was the best feeling of achievement and satisfaction that I ever had from a film.' Away from Arkoff, Price showed everyone there was more to the actor than melodramatic ham.

Critical reaction on the film's release in April 1973 was surprisingly positive for a horror flick, and Price was singled out for the highest praise. 'A triumph of stylish, witty Grand Guignol,' said the *Los Angeles Times*, 'it allows Price to range richly from between humour and pathos as a crazed Shakespearean actor, and his performance revitalises that tired-out adjective, magnificent, indeed, if horror pictures were taken seriously, he would surely be an Oscar contender.' David Pirie, writing for *Time Out*, stated that the film, 'really does give Vincent Price a chance to do his stuff, with deliciously absurd results.'

'A superior film in every way,' said the *Chicago Sun Times*. 'The script has genuine wit and malice, the production is handsome and Vincent Price, whose horror movie roles don't often give him much latitude, gets a magnificent chance to ham it up this time.' *The New York Times* stated that, 'Vincent Price is king of the genre. With all his lush villainy beautifully supplanted by marvellously bombastic Shakespearean recitation. To all involved, in fact, our gratitude for restoring that fine sense of fun to a genre more honoured of late in its exploitation than by a creative exploration of its intelligent entertainment values.' Box office receipts were equally impressive.

Remaining in London for a few weeks once production wrapped on 17 August 1972, Price finally returned to Los Angeles in September 1972 leaving behind a devastated Coral Browne. 'When he went away to America,' said Adrienne Corri, 'she cried an awful lot and said, "I'll never see him again. He's out of my life."'

The opposite was true. Far from forgetting her, Price missed his new woman, and corresponded with her on a regular basis. The irritable behaviour he displayed during Mary and Victoria's visit to London remained with him, much to the confusion of Mary, who still had no idea what was going on. At least the pressure of keeping the affair to himself was alleviated when he embarked on a month-long lecture tour, which enabled him to call Browne almost every day.

Price returned to London for a week to do some post synching work on *Theatre of Blood*. During this time he received an interesting offer from UK-based Canadian animator Richard Williams to do some voice work on his personal movie project *Nasrudden*.

Williams had made his name for his imaginative title designs on *What's New Pussycat* (1967), *Charge of the Light Brigade* (1968) and the *Pink Panther* series. His crowning achievement was *Who Framed Roger Rabbit* (1988), which brilliantly combined animation and live action. *Nasrudden* was a different kettle of fish. Williams began work on his *Arabian Nights* fantasy in 1968. It was a self-financed effort with every frame hand drawn. Williams had envisaged Price for the role of villain Zizag.

Price came over to work with Williams on the preliminary drawings of the character with voice work to follow. 'I'm sitting in a tiny room surrounded by many caricatures of Vincent Price,' recalled Williams. Price enjoyed his involvement in the project, which was very different from what he had done before on film.

Price had other things on his mind, namely his transatlantic affair with Coral Browne. 'He came back to do a voice for a cartoon character,' said Adrienne Corri, 'and that's when they met up again. After that, it was sort of for good.' Price had booked a hotel room in London during his time working with Williams, but he spent every night at her home, and this eventually proved his undoing.

Mary received an urgent call from one of her husband's business associates asking him to get in touch. Mary called the hotel but he wasn't around. As a man who was very meticulous regarding his whereabouts should anyone need to get in touch with him, just vanishing without word was completely out of character. Mary quickly grew frantic, especially when their London friends had no idea of where he was.

When he finally returned to Los Angeles, Mary confronted him about his absence and once again Price remained distant until she asked him if there was another woman involved. He finally confessed (without saying who it was) and a devastated Mary impulsively asked for a divorce, to which he agreed to, much to her surprise.

Things grew more uncomfortable when, in November 1972, Price became the subject of the popular TV show *This Is Your Life*. The surprise event had been previously organised by Mary at the Pickwick Bookstore, where Price was signing copies of *The Vincent Price Treasury Book of American Art*. Surprised by a visit from his friend Hans Conried, Price got a bigger surprise when Ralph Edwards turned up with the famous 'Big Red Book.'

Back at studio, an ill-at-ease Price did his very best to be affable as the variety of guests, including Sam Arkoff and Helen Hayes, turned up to pay tribute.

Mary too gave her own tribute, 'We are very pleased and proud to be Vincent's Family,' ironic since the marriage had ended beforehand.

Later, at a party after the show, Price remained distant with no one else other than Mary being aware of the situation. His daughter-in-law Rini sensed something wasn't right as he propped up the bar for most of the evening, knocking back more than his fair share of booze. The couple finally broke the news to Victoria during a very tense Thanksgiving.

Although the separation wasn't made official until Victoria finished her schooling, the couple began sorting out their legal and personal affairs while Price continued his relationship with Browne, but keeping it quiet from everyone else, especially Mary and Victoria. 'It was terribly cowardly of Vincent not to tell Mary about Coral,' said old friend Roddy McDowall, 'but he didn't want to hurt anyone and wanted everyone to love him.'

Price's public image was always a major concern. Behind the casual exterior was a serious and insecure individual, easily hurt. He remained reluctant to reveal Browne as his new woman as it might have a negative effect to his personal image and career.

'He was always extremely concerned with what people thought of him,' said Victoria. 'To the outside world, he wished never to seem anything other than content and grateful for his life, but in truth, he frequently struggled with feelings of inadequacy, failure, guilt and terrible, terrible worry.'

With 1972 coming to a tumultuous end, The Prices decided to stay together for the Christmas celebrations. During this time, the actor went to Washington to attend a three day event for the Indian Arts and Crafts Board. He arranged for Coral Browne to meet up with him, and once more they resumed their relationship with an intense vengeance.

Returning home, Price shared one last Christmas with his family. 'He was in very high spirits,' said Victoria recalling the day they went shopping. 'I remember our day together being very special, filled with funny, imaginative adventures. Unbeknownst to my mother and me, a week before Christmas, Coral came to LA, where she and my father celebrated the holiday early at the nearby home of Robert Hanley.'

Theatre of Blood became a catalyst for Vincent Price. Starting the year out with many careers uncertainties, he received several life affirming experiences that included the horror role of a lifetime. As 1972 drew to a close, the New Year would bring more changes that finally took him away from the genre. But for now there was one more chiller to make for AIP, marking the end of his career as the transatlantic king of horror.

Madhouse

'Making a horror film is far harder, in fact than making many so-called straight films.
We have to make them believable at all times.
This can be damned hard work.' – Vincent Price

Although he continued to make chillers in his later years, as well as spoof his image on TV, *Madhouse* (1974) closed Vincent Price's tenure as king of horror. He had simply come to the end of his tether with the genre that had made him a star.

'My contract had finished and I hoped (*Madhouse*) would be my last.' For many years Price refused to discuss this enjoyable if undistinguished effort with friends and fans. With *Theatre of Blood* strengthening his desire to return to the theatre, it's rather surprising he agreed to do the movie at all.

At the beginning of 1973 Price escaped the pressures of his impending divorce with a lecture tour, which gave him time out to correspond with Coral Browne. Victoria Price would describe the correspondence as, 'wildly sexual letters.' Later in the month he returned to London to continue his voice work on *Nasrudden*.

Price also took time out to pay tribute to Christopher Lee in the British version of *This Is Your Life*. Looking far more relaxed than he did in his own American edition, he told a funny story about being mistaken for both Lee and Boris Karloff. Lee's *This is Your Life* is unique as it also features Peter Cushing – the three Titans of Terror together on TV for the first time.

These professional excursions to London had more to do with spending as much time as possible with Coral Browne. On his return to Los Angeles he moved to his beach house while the divorce was being finalised, the isolation giving him a chance to think about the future. He also received offer to play Pandarus in a stage production of *Troilus and Cressida*.

Sam Arkoff, as usual, had other ideas, and wanted Price back in London for another British horror flick. Had circumstances been different, Price would have put his foot his down and said no. But as he was in the final year of his contract, and had the chance to spend a few weeks with his new lady, he accepted the assignment without hesitation.

There had been a lot of changes at AIP since the *Dr Phibes* movies. James H Nicholson and Deke Heyward had departed, and the company had moved to cheaper offices. Sam Arkoff now found it increasingly difficult and expensive to mount further film productions in England, and his new number two, Steve Previn, did not share the same ideas about the genre.

'That was the end of the horror cycle,' said Robert Quarry, who was just as disillusioned with the genre as Price was.

Madhouse was loosely based on Angus Hall's 1969 pulp novel *Devilday*. After purchasing the film rights, Arkoff put it on AIP's shooting schedule in 1969 with Gordon Hessler as director; the project was then shelved until November 1971 with Murray Smith providing the script. Shooting was due to start in the summer of 1972 but with Nicholson quitting, the project was further delayed and Smith's screenplay was abandoned in the process.

Devilday remained in limbo during AIP's year-long production break. Heyward's replacement, Peter Katz eventually brought it forward along with several other projects. Re-titled *The Revenge of Dr Death*, it resurfaced in April 1973 with a new script by Ken Levinson, who came on board at Price's suggestion. It was then rewritten by film publicist Greg Morrison. 'They had a very good script,' recalled an unenthusiastic Quarry, 'which Sam Arkoff, with his usual back-handed "brilliance", fucked over!'

Keeping costs down, Arkoff arranged a second co-production deal with

Milton Subotsky at Amicus. For the sake of economy, Subotsky set up a small office at Twickenham Studios where he had access to cheaper stage sets used mainly for television. The company rented studio space for two weeks and arranged for further interior shooting to take place at London Weekend Television Studios in Wembley, the Esso Motor Hotel and London East India Docks. There was also some location work around London.

The main setting for *The Revenge of Dr Death* was Pryford Manor, a 15th Century country residence situated in Woking, which doubled up as Herbert Flay's home. The place was previously owned Sir Archibald Sinclair and was a frequent residence for Queen Elizabeth I. Principle photography began in May 1973.

The cost cutting measures carried out by Subotsky were a clear indication that Amicus was going through similar internal problems as AIP. Despite the success of their portmanteau films, the company had their fair share of box office flops, the situation further complicated by the tense relationship that erupted between Subotsky and Max Rosenberg. Rosenberg appointed John Dark Executive in Charge of Production, but the newcomer's increased involvement at Amicus seriously undermined Subotsky's position.

Changing the film's title to the somewhat vague *Madhouse*, in order to avoid confusion with a film called *Dr Death – Seeker of Souls* (1973), the production got the green light on 14 May 1973. With Robert Fuest passing up the assignment, former editor Jim Clark took the helm on Subotsky's recommendation. Clark's previous work as director were the low brow comedies *Every Home Should Have One* (1969) and *Rentadick* (1971).

AIP's involvement in *Madhouse* was minimal. Leaving Amicus to handle the production schedule, Arkoff stipulated that Price and Quarry should take part in the film, a decision that pleased Subotsky. 'I do wish there were more horror stars available,' he lamented. 'I haven't used Christopher Lee recently because his agents are now asking an enormous amount of money for him and he's become too expensive. Peter Cushing, on the other hand, is good value. I think his agent is very smart; he asks for an amount which is reasonable, but he asks the maximum reasonable amount. And Cushing is very good – he can do anything. In our films we always cast him against his usual type. He loves it because it gives him a chance to do something different. But I would love to have more people to choose from who are considered as horror names.'

Casting Price as washed up horror star Paul Toombes also pleased Angus Hall, who claimed he had Price in mind when he wrote his character in *Devilday*. This is a highly unlikely statement as the Toombes in the novel is described as 'an obese, hairy man' and paedophile who practised black magic, and in all probability did murder his wife. The character couldn't be further removed from the handsome, debonair Price.

Robert Quarry was set to play Toombes' best friend Herbert Flay, but ended up with the thankless role of boorish producer Oliver Quayle. 'Originally I was to play the Peter Cushing role,' he bemoaned, 'but age wise that didn't work out, so they manufactured a part for me.'

With Price and Quarry being part of the AIP deal, Subotsky brought in Peter Cushing, who had been his most regular Amicus star. After two false starts in *Scream and Scream Again* and *Dr Phibes Rises Again*, *Madhouse* is remembered for the long overdue horror teaming of Price and Cushing. Even though the film is a long way off their best work, it began a deep friendship that lasted until Price's death.

With the horror trio in place, Amicus had a free reign in the casting of the female leads, all of whom were taken from the world of horror cinema and TV comedy. Playing Herbert's demented wife Faye was the tempestuous Italian-Scottish actress Adrienne Corri. The talented but explosive star appeared in the chillers *Corridors of Blood* (1958), *A Study in Terror* (1965) and *Vampire Circus* (1971), but is best known for being raped by Malcolm McDowell in Stanley Kubrick's *A Clockwork Orange* (1971).

In the smaller role of ill-fated Elizabeth Peters was Linda Hayden. Hayden first earned notoriety as the orphaned nymphet in *Baby Love* (1969). Her long blonde hair, angelic looks and piercing eyes could register innocence and evil, and that made her a natural for British horror. She appeared in *Taste the Blood of Dracula* (1969) and gave her most memorable horror performance as the demented Angel Blake in *Blood on Satan's Claw* (1971).

As the likeable but tragic PR girl Julia, Natasha Pyne is best known as Patrick Cargill's teenage daughter in the popular sitcom *Father Dear Father*. Benny Hill protégé Jenny Lee Wright appears as Quayle's talentless girlfriend Carol Clayton, and had the original casting of *Monty Python* funny girl Carol Cleveland went ahead, *Madhouse* would have boasted leading ladies from three completely different fields of British comedy – sitcom, slapstick and satire! However Cleveland had to drop out at the last minute so her role as Toombes' wife went to Julie Crosthwaite.

But all was not well from the start. By the time Quarry arrived in London, he wanted out of his contract. 'I was just a piece of meat on a rack to be used. I was under contract, but it was the beginning of the end of AIP, though it lingered on, doing one ghastly film after another.'

Quarry had scant regard for *Madhouse*. 'That was a terrible film! *Madhouse* was ill-fated from the start, thanks to Vincent's shaky status at AIP after years of contract disputes.' This situation became really tense when, on his arrival in London, Price received a phone call from a *Sunday Mirror* reporter asking for an interview.

This published interview described Price as compulsive and broke with the actor stating that, 'I live from picture to picture and on fees from TV quiz shows and the like. Without these I'd have trouble supporting my family and keeping up with alimony. As it is I live very simply and except for an art collection that's far from Sotheby's standard. Whenever I make a picture, I blow any spare money on a work of art that may or may not be valuable one day. Then, of course, I subscribe to various charities, including the tax man.'

The article left the usually easy going Price hopping mad. So much so he barred AIP's press agent Dennison Thornton from assisting the British tabloids in further news items. Price didn't want to risk making his relationship with Coral Browne public while his divorce was being finalised.

Production began on a bad note with Levinson's re-writes causing endless frustration. 'None of us could really prepare for *Madhouse*,' said Quarry, 'because we got the script on the actual day before we were supposed to start shooting. And I read the thing and just said, "You've got to be kidding." What could we do? It was Vincent's last movie at AIP. His contract was up. We never got the script until Sunday morning, and we were to start shooting the next day. This gave us no time to bitch and scream. They knew if they'd sent it to us two weeks before, we'd have called them up and said, "Hey, work this over, as it's terrible." So they were very smart there.'

After the tense atmosphere between the Americans during the making of *Dr Phibes Rises Again*, it is surprising to see them join forces on the set of *Madhouse*. Unhappy with the script revisions, Quarry made his own alterations. 'The script we ended up with was so bad that I started re-writing some of my dialogue.' With his role as Quayle being non-existent, Quarry re-wrote the part to resemble Sam Arkoff as closely as possible. 'At least it gave me something to work with,' he added.

Quarry was equally unhappy with the choice of director. 'Jim Clark may have been a good editor, but he was ill-prepared to direct a movie; he was just gonna shoot what was there. So I changed my dialogue around so it was speakable and then leave the last line, the cue line, in. They never knew what hit them; when I finished talking and gave the cue line, the other actor spoke.'

Quarry's re-writes impressed the disgruntled Price. 'About the second day I told Vincent I had made some changes, so I wouldn't have to speak this shit. He said, "God, help me with my stuff – could you re-write some of this?" I was flattered that Vincent trusted me enough to re-write some of the scenes. I couldn't change the scenes but at least we put a little edge on them ... We didn't really improve on the movie though.'

Price also confided in Quarry about an expenses fiddle he was working on. Despite the inevitable divorce, he was still claiming for Mary and Victoria so he could buy art work on the quiet. 'Vincent told me that if anybody asked if Victoria and Mary were there, I was to say yes, because he wrote it in his expenses. All that expense money for two weeks: first class air fare, food. I said, "Oh, I love it, I love it. Can't you get anybody else on there?" After all, he made a great deal of money for AIP. He was their only superstar. And they should have been damn grateful for him, and they should have paid him more money. Frankly, anything he could steal out the studio, I said, "Steal baby, steal!"'

As confidants, Price continued seeing his new lady while the powers-that-be assumed his wife was with him. Quarry in the meantime bonded with Peter Cushing. Concerned that the actor wasn't eating properly since his wife's passing, he regularly cooked dinner for his new friend at rented Chelsea apartment.

Summing up his time with Price on the film, Quarry said, '*Madhouse* was the only serious work we did together, trying to find ways to do this dreadful picture.'

Peter Cushing on the other hand thought, 'This script is very original.' As one of the cinema's most meticulous perfectionists when it came to acting, he did his own fair share of script re-writes!

Despite their writing collaboration, Price and Quarry never became close friends and basically spent their days off away from one another. Price did however forge his lifelong friendship with Peter Cushing. 'I like Peter very much, and I hear from him always at Christmas. On our birthdays we send each other the funniest cards we can find. He's a very gentle, sweet man. I am very, very fond of him.'

Cushing was equally complimentary towards his friend and contemporary. 'A dear man, with a great sense of humour, strictly a professional, who cares far more about his work than he allows his public to know. I am extremely fond of him and bask in his gentle kindness and warmth.'

Both men were similar in their attitude towards other people. 'One of his qualities as a gentleman,' Cushing said of Price, 'is his manner and attitude to all that come into his orbit. No matter what their status, everyone received the same charming courtesy and attention.'

Price and Cushing have a natural on-screen chemistry. They play off each other so well, it's hard to imagine why a horror teaming never happened sooner. 'The relationship between Vincent and Peter was one of mutual respect,' recalled Natasha Pyne. 'Each had a healthy, objective view of their work that made their living, which helped for an easy, mutually supportive working relationship. They seemed to me to be very good friends.' Because of their similar ages and backgrounds, Cushing looks more at home on screen with Price than he does with his long term friend Christopher Lee.

Pyne further added her own personal enjoyment working with Price. 'It was a delightful experience to work with Vincent and to share stories with him. He had a mischievous sense of humour, and before some of the perhaps less believable sequences he would throw one a naughty twinkle of the eye just before a take. Definitely at the top of my favourite colleagues – an erudite and interesting man. I treasure the book on American art which he gave me upon completion of the film.'

Linda Hayden was equal in her praise for the actor. 'He was something special. He had such a lovely twinkle. We were having this scene when I was on an ocean liner, and I was lying on the bed with this plunging neckline. Then he came over to me and I was lying on the bed. They gave me quite a cleavage, which I didn't actually have, and they taped me with all this double sided tape. God! It took bloody ages to do it! Then Vincent leaned over and saw some of it come unstuck, and it was just hysterical because he was pulling my leg! Every time I saw him after, he always asked if I had double-sided tape. He was just a great man with a great fun element to him.'

TV presenter Michael Parkinson, who was playing himself on the film, also enjoyed his time with Price. 'Vincent was a joy to work with, an urbane man with a deep knowledge of art and a great lover of racehorses.'

During the making of *Madhouse*, the production received a visit from the BBC who were filming for the series *Film 73*, presented by critic Barry Norman. During an interview with Jim Clark, the director expressed his own admiration for Price and Cushing. 'One couldn't work with easier people. They respond marvellously to direction and know instinctively what to do. They're both extraordinary pleasant people to know, and one is terribly lucky to have them.'

Film 73 went further by interviewing Price and Cushing about their association with the genre. The on screen chemistry between them was exactly the same away from the camera:

PRICE: I think the one thing about horror pictures, they are kind of fun, and I don't like to call them horror any more than you do (turning to Cushing). It's a fantasy or gothic tale, is that they don't date. They go on year after year because in the first place they are usually a costume thing or beyond reality, so they don't date.

CUSHING: Like a western

PRICE: Yes, a western never dates. I love to see them really go off and make a real fantasy. I'm anxious to do a thriller for children, where there is no blood, but all those marvellous old things like creaking doors. Kids are the biggest audience in the world.

CUSHING: Look how they love *Doctor Who*. Do you know it? We did two films and it's been such a success on television. I don't think you can make science fiction with that sense of fantasy. I think keeping it in the 1900s, the turn of the century, it is a wonderful time, particularly for the children.

PRICE: I always wondered that the best setting in the world for a thriller, a spooky picture is always London in the fog.

CUSHING: I tell you what, they haven't used for a long time is an old castle. I mean London in the fog with Sherlock Holmes, but an old castle; almost a ghost story.

'I think horror stories end up more successfully if they're done the (Roger) Corman way,' Price said in a separate interview. 'By which I mean to say, letting the audience in on the secret that the actor is enjoying it.' Price and Cushing certainly enjoyed their time together on *Madhouse*.

Jim Clark's own approach to the film couldn't be removed from the fun element Price enjoyed in his previous efforts. 'I have tried to give (*Madhouse*) a quality of strange and brooding tension, with overtones of horror. And there are quite a few murders. But it is not a tongue-in-cheek horror send up like Vincent Price's two *Dr Phibes* films. We never touched on the area of black comedy.'

As production carried on throughout June 1973, Price received an offer from the BBC to play host for a radio anthology series called *The Price of Fear*. On Price's insistence, Cushing was brought in to star in the show's most popular episode, entitled *The Man Who Hated Scenes*. Here Price's host is sitting on a long train journey where he encounters at breakfast Cushing's nervous and timid little man; a chap who tries to avoid making a scene if he can help it.

As the story unfolds, the ineffectual chap turns out to be a cuckolded husband who reluctantly takes revenge on his adulterous young wife. It's a brilliantly played episode featuring an outstanding performance by Cushing. Price may have been the star of *Madhouse*, but it's Cushing who takes the acting honours in *The Man Who Hated Scenes*. According to writer David Miller, 'The *Film 73* interview and the radio work reveals a rapport and genuine friendship between Cushing and Price which is perhaps not so apparent in their film work.'

Despite barring press scoops following the *Sunday Mirror* incident, Price remained his affable self when it came to further interviews, one of which took place in June 1973. During the interview, Frances Horsburgh asked the actor what scared him the most:

'"So you want to know what frightens me? The other night someone rang me up from the States and one o'clock in the morning. Now, I have to get up at six when I'm filming, so I wasn't very pleased. 'Do you ever get nightmares after shooting one of those scenes?' he asked me. 'Yes I do' I said. 'I have nightmares all the time about some silly son-of-a-bitch is going to phone me up in the middle of the night. That really frightens me!'" Mr Price chortles into his coffee. "I guess he hung up after that." The tall elegant 62 year-old actor and I are lunching in his caravan. He looks like a lean Rhett Butler – a man born to sport slouch hat, a silk waistcoat and a brace of aces. Outside, a touch of the Derby Day Fever has gripped the film crew, and the star has given them a pound to place on the horse of their choice. "Whoever wins, I get 10%," he quips. This soft-spoken sophisticate is an enthusiastic Anglophile, with an enviable reputation inside and outside the business for kindness, generosity and approachability. They were calling him back onto the set as Dr Death. Mr Price eyes himself in the mirror. "Do I look human?" He loses a disquieting laugh. "Well vaguely anyway."'

During the filming of *Madhouse*, Milton Subotsky received a visit from Sam Arkoff. Despite his minimal involvement in the production, Arkoff still held the purse strings regarding budget and distribution. On his arrival on the set, he announced a new film adaptation of J Sheridan Le Fanu's vampire novel *Carmilla*. Nothing came of it.

A few days later, several important dignitaries, including Angus Hall, paid a visit to Twickenham. Unfortunately Milton Subotsky made a huge error by introducing Adrienne Corrie as Diane Cilento. Angus Hall later viewed the rushes and expressed his own doubts regarding the way his novel was being filmed.

Madhouse wrapped up in the middle of August 1973, and Price, with his usual consideration to others, sorted out gifts for the cast and crew prior to returning to America. Following his departure, there was a great deal of controversy regarding the final cut.

If Quarry had his own reservations about Jim Clark's inexperience on the set, the director had his own beef with Milton Subotsky. Price received a heartfelt letter from Clark, who was, 'in a miasma of impotent rage,' about the way Subotsky took over the editing of the film. According to Price, 'The director was having terrible disagreements with Subotsky.'

Clark told Price in his letter that Subotsky, 'bulldozed his way into the cutting room and is at this very moment cutting a swath through the film. I feel responsible towards you, and as a friend I shall defend our mutual interest just as long as I can, but I fear, in the end, that we shall both suffer at their hands, and it's your name that will sell the film, and mine that will receive the blame for making a poor picture. They are retaining the action of course, but every time anyone opens their mouth, Milton tries to cut the line, for no reason than "it bores me" or "we don't need it." It is pure butchery and I don't really know why I'm surprised.' Small wonder Clark returned to full time film editing.

Milton Subotsky, on the hand, paints a different story about the final cut. '*Madhouse* was directed by Jim Clark. He's a film editor and did a terrible job. Again, we never liked the script. Then, when AIP got it, they re-edited the picture entirely and I nearly died when I saw it. What they did made no sense at all. I remember when the film editor came back from California and showed it to me, I said, "This is absolutely senseless. Maybe we can disguise some of it by putting music under the whole picture all the way through." He said, "They don't like music under dialogue." I said. "Oh forget it." He cut the picture and that was that. They murdered it. They sent us all the trims, all the cuts, everything from the picture and they re-edited it in California. My editor said he never saw such unprofessional behaviour at the screening of the film. The first time they saw the film, he said people were wandering in and out, they were eating popcorn and peanuts, they were talking, and these were the professionals at AIP. It drove him really crazy.'

To sum up the controversy regarding the making of *Madhouse*, it seems everyone involved was blaming each other for the shortcomings of the end result.

The press screening took place in Los Angeles on 29 March 1974 to a negative response. As a result, the UK release was delayed until November 1974 when it opened as part of a double-bill with Terence Young's *The Amazons* (1974).

Madhouse isn't a bad film, but it's fair to say it should have been better. Using the LWT TV studios for some of the interior shooting gave the production a cheap look. The well-staged death scenes lack the originality of *Theatre of Blood*, and while Jim Clark's direction is better than Robert Quarry and Milton Subotsky would suggest, he does not have the quirky feel of Robert Fuest.

Madhouse was conceived as a murder mystery, even though there is not much of a mystery to solve. One only has to look at Ellen Mason's demise. There's only four suspects – Paul, Herbert, Quayle and Faye – yet none of them have motive for the murder, even years later. Paul is obviously the innocent party being set up from the start, and Faye is an agoraphobic, so it's unlikely she could have ventured into the TV studio to kill Carol Clayton. Herbert and Quayle are the strongest contenders but other than the fact they are played by horror stars, there is no motive, at least until the end when it's revealed that Herbert was responsible all along; he's played by Peter Cushing so there you go!

The main fault is the script. There are many interesting ideas that aren't fully explored, the main one being the relationship between Herbert and Faye. It seems Faye's addition to the story was conceived as an afterthought, and while Adrienne Corrie is superb, one would like to see her character and her marriage to Herbert develop beyond the fact they just live together. There is one interesting scene when Faye says, 'This is my house.' It gives an indication that Herbert isn't the success he claims to be, living off his wife's money, and getting away with 'murder' because she can't venture outside. It's a nice idea that is completely ignored.

Another fault is the feeble effort to pay tribute to Price by screening clips of his old AIP movies at regular intervals. Unlike John Wayne's final film *The Shootist* (1976) which makes good use of the movie clips taken from the Duke's early efforts, what happens in *Madhouse* has more to do with laziness. They don't really add any impact and only serve to show that Price's best horror work was behind him, especially during the fancy dress party scene where a bored looking Price watches a montage of his old movies. At least we get to see Peter Cushing dressed up as Dracula and Robert Quarry donning his cape once more as Count Yorga.

Madhouse also suffers from undercasting. Linda Hayden and Jenny Lee Wright are reasonably effective, but Julie Crosthwaite makes no real impression . As the policeman investigating the murders, John Garrie and Ian Thompson are colourless individuals who lack the humorous charm of Peter Jeffrey and Milo O'Shea from *Theatre of Blood*: giving Garrie a bushy beard and a pipe doesn't make him a Holmesian super sleuth!

There are a couple of interesting performances from Ellis Dale and Catherine Wilmer as Hayden's creepy parents. More interested in making money through blackmail than mourning her death, their comical, almost surreal prancing around is quite sinister. They look like former members of the Meth Drinking group from *Theatre of Blood*, and must have achieved their sobriety following an extensive period with Alcoholics Anonymous!

It is Natasha Pyne who walks off with the acting honours thanks to a beautifully underplayed performance. Pyne is a likable individual who bonds well with Price, and this makes her demise all the more tragic.

And what of the horror stars? Despite the thankless nature of his role, Quarry emerges from the film with some credit, and more than holds his own with a suitably slimy performance, which was achieved on the strength of his unofficial work as script editor.

Cushing is excellent as always, and it's during the climax that he really shines by giving a manic performance of eye-rolling intensity; he re-wrote the fight scene to achieve this. His cool, introverted style compliments Price's flamboyance. Their teaming works so well, one wishes for a better film to make use of their unique talents.

As for Vincent Price, his performance as Paul Toombes remains one of his least interesting. After his excursions on *Theatre of Blood*, he spends most of his time on *Madhouse* looking fed up, and while he doesn't completely walk through the film, his disinterest is apparent. He looks particularly uncomfortable during his interview with Michael Parkinson, and while his death scene gives him the chance to ham it up, his soliloquy makes no sense at all!

The only time he reverts to his customary warmth is during his scenes with Peter Cushing, which leads to their brilliant, final confrontation. That alone makes *Madhouse* worth watching.

In his second autobiography, *Past Forgettings*, Cushing recalled fond memories of working with his friend. 'My antagonist in *The Revenge of Dr Death* was my greatly loved and incredibly funny friend, Vincent Price. What a dear man he is! I came to grief in this piece of skulduggery by falling into a tank full of poisonous spiders, following my titanic ding-dong with the old rascal. With lovely wit he wrote in a magazine about this.'

Price's article illustrated the hilarity of the scene. 'Sometimes, however, a scene is so totally preposterous it is almost impossible to do. Yesterday dear Peter had to fall into a tank of spiders! It's very difficult to fall into a tank of spiders and be Brando!' Luckily Cushing didn't mind spiders at all.

During the fight scene, Price saw another side of Cushing. 'Peter's a very wiry little fellow. But Peter is one of the strongest men I've ever knew in my life. I had to do several fight scenes with him. My God! He can throw you! He doesn't fake it at all. Nobody warned me about this, and I was sorted of battered and bruised. He's a very realistic and very serious minded actor.'

The most bizarre moment comes after the fight scene when Price makes himself up to look like Cushing in order to play Dr Death once more. Seeing the full faced Price merge with Cushing's gaunt features to produce a horror hybrid requires a suspension of disbelief, which, when viewed a certain way, is quite effective as the two genre legends are cannibalised into one.

Madhouse is a film Vincent Price refuses to talk about. This would be understandable if it was *Cry of the Banshee*, but somehow *Madhouse* remains a movie he felt ashamed to be in, and other than his guest spot on Michael Parkinson's BBC talk show two years later (complimenting Parkie on his 'performance'), he's kept quiet about the film ever since.

Marcus Brooks, founder of the *Peter Cushing Appreciation Society* (Price was an honorary member) encountered a brick wall when he interviewed the actor about the film. 'I asked him, "What do you recall from your time making *Madhouse* with Peter (Cushing)?", and his answer was, "I don't really remember that one. No, but I do remember Peter was such a joy. He is such a lovely man. And Christopher (Lee). Do you know we share our birthdays ..." He didn't want to talk about it. Clearly he changed the subject in a beat.'

'That was the most I got out of him on the subject,' Brooks added. 'I did ask him, again and again, he went on about *Scream and Scream Again* – with my prompting. It's easy to see why and on the second try he could see I was trying my luck. He was such an imposing figure, and I was a kid. I was lucky to be there at such close quarters, for that whole working day. He was a really kind and lovely man, and I didn't want to offend him.'

Brooks had his own idea about Price's involvement in *Madhouse* and his other British horrors films. 'Well, I think if you prompted him, all those films to him were money really, and a nice trip to the UK with days off to Paris and Europe on the way home. So you had to talk (with him) about nice things. If I knew him, I could have pressed him on Robert Quarry or Christopher Lee, or such, but I was green and he could have told me to fuck off. He didn't and he acknowledged me the whole day. If I had pressed him on anything else on *Madhouse* he would have closed down I am sure. I don't know, because he *loved* to perform.'

Unlike the positive critical response from *Theatre of Blood*, reviews for *Madhouse* were mixed. The kindest comments came from *Variety Magazine*, 'An inaptly titled but otherwise satisfactory horror entry, with a tepid blend of shivers and snickers … Price is now at a point in his long career where his familiar flamboyance is used to evoke audience sympathy as much as fear … Price and Cushing mellifluously outdo each other as uncharacteristic nice guys. The nostalgia never becomes necrophilic.'

The *Hollywood Reporter* echoed their own praises by describing *Madhouse* as, 'a totally predictable, superbly entertaining horror film, efficiently controlled, adequately frightening and excellently acted throughout. For once Price is not the villain and brings dignity and sympathy to his role.' Leslie Halliwell found this 'in-jokey' horror as 'Quite likeable,' while Leonard Matlin thought it was, 'a good, if uninspired adaptation of Angus Hall's *Devilday*.'

The Times wasn't impressed with *Madhouse*, describing the film as, 'an atrocious Hollywood flick. The makers had the wit to see that their material was ludicrous. The result is not only inept, silly, nasty, but also rather camp.'

Madhouse didn't do very well on its initial London release, taking in a paltry £1,901 in its first week, although it did better around the UK and Europe. The names of Vincent Price and Peter Cushing weren't enough to attract a mass audience.

All was not well with British horror. According to writer John Hamilton, 'If the sixties represented a party for the British film industry, then the seventies were the morning after. By 1970, reality was making an unwelcome intrusion into the offices of the Wardour Street power brokers.'

Tigon had already folded, and having got his knighthood and looking forward to his wealthy retirement, Sir James Carreras sold Hammer to his son Michael, who pressed on only to find that the company was heavily in debt and out of step with the times. The relationship between Milton Subotsky and Max Rosenberg was on the verge of collapse, and even Christopher Lee turned his back on the genre to try his luck in Hollywood.

Sam Arkoff had his own problems with AIP's UK base. 'It's a hard job to get a picture done in England these days,' said Price of the situation. 'It's so expensive, and reason they did them over there was that it was cheaper. I think, also, AIP decided that they were going to be classy. They were trying to go high class, which never worked. That really isn't their forte, or their medium. They should have just turn out good entertainment pictures and let it go at that. But you know they all become grand sooner or later.'

Price's observations were correct. AIP went upmarket with *De Sade* and

Wuthering Heights, and the results were disastrous. There was also a new threat in the shape of a big budget horror extravaganza called *The Exorcist* (1973).

The success of *The Exorcist* gave cinemagoers a new type of chiller. Hammer, Amicus and AIP could not halt the terminal decline of British horror as the studios found themselves all at sea when it came to competing with Hollywood's more expensive productions.

The situation got worse thanks to a cult following generated by a group of low budget horror films that began with George Romero's *Night of the Living Dead* (1968). This was followed by Wes Craven's *Last House on the Left* (1972), David Cronenberg's *Shivers* (1974) and Tobe Hooper's *The Texas Chainsaw Massacre* (1975). These stark and horrific movies introduced a vicious streak that made the average Hammer horror look tame in comparison.

British horror was dying, and although independent filmmaker Peter Walker flew the flag with his own brand of low budget slash fests, it quickly fizzled out by the end of the tumultuous decade.

Madhouse made decent enough business for Arkoff to consider reuniting Price, Cushing and Quarry with a follow-up called *The Naked Eye*. But Price was finished with AIP. 'I didn't see anything that I wanted or needed.' Returning to his beach house in August 1973 to spend some time alone, the additional curtailing of his busy workload allowed him to rethink his professional options. His contract had expired and the actor decided not to renew.

The decision was effectively made for him by AIP. Arkoff closed his London base to pursue blacksploitation horror in the States, and the contract was not renewed. Price's long, successful but tumultuous association with AIP finally came to an undistinguished end.

Price settled his affairs with Arkoff by being loaned out for the woefully unfunny British sex comedy *Percy's Progress* (1974), a sequel to *Percy* (1970), about a man with the first penis transplant. Price briefly appears as wheelchair bound billionaire and art expert Stavros Mammonian. The film was released in the UK in September 1974, and turned up on American shores six years later as *Its Not Size That Counts*!

Price and Quarry never stayed in touch following their stint on *Madhouse*. Quarry's friend David Del Valle recalled a conversation he had with Price while working as a publicist on the film *The Offspring* (1987). According to Del Valle, 'Price brought (Quarry) up in conversation, asking if I knew what had happened to him. After I explained that Bob was still around, Price shook his head and reflected, "This town can be a paradise or a hell, and I have seen it both ways in my career. He should have had a bigger career than he did. Robert was a good character man; he just couldn't carry a tune."'

Hammer horror icon Ingrid Pitt met Quarry many years later when the actors were involved in an unmade adaptation of *The Tell Tale Heart*. She heard her own version of their relationship. 'There were a lot of stories about Bob and Vincent Price not getting on. Bob denied this. He said it was all to do with Price's sense of humour, which, he said, was rather British!'

Quarry never achieved the horror stardom he deserved. Following his break from AIP he continued working but health problems and two life threatening experiences derailed his career. He later kept busy in featured roles for low budget filmmaker Fred Olen Ray until his retirement. Robert Quarry died on 20 February 2009.

Returning to his beach house following his stint on *Percy's Progress*, Price's life was a whirlwind of emotions and changes. He was in love with Coral Browne and looked forward to a new life with her, but could not make it public until his divorce was finalised, so he was biding his time and keeping it quiet. With his busy work schedule slowing down, he could take stock of the situation while enjoying the solace of the ocean.

Professionally, Price was glad to be free of his AIP shackles, although the cessation of his salary proved less pleasant. *Madhouse* ended his horror star career and being in his sixties, fading into smaller roles coupled with diminishing earning capacity can't have helped the situation since his classical style was obsolete in the face of the many changes within the film and TV industry.

The future, though uncertain, looked interesting.

The Intervening Years (1974 - 1980): Part Two

'I like to be seen, I love being busy and I believe in being active. I know some people think I've lowered myself as an actor, but my idea of 'professional decline' is 'not working'' –
Vincent Price

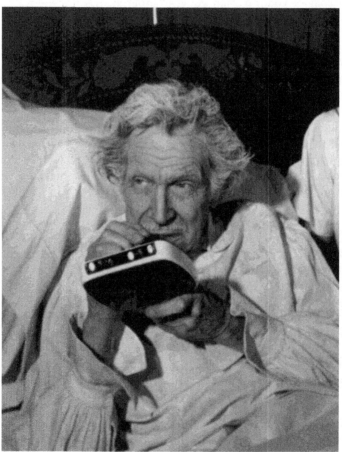

Price in *Scavenger Hunt* (1979)

With his horror career apparently over, Vincent Price's main focus was to put his divorce behind him and marry Coral Browne. Professionally, his association with Browne also led to a return to the theatre. This however, would take time. Price continued to keep his new woman secret from his family and closest friends. Ever the sensitive individual concerned about his public image, he continued to be worried about what people thought about him and desperately avoided any kind of confrontation. 'We kept on hearing that it was this wonderful person that he had fallen in love with,' recalled Barrett. 'But he was always coy about it.'

The relationship was finally made public in October 1973 when an article published in *The National Enquirer* featured the headline 'Vincent Price Admits He's Fallen in Love!' The piece, taken from another interview, had Price admitting that, 'I am certainly in love with the lady – that's for sure. It's a very happy romance. I think that one is never too old to be in love. But I'm going to need an elixir of youth if I am going to around Miss Browne for very much longer.' He later said in the interview that, 'I think I'm going to have to be discreet because I am not divorced yet. The divorce won't be final until about six months from now. I don't feel much like talking about this because I don't want to hurt my family.'

The article was an ill-advised move on Price's part because his estranged wife saw that edition of *The National Enquirer* on display in a supermarket with the cover showing Price and Browne enjoying dinner together.

When the divorce was finalised in April 1974, Price could now do what he liked, and that meant beginning his new life with Browne. After two years of writing letters, long distance telephone calls and seeing each other on the quiet, there was no holding back. First of all, they needed to find somewhere to live.

Price wanted to move to London where he felt there would be more rewarding opportunities in the theatre. Work commitments and the desire to be with his daughter soon put that notion to rest, and Browne, wanting to have a film career, felt LA would be better for her. When the Governor of California, Ronald Reagan, turned La Carillo Beach into a state beach, Price and his fellow residents lost their beach homes. He purchased a modest Spanish style house in West Hollywood while Browne set about moving all her things from London to their new home.

In the meantime Price had one more movie commitment, a Canadian production of *Journey into Fear* (1976), an ill-advised remake of Orson Welles' 1942 thriller that gave the couple a paid vacation in Genoa, Italy during July and August 1974.

Unfortunately this was a production Price would rather forget, when, while going out for a walk with Browne, a thief broke into their hotel and stole $2,000 in cash, his driver's licence and all his credit cards. To top it all, due to various legal wrangles, the film never saw the light of day.

'I just want it to be a love affair for a while,' said Price of the relationship, further adding, 'Coral and I have formed the permissive society for the elderly.' Browne, on the other hand, stated, 'I'm sick of being introduced as Miss Browne.' With time and age not on their side, she was now desperate to become the new Mrs Vincent Price.

They finally tied the knot on 24 October 1974, by which time Price converted to Catholicism to please his new wife while Browne became an American citizen.

'Coral was a devout Catholic,' said Victoria. 'I mean seriously devout. She had converted and attended mass and confession with the fervour of someone who has chosen to believe. My father converted to Catholicism for Coral. He secretly attended classes to surprise her before they married, and he even sent two priests to talk to my mother about annulling their 23 year marriage so that he could marry Coral with the blessing of the Catholic Church.'

'Coral took the covenant of marriage very seriously,' she added. 'The moment she married my dad, she expected both of them to be husband and wife – fully faithful and committed to one another emotionally and physically.'

The Prices looked every inch the Hollywood glamour couple, exuding elegance, grace, sophistication, intelligence and, in Browne's case, a sharp, acid wit that occasionally turned nasty. 'They were giving an art tour in their home,' observed comedian Steve Martin, 'when, with a particular frown, a woman looked at a Diebenkom they owned and snarled, "You have so many beautiful things, why would you own that? What's it called?" And Coral Browne replied. "It's called, 'We Like It. Now get out!'"'

While Price's old friends slowly warmed to his new wife, his marriage to Browne introduced him to her circle of theatrical friends, and this further enhanced his desire to return permanently to the stage. Moving to London to pursue his goal, Browne's encouragement and support gave him renewed confidence. His unpleasant experience on *Journey into Fear* also gave him the incentive to turn down film work that he would previously have taken solely for the money.

One such offer was the criminologist in the cult rock musical *The Rocky Horror Show* (1974), a perfect vehicle for Price to camp it up with total aplomb. This was not part of his long term plans so he turned it down, as did Peter Cushing, who was also seriously considered. The role eventually went to genre favourite Charles Gray.

'He saw another career, another thing happening,' said old friend Norman Lloyd. 'What was the alternative? He'd come back (to England) and make another horror movie, because by that time, that's what was there. And suddenly he had another entrance into a world of theatre that he admired and wanted to be a part of. Any actor of his generation was enamoured of the English theatre. In a sense, both Vincent and Coral saw an opportunity, and who is to say who benefitted, really?'

The opportunity came when the Prices appeared as Count Gaston and Countess Liliane in Lucienne Hill's English revival of Jean Anouilh's *pieces grincante* ('grating' black comedy) *Ardele ou la Marguerite*. 'I'm a sucker for Anouilh,' said Coral Browne. 'I love the way he writes and the things he has to say. It's not an ideal play for Vincent and myself to do because we have almost no dialogue at all alone together. We are husband and wife in the piece, but we're not actually opposite each other; we each have a lover.'

Reviving the play for the West End was her idea and during discussions with producer/director Frith Banbury she decided to put the production together for Broadway with a US tour and then to London. Unable to get sufficient backing in the States, there was a change of plan and the play would just open in London.

For Vincent Price, it was a dream come true. It was his first British play since his days at the Gate, his first serious play since his time on Broadway in the fifties, his first venture into legitimate British theatre and his official London West End debut. 'It's a great luxury for me to do a (London) stage play, even for a short time. I can never believe what stars make at the National Theatre! I think in my career's forty years, I've joined every American attempt at a national theatre and in the process I've done about 50 plays, mostly subsidised by my movies.'

The success of *Ardele* was a golden opportunity to establish himself as an English theatre actor. It also made a permanent move to London a more attractive proposition. He even agreed to do the play for less money than he was used to in the States.

Ardele boasted an excellent cast which included Charles Gray, Allan Cuthbertson, Lalla Ward and Anita Dobson. Unfortunately for Vincent Price, the thrill of being in a West End production at his age quickly turned to nerves. After years of playing up his persona in films, he now had to immerse himself in character once more, and in a demanding role. Realising he didn't have the range, he quickly floundered during rehearsals.

'Vincent and Coral weren't from the same world of theatre,' observed Banbury. 'Vinnie started there but then went off into films. Sad to say he was rather lost on *Ardele*. During the first week of rehearsals Vincent kept looking at the other actors and saying how good they were in their parts and I said, "Think about yourself." But after three or four days, Coral came to me and said, "What are we going to do? He can't do it can he?" I told her that I thought it was a bit early to know that, but Coral said, "You and I have to support him in every way we can." Coral's feelings were correct.'

Banbury noticed the situation getting worse. 'For about twenty minutes he had to carry the whole thing on his shoulders and he couldn't cope with it. If he hadn't gone to Hollywood and had remained a stage actor, he could have coped with it, but he was 64. Vinnie never got fussed, but I had to give him the sort of direction one doesn't expect to give an international star. We had a session alone and Vincent took it as a first-term student. Vinnie was a commodity and that blunted his sensibilities as an actor.'

Prior to the West End opening, *Ardele* had a try-out at the Theatre Royal in Brighton, which, being in a smaller theatre, should have helped Price's nerves. The opposite was true. According to Victoria, 'Vincent was given the wrong cue, and for the first time in his life, he went up on his lines, skipping four pages of dialogue. Given his generally excellent memory, this was more terrifying than anything. He began having nightmares and soon found that he had to take sleeping pills every night to calm his anxiety.'

The situation got worse when he developed stomach pains that turned out to be a malignant tumour in his digestive track. The tumour was successfully removed and Price returned to his hotel for complete bed rest for at least two weeks, but the inactivity got the better of him and a visit to a local museum ruptured his stitches, forcing him back into bed for a while longer.

Ardele got its West End opening at the Queen's Theatre on 18 June 1975, and it turned out to be a resounding flop, although not all of it was down to Price. Helen Dawson of *Plays and Players Magazine* commented that, 'The director, Frith Banbury, has sugared the pill under the layers of candy floss, and just about smothered it.'

Price simply could not measure up to the demands of the play. 'Vinnie never behaved like anything but that terrible expression, a gentleman,' said Banbury. 'It was a flop, but I wouldn't put it down to him. Vincent wasn't a draw for a stage play. There was a queue at the stage door waiting for autographs, but one felt they hadn't bought tickets to the play. Vinnie later wrote to me, '"I feel as though I let you and Coral down." But Coral was not disappointed in him as a human being, but rather in herself for having miscalculated.'

The failure of *Ardele* may have been a devastating blow to Price, but the actor, affable as always, took a philosophical view about the whole thing. 'Coral and I have survived a play together so I guess this marriage will last forever.' Price also received a congratulatory message from his first wife Edith Barrett: the ill feeling between the couple had eradicated over the years.

Edith Barrett died on 22 February 1977, alone, and in a nursing home in Albuquerigue, New Mexico. Her final years were not kind to her as she was virtually destitute due to her alcoholism, drug addiction and mental health problems.

Ardele wasn't a complete waste of time for Price. His marriage allowed him to mix with the UK's theatre greats Laurence Olivier, John Gielgud, Ralph Richardson and Alec Guinness, so the opportunity to establish himself on the English stage remained a possibility, if it wasn't for the income tax increase imposed by the Labour government that had prompted Christopher Lee, Sean Connery, Michael Caine and Roger Moore to leave the UK for foreign parts. The Prices did the same, although he retained his anglophile links to the end.

Back in LA, the Prices socialised a great deal, attending lavish parties and hosting many of their own. There was plenty of travelling around the world too, which they achieved through their various endorsements to hotels and cruise liners. To keep things on an even keel financially, Price had plenty of TV work, whether it was guest spots on popular shows or appearances in several commercials, all of which guyed his Uncle Vinnie persona. Such efforts were beneath the dignity of a great man, but they served him well until something better came his way.

Theatre-wise the couple appeared in Roddy McDowall's production of *Charley's Aunt* co-starring McDowall, Annie Potts and Joanna Gleeson. Price still found it a struggle to project himself in character without resorting to his familiar mannerisms, much to his wife's dismay. According to McDowall, 'When Coral did *Charley's Aunt*, it was an act of great generosity. And she did it just because she wanted Vincent to be legitimate. That was her big quest. And I must say she did achieve that. Her fury about the fact that "the old boy" was wasting his gifts in "these fucking horror films!" She couldn't stand that. I mean, there's no doubt the fact that she loved him and admired him, and one thing that Coral couldn't abide was the fact that she felt he'd squandered his acting talents. She was right because, even when we did *Charley's Aunt*, he still wasn't really with it. He was still trading on his personality. I don't think Vincent, in that sense, was an actor. By the time of the Poe films, he was immersed in a preconceived notion and had given in.'

Charley's Aunt did much better than *Ardele*, as the humour suited Price's style despite his obvious difficulties in achieving a convincing performance. It was also the last play the couple appeared in. 'I don't think it's a terribly good idea to do plays together,' said Browne. Price continued working on the stage, repeating his role as Fagin in *Oliver* and working with McDowall in *Damn Yankees* when he returned to St Louis. Remaining busy with his lecture tours, the British link continued when he narrated Roger Glover's excellent rock opera *The Butterfly Ball*.

Horror roles continued to pursue Price but thanks to his wife's influence and his desire to reinvent himself on stage, they fell by the wayside. One offer was the Anglo-Canadian portmanteau *The Uncanny* (1977), written by Michel Parry and produced by Milton Subotsky, who had quit Amicus following a final acrimonious fall-out with his partner. 'Rene Dupont made a deal, I got a co-producing credit and editing rights so I went to Montreal to work on the cast. Vincent Price turned me down. So did Peter Cushing and Christopher Lee. Cushing relinquished when he found out it was one of my pictures.' Judging by the end result. Cushing would have been wise to stay away too.

Another horror project that would have reunited Price and Cushing came from Robert Fuest. But Price was unenthused by *The Coming*. 'Bob sent me a script that was dreadful. Absolutely dreadful! It didn't make a word of sense. It was a sort of mishmash. I mean you will go along with a script if you think a director is going to bring a lot to it, but it was not a question of that because there was nothing he could bring to it. It was just not a good script. I understand he had some money to make it in Italy, and then it fell through.'

Price worked with Cushing during the autumn of 1976, but this time on BBC radio, which prompted a welcome return to the UK. By this time Cushing had gained a new generation of fans following his brilliant turn as Grand Moff Tarkin in *Star Wars* (1977), a film Price enjoyed immensely. 'I would have loved to have been in *Star Wars*. Peter Cushing was really marvellous in that. Of course when you're talking about (Steven) Spielberg and (George) Lucas, You're talking about really popular pictures.'

Aliens of the Mind was developed by *Doctor Who* script editor Robert Holmes and was set in Scotland where a genetic mutation on the Island of Lewigh evolves into powerful telepathic aliens. Price plays brash American bohemian Professor Curtis Lark while Cushing is the ever so prim British brain surgeon Dr John Cornelius. While dealing with all this paranormal activity, Cornelius is teaching Lark the finer points of British life.

The series proved popular when it was screened in January 1977. During this time Price kept up his British links by guesting on Michael Parkinson's BBC1 chat show, doing TV commercials for Haywards Pickles and making an enjoyable guest appearance, spoofing himself once more, in *The Muppet Show*.

In the mire of TV guest spots, talk shows and regional stock theatre, Price received an offer that defined his stage career, a chance to play Irish writer, author, playwright, poet and bohemian Oscar Fingal O'Flahertie Wills Wilde. Once again it was due to the encouragement of the ever loyal Coral Browne.

Diversions and Delights was the brainchild of playwright John Gay, who took advantage of his enforced unemployment during a strike by the Writer's Guild of America to work on a subject that had long fascinated him.

'Wilde still has a lot of relevance for people today,' said Gay, 'not just because of gay liberation, but on matters of art, politics and economics.' Gay's idea of bringing his project to the theatre was to have a humiliated Wilde, in poor health and his reputation destroyed by scandal, giving a lecture in a tacky old hall in Paris' Rue de la Repinier. The idea was to present Wilde in a one-man show, and Gay split it into two acts, the first act presenting the arrogant wit and humour of the man while the second sees a broken, drug addicted and alcoholic Wilde, wallowing in self-pity as he examines his ill-fated relationship with Lord Alfred Douglas, the estranged son of The Marquis of Queensbury, which inevitably lead to Wilde's downfall in the face of convention.

Being a one-man play, all that was needed was an actor to portray Wilde, not an easy task considering the flamboyant intellect and humour that encompassed him as a person. Gay needed an actor who could capture the personality of Wilde, but must also be an individual actor with his own unique qualities that could make it work so well.

With Roger Berlind, Franklin Levy and Mike Wise as producers, and Joseph Hardy as director, Gay set his sights on Vincent Price. While the play was being cast in Los Angeles, Gay recalled that the producers, 'kept coming up with all sorts of Hollywood type actors, and (Hardy) said, "Look: Vincent Price!" Everyone looked blank, then said they were sorry they hadn't thought of it first.'

Hardy felt Price was a perfect choice. 'While on the surface Price and Wilde had nothing in common, both men had a "take or leave it" attitude to their work.'

Now it was time approach Price. 'Joseph Hardy asked me to read the play, which was written by a very good writer called John Gay. Hardy felt I would be right as Oscar Wilde, and I found it was something I really wanted to do.' With the failure of *Ardele* damaging his confidence, Price wasn't sure if he had the ability to take on such a challenging part. Price was also much older than Wilde (who died in 1900 aged 46) so miscasting was a factor. In addition to his health scare during *Ardele*, the success of the play wasn't guaranteed; another failure could finish his stage career.

Price trusted the instincts of Coral Browne, who said, 'Go stick your neck out.' It was a challenge and Price spent several gruelling months devoting himself to careful research into Wilde's life and carry out extensive preparation for the play in order to create the poet's personality. 'I'm trying as hard as I can to be as close to Wilde as I can. Wilde had a very peculiar speech pattern, an Irish Protestant accent. A kind of meticulous pronunciation of every single syllable. I also raise my voice a different pitch. I'm terribly well known for my voice and I don't want to have that voice because I'd still be Vincent Price.'

'When I created the part,' he added, 'I found it very difficult to know too much. You should enter a part with a kind of innocence. I did the research at the time, and since, a lot during the rehearsals and after we started trying it out.'

Diversions and Delights opened on 11 July 1977 at the Marines' Memorial Theatre in San Francisco. Thanks to Wilde's reputation in the city's gay community, the play proved an instant hit with audiences and critics taken aback by Price's performance. Few people could even see Price as Wilde, despite creating a convincing appearance of the man – curly wig, velvet jacket, green tie and tweed trousers, and no trademark moustache!

'Price never would have struck me as the man for the role,' admitted critic Sidney Harris, 'but he controvertibly is, hairpiece, costume, facial expression, bodily movement and all. He senses who and what Wilde was, at a level deeper than merely verbal and visual, projecting the essentially likeable man beneath the poseur.'

If anyone involved in *Diversions and Delights* had their doubts about Price pulling it off, they were happily surprised. 'Vincent Price was a marvellous choice,' enthused John Gay. 'You felt that it was Oscar Wilde was up there.' Joseph Hardy concurred as he felt the performance worked, 'because of the space he fills – his size, his age, everything about him – is perfect to fill Oscar's. It's a dignified space.'

Price expressed his own joy of playing such an iconic and controversial figure in English literature. 'I believe my role as Oscar Wilde was my greatest achievement as an actor,' he said. 'It has really been the most critically acclaimed play I've ever done. It's great fun to be able to lose myself in the character. Wilde probably had the greatest command of the English language, as far as wit is concerned, of any man who ever lived.'

The audience loved it, especially one particular person. 'We had one woman in San Francisco who saw it 33 times,' he recalled. 'I couldn't believe it. Every time I came out, she'd be there, and I would just about faint! My god, she could have played it herself. She probably would be very good as Oscar Wilde!'

Diversions and Delights was a critical and commercial success in San Francisco. It was followed by a tour across the major cities. It met the same positive response in Chicago and was a resounding success at the Ford Theatre in Washington DC. Such was the audience reaction in the city capital, the four-week run got extended another week. The next step was Broadway.

If *Ardele* dented his confidence in London's West End, facing a Broadway audience must have been equally frightening, considering he hadn't performed there since *Darling of the Day*. The stress affected him badly. Opening at the Roundabout Theatre, the gods were not smiling. According to the play's stage manager David Clive, 'He was so terrified by the thought of a Broadway opening that he gave his worst performance ever in the role. The show was roundly roasted and we closed after only two weeks. There had been a rash of one-character productions, and the critics jumped on us as the latest boring trend. Even if Vinnie had been brilliant that night, I suspect the result would have been pretty much the same, but he blamed himself and was devastated.'

Diversions and Delights never took off on Broadway simply because the play needed more intimate surroundings. Deeply saddened by the lack of success in New York, the producers took the play back to San Francisco. Its opening at the Geary Theatre proved a huge success; it ran for over a month. The play then went on the road, touring California, Nova Scotia and Ohio. In addition to the theatres, the play also performed at various colleges before finally ending its amazing run in Minnesota in December 1978.

Of course *Diversions and Delights* never ended there as Price spent the next decade playing Wilde in several small scale tours that took him all over America as well as Canada, Australia, New Zealand and Hong Kong. According to Victoria Price, 'Touring with his one-man show gave him back the theatre.'

Price had his own feelings about performing in such an incredible production. 'Wilde is a joy to play. For his personal tragedy is a universally appealing as his private-public wit is individually enchanting.'

More importantly, *Diversion and Delights* had given Price long overdue recognition as an actor. 'It was really extraordinary. It was the first time I really, completely fell into the character. I was really able to escape into the wit and brilliance of the man. A divine feeling.'

Other than recording the Alice Cooper album *Welcome To My Nightmare*, Price spent 1978 touring with *Diversion and Delights*. With the start of the New Year, he looked incredibly relaxed, and in the spring of 1979, Price and Coral Browne began work on a new TV series for CBS called *Time Express*. The intriguing premise is set on a Pullman train (the *Time Express* of the title) that travels back in time – through lots of fog!

Certain passengers are handpicked (by the unknown and unseen Head-of-the-Line) to embark on their journey. The passengers go back in time to relive a particular moment in their lives, and are given the chance to change that moment and see the outcome of their decision.

The Prices play Jason and Margaret Winters, the sophisticated hosts of the *Time Express*, exuding class and elegance, and a natural chemistry that wasn't so apparent in their stage work. They are clearly having a fun time of it, especially Price following the rigors of *Diversions and Delights*.

The show's TV screening in April 1979 didn't win over the critics with the kindest comment being, 'Let's say five nice words about *Time Express*: Vincent Price and Coral Browne.' The style of the format wasn't enough to sustain a series, and it got cancelled after four episodes. The time travel theme was successfully explored years later in *Quantum Leap* and *Sliders*.

In April 1979, Price appeared in the screwball comedy *Scavenger Hunt* (1979). Boasting an impressive cast that included Richard Benjamin, Roddy McDowall and Robert Morley, Price is among a roster of guest stars that includes Scatman Crothers, Ruth Gordon, Arnold Schwarzenegger and Meatloaf.

Price's role of eccentric board game tycoon Milton Parker is tiny but pivotal to the story. In the opening scene an aging and decrepit Parker is playing what could be described as an electronic game of life for frogs with Carol Wayne's sexy nurse. Speaking only in grunts, when Parker's frog 'croaks,' so does he! Later his voice turns up on a tape recorder explaining the scavenger hunt to his greedy relatives. If they are to inherit Parker's $200 million estate, they must follow the rules of the hunt.

The film is more annoying than silly, and died a death at the box office. More satisfactory was his next effort in July 1979 when he narrated the feature length documentary *Day of Fury* that showed all the natural disasters that changed the world.

With the start of the new decade, The Prices were jointly awarded at the Eleventh Annual Los Angeles Drama Critics Award. During the tribute there was a special screening of *Theatre of Blood*!

The new decade also allowed Price to fulfil one of his ambitions, to star in a horror film for kids!

The Monster Club

'I'm not really the kind of actor who hides away. I think I've had a wonderful and very public life. It doesn't bother me at all to be recognised when I go out. The only people I can spot like a bird dog are drunks!' – Vincent Price

VINCENT PRICE RETURNS TO HORROR AFTER A SIX YEAR ABSENCE! thundered *The Sun* newspaper. The article featured Price posing with a few ghoulish co-stars from his new movie *The Monster Club*.

To his many fans it was something of a surprise that he'd been absent for so

long. With his older horror films constantly being shown on television all over the world, it was as though he'd never been away in the first place.

British horror film production had changed over the years, and by the time *The Monster Club* saw the light of day, many of those associated with the genre in the sixties and early seventies had all but vanished.

Shortly after closing his UK base, Sam Arkoff carried on with AIP, producing low budget quickies, and distributing many more until he sold the company to Filmways (which was taken over by Orion). He later felt his decision was a big mistake. 'They wanted to change everything AIP stood for,' he lamented.

Arkoff continued as a consultant at Filmways before selling his shares and retiring. But you can't keep a good schlock producer down! Coming out of retirement he founded Arkoff International Pictures (keeping the famous initials!) and continued as an independent until his death in 2001.

For Hammer Films, the demise was much sadder. After taking over from his father, Michael Carreras could not compete with the Hollywood majors and found himself pushed out of the American cinema circuits. Now heavily in debt, the company folded following the failure of *The Lady Vanishes* (1978) leaving Carreras a broken and bitter man, reluctant to talk about his time with Hammer.

Amicus were luckier because they changed direction at the right time with the monster movies *The Land That Time Forgot* (1975) and *At The Earth's Core* (1976). Relations between Milton Subotsky and Max Rosenberg had fallen apart with Subotsky resigning his position in 1975. This was followed by a series of acrimonious lawsuits between both men. Amicus continued but the success of *Star Wars* (1977) finished the dinosaur genre – at least for the time being!

Subotsky continued as an independent filmmaker. He moved to Canada to produce *The Uncanny* (1977) and *Dominique* (1978), but neither made much impression at the box office. As a man who never admitted defeat in the face of changing cinematic tastes, Subotsky returned to England and his beloved horror anthology.

Subotsky's extensive list of reading matter included the novels and short stories of Ronald Chetwynd-Hayes. Born in 1919, Chetwynd-Hayes' first published novel was *The Man From the Bomb* in 1959. He went on to become a prolific horror and fantasy writer. Four of his terror tales were adapted for the Amicus portmanteau *From Beyond the Grave* (1973). Subotsky wanted to adapt further stories, but the film's failure at the box office and his fragile position at Amicus meant forthcoming adaptations were put on hold.

Subotsky commissioned a script based on Chetwynd-Hayes' 1975 novel *The Monster Club*, which told of a vampire inviting a passing stranger to a club inhabited by monsters. The vampire related five stories to his friend, *The Werewolf and the Vampire*, *The Mock*, *The Humgoo*, *The Shadmock* and *The Fly-By-Night*. Subotsky's attraction to the book was Chetwynd-Hayes' idea of cross-breeding monsters; a werewolf who mates with a vampire becomes a were-vamp, and so on.

The Monster Club was scheduled for production in January 1978, but lack of funding delayed things until late the following year when Subotsky's Sword and

Sorcery Productions went into a co-production deal with Jack Gill's Chips Productions. Gill had recently produced *The Hammer House of Horror* TV series and was keen to move into cinema features. Gill's associate, Lord Lew Grade provided a reasonable budget of $1,7million and guaranteed overseas distribution with his company ITC Productions. Subotsky then commissioned writers Edward and Valerie Abrahams to write a script.

Subotsky's ultimate dream, aside from doing a horror film for the kids, was bring together all the genre favourites – Vincent Price, Peter Cushing, Christopher Lee, John Carradine, Donald Pleasence and Klaus Kinski – the whole lot!

Having Pleasence involved was a good move on Subotsky's part. After years of being a part-time horror star, Pleasence sealed his genre status as Dr Sam Loomis in John Carpenter's *Halloween* (1978), a role previously turned down by Lee and Cushing. Subotsky also had the in-jokey idea of turning the passing stranger from the original novel into R Chetwynd-Hayes himself!

Subotsky wanted Peter Cushing and Christopher Lee to play Chetwynd-Hayes and Eramus the vampire, with the other horror stars providing solid back-up. However the casting didn't go according to plan.

Lee had long abandoned the genre by the time *The Monster Club* went into production. Moving to Los Angeles to seek more eclectic film work, Lee had done his best to distance himself from Dracula and his other monsters, playing supporting roles in a variety of big budget Hollywood or international ventures. Horror roles still pursued him but he turned them all down, including Dr Loomis in *Halloween*, which he later admitted was a big mistake.

When Lee received an offer from an old associate to star in a British-made horror, he gave it some consideration. 'I got a message from my agent asking me if I would consider doing a picture with Milton Subotsky, and I said, "Yes. After all these years, what does he have planned?" So he told me he's going to produce a picture called *The Monster Club*. I said, "That's enough. We need go no further!"'

Undaunted by the setback, Subotsky approached his second choice, Vincent Price. Receiving the script in January 1980, Price was clearly excited. 'I haven't been offered a script as good as this for years. I thought it had possibilities. The stories were good, the whole description of the monsters was funny. I see *The Monster Club* as a sort of vampire disco, as a fun picture for children. It is scary but not frightening. My vampire for instance is quite kindly.'

Price was far from impressed with films like *Halloween*. 'I go to see those films, because I know people are going to ask me what I think of them. I find that they have no surprises. They throw so much violence at you, that there's no suspense. You know, violence is something you can only have a little bit of. You can't have somebody ripped apart at the beginning of the show! Where are you going to go from there? They also have no sense of humour, whatsoever! Also, I know how it's all done, so consequently they don't frighten me. I find that some of the old ones that were made with a sense of suspense are far better. You didn't know what was going to happen. There is such a thing as suggesting something.

It's like nude women. Very few women should be caught nude. They should be perfect if they're going to be caught nude.'

If Lee wasn't willing to get involved, the idea of Price locking horns with Peter Cushing again held great possibilities for Subotsky, if Cushing hadn't decided to turn down the movie too!

Unlike Lee, Cushing continued his involvement in British horror until it finally collapsed at his feet. His later output included several increasingly obscure features made in Europe but barely seen elsewhere. Even his superlative performance as Grand Moff Tarkin had no long term effect on his career, making his decision to turn down Dr Loomis equally ill-advised. By the time he was offered *The Monster Club*, Cushing had gone into semi-retirement.

'I offered Peter the part of Chetwynd-Hayes,' recalled Subotsky. 'But he turned it down saying he didn't like the script. I then offered him the part of the Innkeeper, but he turned me down. I then offered him a guest spot, but he turned me down. He turned down three roles because he didn't like the script. I don't know. I guess he thought it was a gruesome horror film and not one for the kids.' Filling Cushing's second role as the Innkeeper was genre favourite and Amicus regular Patrick Magee.

The part of Chetwynd-Hayes finally went to John Carradine. The author liked the idea of an actor playing him on film, but wasn't too happy with the casting. 'Although greatly admiring Mr Carradine over the years and appreciating the fact that having anyone playing me was intended to be a joke, I still would have preferred someone a little younger. Mr Carradine was then 74 and suffering from severe arthritis. At a preview of the film, one lady commiserated with me for being so afflicted with this painful ailment. I had to stress that it was to the distinguished Mr Carradine she must direct her sympathies to, not me!'

While Donald Pleasence was happy to play Inspector Pickering in the second tale, Klaus Kinski turned down the role of Lintom Busotsky's vampire father. He was replaced by Richard Johnson, who recently achieved horror immortality in Lucio Fulci's *Zombie Flesh Easters* (1979). . Other actors who had previously worked with Subotsky were Britt Ekland and Geoffrey Bayldon.

With the cast in place, Subotsky brought in as director another old face from British horror, Roy Ward Baker. Following a varied career, that included Hollywood success, Baker established himself in the genre following his excellent work on Hammer's *Quatermass and the Pit* (1967). After several chillers for Hammer, he directed the Amicus portmanteau *Asylum* (1972). 'Milton and I now established a solid working relationship and I directed two more pictures for him.'

Baker had nothing but praise for Subotsky. 'Milton was one of the nicest people I ever worked with. Shy, honest, modest – not the popular image of a film producer. Milton was no good at publicizing himself, never put himself about. Always anxious to give the credit for a success to anyone but himself. He was an innovator. He filmed Harold Pinter's *The Birthday Party* (1968), directed by William Friedkin. He revived the magazine format with macabre stories. His productions were in the same field as Hammer but were always somehow different. An admirable man. He loved stories and he loved film, it wasn't just a business.'

Baker was in semi-retirement when he was offered *The Monster Club*. Not only did he jump at the chance to work with Subotsky again, he re-established contact with Price, who he knew from his Hollywood days. 'I directed one more picture for Milton, *The Monster Club*, with Vincent Price and John Carradine and another distinguished cast, which again included Britt Ekland, a much underrated actress. Vincent and I exchanged some reminiscences of Hollywood in the fifties. Vincent was disdainful about Darryl F Zanuck: "A common little man," he said.'

The Monster Club began filming at Elstree Studios in April 1980 on a five-week shoot. Price and Carradine's scenes were filmed over a single week in early May. Due to budget restrictions or the fact the novel could not be adapted adequately to the big screen, *The Mock* and *The Fly-By-Night* were jettisoned leaving three tales and the linking story more or less intact following some extensive re-writes.

The Monster Club featured on an episode of the popular children's movie series *Clapperboard*. The show's presenter, Chris Kelly, interviewed Price and Carradine during filming, with Peter Cushing also turning up for a chat (no doubt regretting his decision not to take part). Price looked happy, relaxed and clearly enjoying his time on the set. As a film for the kids, *The Monster Club* had a lot going for it.

Filming went without a hitch, and while relishing the chance to play a vampire for the first time, wearing the fangs posed a few problems when it came to speaking. The decision was made to have the fangs 'retractable when not in use.' 'It was Milton Subotsky's idea not to! Saves me having to wear them! This was necessary because I found I couldn't talk with the vampire fangs in my mouth.'

Price did have one issue about the film. 'The thing that went wrong with *The Monster Club*, was that Milton Subotsky had found some man, who was a milkman that had a hobby out of making masks. Well he hired this fellow, and thought they would look great, but they were terrible, just terrible! It looks like amateur night. They should have been wonderful, elaborate masks, that look real, but these look like some kid made them! You can have a low budget, but that doesn't mean that! You can still go out and rent them!'

Vic Door, who designed these 'terrible' masks, was not Subotsky's milkman. He was working at a milk processing plant but was freelancing as a make-up artist when he was commissioned at the last minute to design the masks. *The Monster Club* is his only screen credit.

Price's other gripe was the music. 'The rock 'n' roll music was no good. There were no good names. The stories were excellent though. We were the bridge between these stories. (John Carradine) and I had fun, but we were so shocked at the rock 'n' roll music. I have a great admiration for rock 'n' roll, but not when it's done badly. My god!'

Roy Ward Baker shared Price's feelings about the music. 'Everything was going for us, but there was one fatal flaw in the project. The envelope was *The Monster Club* where Vincent and John introduced the stories. Also in between them was a cabaret of rock bands. The flaw was the terribly short duration of the bands' popularity, compared to the time it takes to complete a film. Anyway, all the money in the world wouldn't have got us The Beatles or The Rolling Stones.'

For Milton Subotsky, *The Monster Club* was a personal in-joke regarding his time at Amicus. Vampire film producer Lintom Busotsky (Anthony Steel) introduces his new film called *From Beyond the Tombstone*, which is clearly inspired by *From Beyond the Grave*. The film's producer is Dark John, an unsubtle reference to former Amicus producer John Dark, who Subotsky never got on with.

To tie in with the 1980 *Cannes Film Festival*, Pioneer Press published a promotional graphic novel adaption written by Dez Skinn with illustrations by John Bolton and David Lloyd. The magazine was distributed during the festival – 1,000 copies in total. Very much a collector's item, some of the artwork resurfaced in the paperback edition of R Chetwynd-Hayes' collection, which came out in 1981 and was later reprinted in 2013.

The Monster Club wrapped in 24 days, with Subotsky doing the editing straight away. 'Milton broke all the records in delivering the picture,' said Roy Ward Baker, 'doing all the post-production work in about four weeks.'

The end result did not impress Chetwynd-Hayes. 'I thought, and still do, the so-called humour in the film was downright silly. The only attempt to keep to my original was in *The Humgoo*, and the only horror was the really horrible pop music they inserted into it. When I think what could have been done with it! My first story, *The Werewolf and the Vampire* was ignored while another was completely ruined! I was all but struck dumb when actor Richard Johnson pulled a stake from his heart and said "I was wearing a stake proof vest – and look, tomato ketchup!" Awful! Milton Subotsky was a very nice man, but he should have accepted advice from a scriptwriter – or me! I was not surprised that the film was a disaster at the box office!'

The Monster Club received its UK release on 24 May 1981, only couple of days before Vincent Price's 70th birthday. However, the collapse of Lew Grade's ITC Productions shortly after the film's completion meant it couldn't get distribution in the all-important American market.

The situation was further hindered by the film getting an AA certificate in British cinemas making it off-limits to kids under 14: the intended audience. After a few alterations, *The Monster Club* received an A certificate (no one under 5), but with most kids preferring to sneak into cinemas to see the stalk and slash antics of Jason in *Friday the Thirteenth* (1979), flesh eating zombies in *Dawn of the Dead* (1979) and the famous exploding head in *Scanners* (1980), *The Monster Club* looked too out of step with the times.

Critical evaluation was hardly positive. While *Time Out* described *The Monster Club* as a, 'rather jolly horror compendium,' Leslie Halliwell considered it a, 'A spoofy but not very entertaining variation on a too-familiar formula.'

Variety had their own feelings on the film, 'The Milton Subotsky production, alas, has all the aspirations of its budget – low. Strictly a program entry with limited prospects. Vincent Price seems to have an enjoyably hammy time as a jovial vampire who spins three yarns.'

The Monthly Film Bulletin puts the facts down in the face of critical disdain. 'With a cast topped by such veteran blood-curdlers as Vincent Price and John Carradine and a character list that includes two horror filmmakers (Milton Subotsky and Roy Ward Baker), one might have hoped for a touch of sophistication.'

The Monster Club is not a great film, it's not really a good film. In fact it is pretty poor stuff. Roy Ward Baker's direction is tired and the script doesn't really cut it. And while the two serious tales have their moments worthy of an Amicus anthology, the linking story and the vampire tale are too silly to be enjoyed as camp, even if that was the main premise of the film.

Viewed in the right frame of mind, there is a lot to enjoy, and the film is an adequate time passer for those not wanting too much from their evening entertainment. The music isn't that bad and the actors are having fun, with Price making the most of his role, camping it up with a spirited comic performance.

According to Price's biographer, Lucy Chase Williams, Price sounds, 'smoother and even more mellifluous,' from his spell as Oscar Wilde. Finding his mojo again, the actor is having a ball. It takes just a knowing wink at the audience to make it all work beautifully, even in a silly film like *The Monster Club*.

While *The Monster Club* would have worked better if Peter Cushing had played Chetwynd-Hayes, John Carradine is an agreeable substitute, despite the author's reservations about the actor's age and health. Price and Carradine play well off each other and form an agreeable chemistry that could only come from two old masters. After working many times together during their Hollywood years, *The Monster Club* marks their first horror teaming.

Price had nothing but immense admiration for his friend and co-star. 'He was an extraordinary man. He told me that he had done 450 feature films. I believe him because when I was under contract to Fox, John used to do, maybe, 20 movies a year, whereas everybody else was doing two or three, because he played very small but very good parts. He was a good Shakespearean actor; he would quote Shakespeare at the drop of a hat. In the old days he used to stand on Hollywood Boulevard with a cape over his shoulder. He was very theatrical, kind of a take-off of (John Barrymore). But he was a very nice man. How he put up with that arthritis I just don't know because he had it for years. He hands were terrible, terrible – and terrible pain – you'd see him begin to knot and up and then he had some pills that helped it, but not too much. I liked him very much.'

Donald Pleasence and Patrick Magee also have an enjoyable time with some classic scenery chewing. Magee is especially wild eyed, despite having only eight lines of dialogue, and Pleasence has ham-slicing fun as the dreaded Inspector Pickering.

The comic antics of the horror veterans are well balance by a moving performance from Australian actor James Laurenson as Raven the lonely Shadmock. He plays the role with pathos even though he doesn't look remotely ugly or scary. All he needed was a decent make-over and a better hair stylist, and he would have been fine. Other performances are adequate enough to carry the film.

Despite its commercial failure, *The Monster Club* has achieved a cult following in America with the 1985 video release hosted by Cassandra Peterson AKA horror hostess Elvira.

The Monster Club was Milton Subotsky's final film as an independent producer. Undaunted as ever, he had the foresight to buy up the film rights of several Stephen King stories as well as *Conan the Barbarian* and *The Incredible Hulk*, which he sold to the Hollywood majors at a considerable profit. Maintaining co-producer credits on *Cat's Eye's* (1985), *Maximum Overdrive* (1986) and *The Lawnmower Man* (1992) meant he didn't have to work again.

Milton Subotsky died on 1 June 1991; his final two Stephen King movies were released posthumously with his producer credit. *The Monster Club* is not regarded as his best work in the horror genre, but it is a fitting swansong for one of the most influential figures in English gothic.

Following his stint on *The Monster Club*, Price toured again with *Diversion and Delights* and spent the rest of the year devoting his energies to the Vincent Price Gallery at East Los Angeles College, where there had been problems with finance. In November 1980 he received an offer from the Public Broadcasting Service in Boston to be host for the popular series *Mystery!*

Mystery! was an American showcase for several popular British television crime thrillers and detective stories that included *The Adventures of Sherlock Holmes*, *Agatha Christie's Marple* and *Poirot*, *Inspector Morse*, *Cadfael* and *Prime Suspect*. The original host, film critic Gene Shalit dropped out after the first series and Price was announced as his replacement.

Travelling twice a year to Boston to record the opening and closing segments of the show, Price regarded his time on *Mystery!* as the happiest in his long career. 'I'm a grand fan of English mystery movies. All the great mystery writers are English. American mystery writers are a bit too obvious. I think the English do it better than we do – ours is full of car chases. But theirs are so extraordinarily well thought out.' As an actor who could host any kind of TV show, his elegance and charm served him well during his 9 year stint on the series.

In May 1981, Price received a letter of introduction from Walt Disney Studios to meet an ambitious and talented animator named Tim Burton, who was putting together an animated short called *Vincent*, the story about a little boy who wants to be Vincent Price. 'Vincent was like my psychologist when I was growing up,' recalled Burton. 'He helped me get through the abstractions of the early years.'

Price went to the Disney studios to meet Burton and his producing partner Rick Heinrichs. He narrated the poem for the 6-minute short, but more importantly it led to a significant friendship with Burton. 'I was really struck by his charm and enthusiasm,' he said of the director. 'Tim is really in love with (*Vincent*) and is a wonderful kind of mad fellow.'

Burton saw Price as a major influence on his career. 'Vincent was always a great inspiration to me. It would have been devastating to me if he hadn't been so responsive. He really shaped my life when I was starting out and gave me hope to grow. He's a really wonderful person.'

Production on *Vincent* was completed the following year. It led to a string of awards including Best Short Subject at the *Chicago Film Festival*. In the meantime Price was back in England playing Sir Despard Murgatroyd in a TV adaptation of Gilbert and Sullivan's opera *Ruddigore*.

'That was great fun,' he recalled. 'I was in England and they decided to do all the Gilbert and Sullivan operas (for television) and they asked me to play in *Ruddigore*. It was really a challenge because the English know how to do it better than anybody. After all, they wrote it. Doing *Ruddigore*, the marvellous thing about it was that it was pre-recorded, so there was no chance of the orchestra winning while I was there. They had already won, before I got there. I've done a lot of musical comedy, although I'm not really a singer, I just fake it!'

House of the Long Shadows

'These horror films are pure fun. People love them because they love being scared. But for us actors and technicians involved, making films like these is a very serious business indeed. We would be lacking in all responsibility to our public if we allowed ourselves to say that they are rubbish.' – Vincent Price

Clockwise: Christopher Lee, Vincent Price, Peter Cushing, John Carradine

On 22 June 1982 Vincent Price was the main guest star on an episode of *Wogan*, a BBC1 talk show hosted by radio DJ and TV presenter Terry Wogan. During the interview, where Price exuded his usual charm, wit and humour to the delight of the audience, Wogan asked a question that equally delighted the actor's long-time fans.

'You're doing a new film with two of your old mates, Christopher Lee and Peter Cushing?'

'Yes it's wonderful,' replied an enthusiastic Price. 'I really can't wait to get together with them again. It'll be such fun.'

House of the Long Shadows originated from a 1913 novel by *Charlie Chan* author Earl Derr Biggers called *Seven Keys to Baldpate*. The story tells of William Magee, a hack writer with dreams of producing a literary novel. To achieve this, he spends his solitude during the winter months in the deserted Baldpate Inn, situated in upstate New York.

However, his peace and quiet is quickly interrupted by a number of mystery guests, each with a dodgy explanation to their presence, but all of them, for equally dubious reasons, are trying to get their hands on $200,000 hidden somewhere in the inn.

Seven Keys to Baldpate is a hokey, melodramatic work that has an interesting idea of Magee's adventures becoming the book he will write. The moral of the story is that Magee should stick to the type of sensationalistic writing he's made his living from, instead of trying to be the literary genius that is in reality is out of his reach.

A stage version had first opened in 1913, and it had been previously filmed several times, however the screenplay had become dated so when producers Menahem Golan and Yoram Globus envisaged a new film version, it needed to be re-written as a nostalgia piece and tailored made as a vehicle for the four surviving horror greats – Vincent Price, Peter Cushing, Christopher Lee and John Carradine. 'This is historic!' exclaimed screenwriter Michael Armstrong. 'Four legends in one film. If nothing else, we're guaranteed posterity.'

House of the Long Shadows marked the return of British horror's most infamous auteur, Pete Walker.

By the early seventies, British film production was going through a turbulent period. Horror films remained a sure sell at the box office and Peter Walker took his first step into the genre with *The Flesh and Blood Show* (1972). This was followed by *House of Whipcord* (1974), *Frightmare* (1974), *House of Mortal Sin* (1975) and *Schizo* (1976). After directing *Home Before Midnight* (1978) and being briefly involved with an abortive project about The Sex Pistols, he retired from films and moved into property.

By 1982, Walker was itching to get back into filmmaking. His old friend and collaborator Michael Armstrong had written a script called *Deliver Us From Evil*, which he described as 'very Pete!'

Unable to secure finance in the UK, Walker took Armstrong's script to Hollywood, where he became friends with actor Desi Arnaz Junior. He then hired additional writers to work on the script; among the changes considered was a shift of location to either Mexico or the South of France. Despite the initial optimism, the Hollywood studios lost interest and Walker returned to London where he approached Israeli producers Menahem Golan and Yoram Globus at Cannon Films in London. 'We had contact with Cannon,' said Armstrong, 'and we took *Deliver Us from Evil* to Menahem.'

The Golan-Globus/Cannon Empire was varied, and successful. Following on from the low brow Israeli based *Lemon Popsicle* series, the cousins produced the period dramas *Lady Chatterley's Lover* (1981) and *Mata Hari* (1985), both of which had added sex. The G-Gs stepped up their game with more serious work that included John Cassavetes' *Love Streams* (1984) and Franco Zeffirelli's *Othello* (1986).

With the films being successful in the UK, Golan and Globus set up Cannon Cinema and purchased several British cinema chains. They also founded the video mail order company Videolog. The start of the eighties was an encouraging time for British Films with the success of Handmade's *The Long Good Friday* (1980) and Goldcrest's *Chariots of Fire* (1981), the latter getting the Best Screenplay Oscar for Colin Welland, who proudly proclaimed 'The British are coming!'

The prophecy turned out to be false and UK film production hit an all-time low: even Handmade and Goldcrest never achieved their early promise. With Cannon setting business up in London, the cousins saw themselves as the saviours of the British film industry.

And one of their proposed cinema projects was an old fashioned chiller in the Hammer tradition, and Peter Walker's eventual meeting with Menahem Golan came at the right time to discuss the idea.

'I was working on a script at the time called *Deliver Us from Evil*, which Michael Armstrong had written. I said (to Golan) that this was about an abortive foetus that has come back to Earth to claim its life. There was a silence and then Menahem said, "We don't know what you're talking about. This is not a horror picture. We want Boris Karloff and Bela Lugosi." I said, "They're dead Menahem," and he said, "We'll get some footage." So that's where the idea was born, an old fashioned horror movie and they would have the horror names around: Vincent Price, Christopher Lee and Peter Cushing.'

With *Deliver Us from Evil* falling by the wayside, Walker went back to Michael Armstrong with a few ideas about this new project. 'Peter called me, and said, "We're doing a picture but we got these horror stars." I thought, "brilliant," to write for these stars, especially Vincent.'

'We were both excited about the prospect,' Armstrong continued, 'and our first thought was a remake of *The Old Dark House* (1932).'

'We could not get the rights to the *Old Dark House*,' said Walker, 'because someone else had the rights to remake it but never did, but we couldn't get it, so there was this old movie called *Seven Keys to Baldpate* that had been made three or four times. It wasn't a horror movie but it had a kind of mystery, and had a kind of dark twist to it, so the idea could form the basis of our movie.'

With an updated version of *Seven Keys to Baldpate* on the cards, Michael Armstrong set to work. 'I then did the treatment virtually overnight, which was shown within a few days to Cannon, and they said they were interested.'

Armstrong set to work on the idea. 'All we really used was the beginning and the end. We took the premise to make a picture that is the pastiche of all the thirties and forties fear films. Very stylish, gothic and creepy – but fun.' After he finished his twenty page treatment, Walker then took it to Hollywood to show Price and Carradine, who both agreed to take part subject to seeing the finished script.

'Vincent Price said he loved to do it,' said Armstrong, 'and I said the script was almost finished, and I'll have for him next week. I hadn't even started on it yet! Oh shit! So I locked myself away for two weeks. The result was virtually the script that was filmed.'

Then Walker pitched the film to Peter Cushing. The actor had previously turned down Walker's *House of Mortal Sin* because of the level of sadism, so trying to convince him to take part in another one of his movies proved a harder task, a situation further complicated by the fact that Cushing had recently fought off prostate cancer. He recovered sufficiently to take up the offer. After missing the golden opportunity to work with Price in *The Monster Club*, he could now make amends.

Christopher Lee was the last to accept. He was relieved that Armstrong's treatment did not feature, 'an axe sticking out of someone's face every ten minutes.'

'It is not, in any sense, a horror film,' Lee added, 'and I have told the producers, I am not interested in doing a horror film. There is some violence, but there's no graphic mutilation or any of that nonsense. And there is a lot of comedy; not slapstick but natural humour.'

With the stars provisionally accepting their roles on the strength of Armstrong's treatment, Walker telephoned the writer to say he needed a completed script as soon as possible. 'I hadn't even started it!' he exclaimed. 'So I wrote the script in two weeks, with the last batch of pages being delivered to Pete about two hours before his flight to LA was due.'

Armstrong wanted to capture the style of Gothic melodrama that appealed to the distinguished cast. 'Let's take every *Old Dark House* cliché we can think of, and let's put the whole lot in one film and make it into a pastiche; a film buff's dream.'

'It's a gothic suspense thriller,' he added, 'a pastiche of the thirties and forties. Its creepy and perpetual thunderstorms. We wanted to bring all four of them together for the first time, and the characters were written totally for them.'

To write such a script for those legendary luminaries was a dream come true for Armstrong. 'With the dialogue, I wanted to use every cliché that is possible. It was the opportunity to write that kind of dialogue, especially for Vincent; that he had on the Roger Corman movies. Who else could say, "I have returned?" That line I wrote especially for Vincent. I knew that had to be his opening line.'

Armstrong further commented that the actors 'were complimentary of the writing.'

Walker felt that, '*House of the Long Shadows* was exactly the sort of film we intended to make, that we had to make. Menahem and Yoram ordered a horror film with all the old horror stars and I thought that with those old horror stars you couldn't deliver a horror film that would be a horror film because times have gone on and they belong to an era twenty years past. So we had to create a project to satisfy Menahem and Yoram initially, and then we had to say, "Well, we can't go and make a gothic film that's going to be taken seriously, so what we'll do is a little self-satire." And that's exactly what we did. Because it wasn't my money we thought, "We'll make the best film we can – they had the money, Menahem and Yoram, so we were limited by budget – but it would have been stupid if in 1983 we had made a film that Hammer was making in 1967. So we just had a nostalgia piece and say, 'We're doing it for film buffs'".'

With Price talking about the film on Terry Wogan's chat show and the trade announcements of the historic horror teaming coming out in June 1982, the budget was set at just under a £1 million with shooting to take place between August and September 1982.

Once the paycheques were sorted out for the stars, there was little money left for other things, and to avoid an expensive studio, Walker, through his friend Alfred Shaughnessy, arranged location shooting at Rotherfield Park Manor in Hampshire. This magnificent house, which was later used in *Four Weddings and a Funeral* (1994), had the perfect gothic splendour to double up as the Grisbanes' creepy ancestral home.

With the legends in place, Walker wanted to keep the nostalgia trip going when he set his sights on Elsa Lanchester to play creepy matriarch Victoria Grisbane. The British actress who scored her own piece of horror immortality as the title character in *The Bride of Frankenstein* (1935), was too ill to make the trip to London, so Walker turned to one of his favourite actresses, the indomitable Sheila Keith.

The London born, Aberdeen raised, Keith had a solid career on stage and screen (she had previously worked with Christopher Lee in repertory theatre). Her association with Walker had made her a genre favourite in *House of Whipcord*, *Frightmare*, *House of Mortal Sin* and *The Comeback*. Keith's formidable presence could easily hold her own opposite her distinguished co-stars.

Walker then set about casting the juvenile leads. Aware of the international market, the director turned to his friend Desi Arnaz Junior. 'We wanted someone nice looking, clean cut and Desi fit the bill.'

The son of Lucille Ball and Desi Arnaz, Arnaz Junior had been an actor since childhood. Also a drummer, he worked with his mother in the sitcom *Here's Lucy* from 1968 to 1974. When the show ran its course, Arnaz remained busy in film and television.

For Arnaz, it was a dream come true working with his heroes. He acted alongside Vincent Price on *Here's Lucy*, and worked with John Carradine's sons David, Keith and Robert on various film and TV projects. As a child he grew up watching Peter Cushing and Christopher Lee in their various Hammer horror pictures.

For the main female lead, Walker wanted someone, 'blonde, bubbly and could compliment Desi.' After trying out a couple of actresses, he settled for Julie Peasgood. A veteran of the Royal Shakespeare Company, Peasgood was thrilled at the opportunity to work with the horror icons. 'I just had a baby and wasn't taking on a great deal of work at the time, but when this offer came to work with Vincent Price, Peter Cushing, Christopher Lee, I would have been bonkers not to accept.'

Smaller roles went to Richard Hunter and Louise English as Andrew and Diana Caulder. 'When I was offered the role,' recalled Hunter, 'Peter wanted my character to be like Brad from the *Rocky Horror Picture Show* (1975).' Former Pan's People dancer English, had established herself as member of Benny Hill's 'Angels' in his popular TV show; she rose above the sexy dance routines thanks to her phenomenal range as a comedy actress and singer. Hill had been friends with Walker for many years, and the comedian used his influence to help secure his young protégé the role of Diana.

Rounding off the cast were two veterans of the British cinema. Richard Todd, an old friend of Walker, who had worked with him in *Home Before Midnight* and, according to the director, 'was only a phone call away.' Playing the creepy, but often overlooked role of the station master was Norman Rossington, a familiar face in British films of the sixties, who had also appeared with Christopher Lee in the horror film *Death Line* (1972).

Walker assembled his technical team, all battled hard veterans of British horror. Norman Langley was cinematographer, and had previously worked with Walker on *Die Screaming Marianne*, and was, in the director's eyes, perfect for what he wanted. 'Peter wanted (the film) lit low,' said Langley. As composer was newcomer Richard Harvey, who was grateful to get this wonderful opportunity to work on a high profile feature. 'It wasn't a Hollywood orchestra, but it wasn't a TV orchestra either.'

With the cast and crew in place, the production moved to Rotherfield Park in August for the scheduled five week shoot in glorious sunshine.

And a happy shoot it turned out to be, not just for the horror veterans but for the young cast, all of whom were in awe of these great men. 'The cast loved the humour of it,' said Armstrong. 'They clearly enjoyed it and they were great to write for.'

'We've all worked together before,' recalled an enthusiastic Price, 'but never as a foursome. It was a sort of joyful class reunion. This isn't a horror movie. Today's horror films are just too far out and gruesome for people like us. This is an old fashioned thriller.'

'The story of our lives as actors really,' said Lee of their class reunion. 'One spent so much of one's life dignifying material that was not worthy; giving our very best as professional actors of experience and knowledge and, if I may say so, a certain degree of talent, saying, "Well, this isn't very good. But we'll make it the best we possibly can because that's the way we are." I don't think we've done anything as actors of which we should been ashamed. We've been in films which we shouldn't been in.'

'I just love to see Chris bleed,' Price said of his formidable colleague. 'We're great friends. We both find each other hysterically funny. Before we met, I heard he was very pompous, and I was worried about meeting him. It was on *The Oblong Box*, the first film we did together. Well, we took one look at each other and started laughing. We spend our lives screaming and laughing at each other, and having such a wonderful time. I'm really devoted to him. I think he's one of my few good friends in the business.'

'I think as actors,' Lee added, 'Vincent and I were similar in many ways. We were proud of our profession, and we did the best we possibly could. Vincent already had a wonderful career behind him in which he played in a number of very, very big pictures in major roles, before he got into this gothic genre. I virtually made my name in it. We frequently found ourselves saddled with scripts, direction, and so on which, well, could have been a great deal better, to put it politely. All of us – Peter Cushing and John Carradine, Boris Karloff as well, and Bela Lugosi too. If you got the best script, the best director, the best cast, the best of everything, you'd have to be a terrible actor to make a mess of it. We never had the advantages in these films. We really had to create the proverbial silk purse out of the proverbial sow's ear. We did it because of the kind of people we were, as people; we were proud of our profession, we were dedicated and very, very determined. And in spite of all the setbacks and the problems and the difficulties, and there were many of them, for both of us, over the years, for all of us, we weren't going to let it get to us.'

Price was equally fond of his other illustrious co-star John Carradine. 'John is an adorable character, who I've known for about 40 years. I worked with him a lot, as a matter of fact. He was a very eccentric fellow, but fun to be with. I'll never forget we were talking on the set about the number of films we done, and somebody said, "The four of you ought to do another film together." I said, "You better be quick." John asked, "What do you mean by that?" and I explained, "Because we'll all be dead by the time they get through this one!" He said, "Oh no, no, no! Don't say that." He was a very superstitious man. He was also an extraordinary man.'

Price enjoyed working with Peter Cushing and knew about the actor's deep sadness. 'Peter is unfortunately a little gloomy, because of his wife's death, but still a sweet man. It's very sad. He's just waiting to die, but he's going to have to wait a long time. He's going to live to be 100 years old.'

According to Michael Armstrong, the horror stars, 'were all crafty,' adding that, 'Vincent could camp it up as if it was no tomorrow. Very theatrical with a great sense of fun.' Peter Walker agreed, describing Price as, 'very unactorish, for a man who came from the golden years of Hollywood. (Price, Cushing, Lee, Carradine) were all just fun. It would have been marvellous to have film students sitting there watching them. You don't direct them. Actors like that have a sixth sense.'

'I suppose I was expecting some bitchiness and prima donna behaviour,' Walker added, 'but that never happened. They are consummate professionals; they never blow a line or miss a mark. You learn in this business that you get what you pay for, and they are going to give you value for money.'

Price's sense of fun rubbed off on the rest of the crew. 'Vincent Price was a wonderful character,' said Norman Langley. 'He was fun and was great to have around. He was always sending up the other actors.' Wardrobe supervisor Alan

Flying agrees. 'Vincent was so full of jokes and funny surprises. A very sweet man.'

Producer Jenny Craven also enjoyed working with Price. 'He had a naughty sense of humour, which he brought to the set. A true gentleman.'

Christopher Lee recalled his own funny incident during filming. 'We filmed in this house which had several floors and our make-up and dressing rooms were right at the top of the building, needless to say, with four elderly gentlemen! I remember Vincent telling me, "My damn knees! My legs!" He was having problems going up the stairs; well, were all having them! One day, somebody said, "Get Mr Price down, we want him to set up the scene," and so we waited and we waited. "Is Mr Price coming down?" "Yes he says he's on his way." And he appeared in front of everybody on the set, ready to do the set-up, but he was not wearing his trousers. He was immaculately dressed, including his jockey shorts, but no trousers. Bow tie. No trousers. He said, "Yes, I'm ready when you are. What's the hold up?"'

The young cast responded positively to the quartet. 'There was a great respect between the four of them,' said Louise English. 'When you act with such professionals, it makes you more professional.'

'Vincent was lovely to me,' she continued. 'I was quite shy and I remember my first day, I was very nervous and he immediately put me at ease.'

Julie Peasgood experienced the same kindness from the actor. 'I loved working with Vincent Price. The first day that I met him, he took my hand and held it for quite a time and said, "You remind me very much of Jane Asher," which was quite a compliment as she is such a wonderful actress.'

'He was always funny,' she added. 'Very extrovert, perhaps more extrovert than the others from the cast. He always kept things bubbling along. What was interesting about the actors is that they always had time for you. Vincent Price and Peter Cushing especially had time for you.'

'Vincent Price, a very funny man,' said Richard Hunter. 'Sometimes for lunch we would go to a local pub. We were all sitting at the table having lunch with these great actors and the banter they had between them, winding each other up. We had left the restaurant one day and I was at the bar waiting for all of us to come out to the taxis. There was a couple there having lunch, obviously on their way to their holiday. I was at the bar and Peter Cushing came in, and I can hear this lady saying to her husband, "Isn't that Peter Cushing?" and her husband said, "Don't be silly. What would Peter Cushing be doing in this pub?" And at that point Christopher Lee walked into the pub, and she said, "That's Christopher Lee, surely?" Her husband replied, "I don't think so," and Vincent came in from another point and overhearing the conversation, and saying, "It is!" It was mind blowing! There was this couple seeing all these incredible actors.'

With the veterans having a whale of a time, and the cast and crew, enjoying their presence, *House of the Long Shadows* was a fun film to make. Budgetary problems meant the production ran out of money after three weeks leaving Walker to hastily shoot his remaining scenes, not that he had much problem with the stars getting the job done. 'They were very professional,' said Desi Arnaz, 'very proper, and we finished the movie with each scene only requiring the minimum of takes.'

'It was a marvellous experience for the four of us,' said Christopher Lee, 'we had a wonderful time, but, unfortunately...'

House of the Long Shadows may have been a happy shoot for all concerned, with the stars' long overdue teaming bringing in plenty of advanced publicity, but sadly studio interference during post-production torpedoed what could have been a nostalgia classic, which was the film's main selling point.

'Menahem never came on the set,' said Walker, while preparing the final cut. 'Neither of them (Golan and Globus) ever read the script. Under the terms of the contract, Menahem had the final cut approval. He'd never seen any of the rushes and I remember it was pulling teeth to get him to see the final cut, my cut. We got him out of The Inn on the Park at 9:00 am on a Sunday morning to run it with the editor. He sat there for two hours watching everything and he made five suggestions. Three of them were bloody good suggestions, things that somebody looking freshly would see, and we acted on them and the picture was done.'

Golan and Globus found themselves with a film they weren't sure on how to market – was it a comedy or was it a horror film? Facing the dilemma, they gave associate producer Jenny Craven full discretion with the final cut. Craven decided to cut out the comedy elements to market it as a horror film.

Michael Armstrong was far from happy with the revised version. 'It was funny, absolutely delightful,' he said of the original cut, 'and when I finally saw the finished edit, I wondered where it had all gone. Great chunks had been cut out or fiddled around with. It was silly because it killed off the people who wanted to see it and have a good laugh and it disappointed the people who had gone along to be frightened.'

Armstrong wasn't alone in his feelings. Vincent Price wasn't happy with the final cut either. 'We all thought it was good until this woman took an axe to it! I really don't know what she was doing. She called me up and said, "Will you go out and promote the film," and I said, "if you show the film that we shot!" because it's just not the same film. She cut out all the comedy payoffs to everything. As you know, we're all hired actors to scare Desi Arnaz Jr out of the house, people who just came in to do a job. After everything that happens in the house, Chris getting killed, and all the other things, suddenly we all come out and take a bow, and it's revealed to Desi that we are all actors. We had these marvellous comments on all the things that happened, and that was all cut out. They tried to turn it into a horror picture and destroyed it.'

'I think there was also way too much of Desi Arnaz in the beginning,' he added, 'and it does take too long to get into the story, so I don't quite understand it. I don't know if it was Golan and Globus who wanted it as a horror picture, or what. If they did, then why did they shoot a comedy?'

Unhappy with the way Cannon marketed *House of the Long Shadows* as a chiller, Michael Armstrong persuaded the producers to allow him to market the film as a comedy when it got its release in East Anglia, and the response turned out to be far more positive.

'What I did was to sell it totally as a comedy right from the word go so they knew it was a spoof. And it was amazing. The second the thing started, they were laughing and they loved it, applauded, cheering, roaring with laughter.'

One can only assume that the audience in East Anglia had either seen Walker's original cut or were simply easily pleased because *House of the Long Shadows* is a lousy effort that doesn't work as a horror film or as a spoof on the genre. The movie fails to achieve any kind of prominence, other than wasting the talents of four great men who have little to do but play to their outstanding reputations.

The blame for such a poor effort falls squarely on Armstrong's screenplay and Walker's direction, both of which sink any kind of originality the film could have had.

It is clear that Armstrong was not the right choice to take on what was meant to be a nostalgia piece. More at home with Walker's earlier efforts, Armstrong's style does not suit the old gothic horror format; perhaps the script should have been provided by a more familiar genre name such as Milton Subotsky or Richard Matheson.

If the script falls between two stools, Walker also misses the mark. A very technical director who can get a film finished on time and within budget, his style doesn't suit the old fashioned gothic chiller. Like Roger Corman, Walker lets his actors get on with it, but fails to keep control of them. Of course the horror veterans know their stuff so they don't need much direction, but at the end of the day actors need discipline, and this is lacking with the supporting cast.

And that fault is reflected strongly by the performances of the principle juvenile leads Arnaz and Peasgood. Despite the actors enjoying their time working together, there is no chemistry between them.

Thanks to Richard Harvey's excellent music and Norman Langley's suitably atmospheric photography, each horror star is given a grand entrance, effective enough to bring smiles and chills in equal measures to their loyal fan base.

With his plumed fedora hat and red bow tie, the moment the overtly theatrical Price announces 'I have returned!' audiences will expect flamboyant self-parody at its very best. His over-the-top soliloquy quickly establishes the mocking tone reminiscent of his work with Roger Corman. It's beautifully played high camp acting, which is his stock-in-trade. If there is actor who can ham it up and get away with it, it is definitely Vincent Price.

Sadly Price only has a couple of good jokes at his disposal. While he gets quite a lot of dialogue, it mostly consists of repeating the same tired old guff about fate, destiny, and what happened 40 years ago instead of being allowed to throw in a few corny one-liners and hideous puns, which the film desperately needs. In writing the script, Michael Armstrong should have watched *Theatre of Blood* at least once to see how it all worked. Instead he has Price ready to do stand-up but forgetting the punch-lines.

At the opposite end is Christopher Lee, taking things far more seriously. Immaculately dressed in his evening suit, his entrance into Baldpate Manor makes him look typically imposing, and very Dracula in appearance. Always a towering and formidable presence, and with a voice that can tremble mountains, Lee plays it straighter than Price and gives by far the best performance of the quartet. Unlike *The Oblong Box*, Lee plays opposite Price several times and their acting styles, whilst completely opposite in approach, complement each other perfectly. And even when his true identity is glaringly obvious, Lee convincingly lets the audience guess with a simply change of facial expression, from confident authority figure to twitching psycho, something he has perfected from his many years of big screen villainy.

While Price and Lee trade on their familiar personas, Peter Cushing on the other hand never had a specific horror image. What made Cushing unique was his versatility and the ability to tackle any kind of role. And Cushing never gave one bad performance during his 50 year career. Usually cast as a character with a steely resolve, it's refreshing to see him play a cowardly figure who drinks far too much hot punch to cope with the guilt of his actions. Always an instinctive actor, a bout of bronchitis during the making of the film gave him the idea of mispronouncing his 'R's' to hilarious affect. 'If I had of known,' said Armstrong, 'I would have written him more dialogue with the letter R.' Cushing gives a typically splendid comic performance.

House of the Long Shadows got its UK release on 13 June 1983, and while critics expressed their joy at seeing the horror stars together, the majority weren't happy with the film. One of the kindest comments came from *Screen International* who described it as, 'a fun film for middle of the roaders and all addicts of the vintage gothic horrors in which the four principles have so often starred. The assembled masters glide through with all the elegant menace at their command.' Leonard Matlin however felt that the film was, 'notable for a historic teaming, all wasted in small roles.'

'The old folks are at least professional,' wrote David Robinson of *The Times*, 'which is more than can be said for the sloppy script they have to cope with or the juvenile supporting players.' Leslie Halliwell felt it was, 'too restricted in script and production to be really effective.'

Giovanni Dadomo of *Time Out* was less than impressed. 'A jumble of dark house clichés which stacks up the zzzzz for a good hour before even admitting it's a spoof. Thereafter, two gags for Price, the unavoidable sad ghoulishness of Carradine's mere presence, and a Christopher Lee so wooden that it's hard to tell if he's in a coffin or not. Only Cushing retains any dignity, even coming up with a fresh characterisation – a lisping, drunken rendition of the upper class twit at 70 – that might turn Michael Palin green. The rest is vacuum: bus-ticket script, the usual faceless juvenile support, and bath-chair direction.'

The film's most negative comments came from Derek Malcolm of *The Guardian* and celebrated horror writer Kim Newman. Malcolm stated that, '*House of the Long Shadows* brings together Vincent Price, Christopher Lee, Peter Cushing and John Carradine for the first time. It then proceeds to waste them utterly. The worst thing about the film is its total lack of ambition; it's a horror flick that basks in the Hammer tradition without in any way understanding it.'

For the *Monthly Film Bulletin*, Kim Newman, wrote, 'Golan and Globus seem to have inherited Lord Grade's habit of assembling advertising packages with movies appended as an afterthought. The main selling point of the film was the return of these particular horror actors, which in turn became a major surprise and disappointment, is that the film should waste these grand old icons on an entirely superfluous remake of *Seven Keys to Baldpate*. The preposterous twist ending showed Walker and Armstrong display an appalling contempt for the audience, and that the ending turned a disappointing project into an infuriating one.'

The most contemptuous comments came from two of the stars. 'There wasn't a single marvellous speech to share between us,' said a disgruntled Lee. 'The direction was blank, and we agreed with the critics who shredded the film.'

Price was even more outspoken. 'A disaster, because the man, whoever – I can't even remember his name; psychosomatically I've forgotten it – the guy who directed it and the editor who cut it, they just cut all the comedy out of it. I hated it! Desi Arnaz, who was very good in it – they just turned it all over to him so that you never had the four people you wanted to see ever doing anything at all. That was a stupid director'

Interestingly enough, the DVD release has a special feature where Peter Walker, Julie Peasgood, Norman Langley and author Derek Pykett return to Rotherfield Park Manor to relive their memories of the film and their time with the horror stars. During their interviews, Walker and Michael Armstrong talk about how the actors enjoyed working with them, which contradicts the comments made by Price and Lee about the film, and of Walker's direction.

Whatever the controversy, *House of the Long Shadows* failed at the box office. Cannon Films' inability to market the movie properly meant it was dead on arrival. Had it been promoted as a comedy, it might have done better, but not by much, and as a horror film, it was out of step with the times. Critically and commercially, the movie did very well in Europe, especially in France, where it received an award in Paris for best film. Meanwhile, at the *Stiges Film Festival* in Spain, Michael Armstrong won best screenplay while Vincent Price and Peter Cushing picked up acting awards at the same event.

During their many press interviews, the horror stars were asked if they would come back together for another film, and the reply was always yes. Sadly this never happened. While they all stayed friends, professionally they went their separate ways. Cushing went straight to another Cannon Film, *Sword of the Valiant* (1983) with Sean Connery and Trevor Howard. That too wasn't a success and Cannon collapsed soon afterwards. Both Menahem Golan and Yoram Globus continued on as producers while Peter Walker and Michael Armstrong retired from film work altogether.

Cushing eventually retired from acting, while Christopher Lee carried on his eclectic movie output.

John Carradine also remained prolific if not quite as high profile as Lee, working to the end in a slew of cheap horror films, mostly for his loyal friend Fred Olen Ray. He died on 27 November 1988 at the age of 82.

For Vincent Price, the joyful class reunion was over. It had been fun working with old friends but now it was back to the States where he returned to Oscar Wilde for further tours of *Diversion and Delights* interspersed with the financial rewards of voice over work, TV commercials, and his long running stint as host of *Mystery!*.

Price also received an interesting offer that would introduce him to a new generation of fans worldwide. In April 1982, Michael Jackson began recording his album *Thriller*, and for his horror-related title track, he brought in Price to record a creepy monologue. He was paid his usual fee and received no profit participation. This turned out to be one giant financial misstep.

Released in November 1982, *Thriller* was a worldwide smash selling over 50 million copies and spawning several hit singles. The title track featured an epic 14 minute video directed by horror maestro John Landis. Regarded as one of the greatest albums ever made, *Thriller* did not enhance the commercial prospects of *House of the Long Shadows* (if Cannon marketed the film properly, the free publicity would have been amazing). Worse still, because Price was only paid a flat fee, he made nothing more from the album.

Publically, Price was good humoured about his financial remuneration on *Thriller*, but privately he was seething, both at himself for not arranging a better deal and towards Jackson, who he felt should have acknowledged his specific importance to the album's success. To make matters worse, when Price's agent tried to get more money for the video, he was refused point blank.

When word got out to Jackson, he tried to make amends, albeit poorly when he sent his entourage to Price's house with a letter of thanks, a framed poster of the pop star and three albums, one gold and two platinum. 'He didn't know whether to laugh or cry,' said Victoria when she presented the gifts to her father. 'At first he opted for the former by turning it into a faux altar surrounded by candles and flowers.'

'There were a few things that totally displeased him,' said Price's personal assistant Reggie Williams, 'but one item of memorabilia around the house began to rile him – the framed gold and platinum records for his contribution to *Thriller*.' Price auctioned off the albums and gave the proceeds to his beloved gallery.

House of the Long Shadows is something of a curate's egg. It's a film that fans love and hate at the same time. It's not a good film, but it is looked upon with warm affection because of Price and his brilliant co-stars. It is a fitting tribute to the wonderful actors who have entertained movie goers for over 40 years, and that alone is a true legacy to be remembered for.

Bloodbath at the House of Death

They'll have to bury me before I retire and even my gravestone will read 'I'll be back!' –
Vincent Price

In addition to playing Oscar Wilde on stage and his extensive television work, Price continued his lecture tours. He also had to deal with Coral Browne's health problems after the actress had to undergo surgery for a cancerous tumour in her leg.

In 1981, Browne received an interesting script from her old friend Alan Bennett, entitled *An Englishman Abroad*. Many years earlier Browne had told Bennett a story of her time with the Shakespeare Memorial Company and its tour of Russia in 1958. During the company's spell in Moscow, Browne met the famous British traitor Guy Burgess, whose work as a Russian double agent led to his well-publicized defection to the Soviet Union. The play centred on the elegant actress' time with the exile, now a pathetic alcoholic living a seedy existence in a dingy Moscow flat, and his request to her to buy him a Saville Row suit. Browne kept Burgess' letters, which Bennett used as the basis for his play.

Bennett worked with Browne on casting the pivotal roles of herself and of Guy Burgess. According to Bennett, 'We talk about the Burgess piece and discuss who should play him, and we go through various names while it becomes increasingly obvious that we haven't talked about who should play her.'

After much consultation, Bennett decided that Browne should play herself, despite the fact she was much older. 'Age didn't come into it,' he said, 'and she loved the idea of playing herself.'

'I was scared of her,' Bennett admitted, 'but I wouldn't have dared say no. And I can't think of anybody who could have played her and also anybody who would have dared have played her. And I was very glad she did, obviously!' Also playing himself was Browne's old friend Charles Gray.

Bringing in John Schlesinger as director and Alan Bates as Burgess, production began in January 1983 with Glasgow and Dundee doubling up as Moscow for location shooting. Price stayed in Los Angeles to spend time with his daughter. Before filming began, he received a phone call from his wife, concerned about a growth on her arm, which turned out to be a malignant tumour, but was assured by her doctor that it would be okay for her to have surgery.

To take his mind off his wife's health problems, Price continued to keep busy, and that included another British horror spoof. This new production was a cinema vehicle for an anarchic and surreal radio DJ and TV comedian called Kenny Everett.

Liverpool born Everett was a one-of-a-kind talent. He began his radio career with the pirate station Radio London where he presented *Kenny and Cash* with fellow DJ Dave Cash. This led to stints on Radio Luxembourg and BBC Radio One.

Everett's often controversial style did not adhere????? him to the Establishment, and comments about campaigner Mary Whitehouse and the then-Transport Minister's wife got him sacked from the BBC. It was his move to independent radio where he distinguished himself, especially on London's Capital Radio, where his unique brand of comedy made him a hit with listeners.

Moving onto television in 1978 with his own music/comedy series for Thames Television, Everett developed into a very funny, surrealist comedian, creating characters such as the punk Sid Snot, French aristocrat Marcel Wave and, in the best possible taste, diva movie actress Cupid Stunt. Everett wrote the sketches in collaboration with Ray Cameron, Barry Cryer and Dick Vosburgh, and the shows featured a string of popular guest stars such as Cliff Richard, Rod Stewart and lifelong friend Freddy Mercury. In addition to music from The Boomtown Rats and The Tubes, the risqué dance routines were provided by Hot Gossip, one of its dancers being future stage star Sarah Brightman.

At the peak of his fame, the possibility of a feature film was always on the cards. Thanks to his success, Ray Cameron and Barry Cryer were offered several potential film projects. They eventually worked on a script in 1982 for a proposed star vehicle called *Suicide – The Movie*.

Unfortunately, obtaining finance for *Suicide – The Movie* floundered after a year. 'The movie just wasn't there,' lamented Ray Cameron. Since horror was always a popular genre, Cameron and Cryer decided to write a new script. After arranging a deal with Wildwood Productions, Cryer enthusiastically stated that *Bloodbath at the House of Death* would, 'do for the *Friday the 13th* (1979) slash/horror movie genre what *Airplane!* (1980) did for disaster films.'

Finance for *Bloodbath at the House of Death* almost fell through but theatre impresario Laurence Myers agreed to produce the movie. Once the logistics were sorted out, filming began on 13 June 1983 with location work taking place in a deserted mansion in Potters Bar, Hertfordshire. In addition to co-writing the script, *Bloodbath at the House of Death* marked Cameron's directorial debut.

Everett's popularity with his fellow performers meant Cameron and Cryer could assemble a good cast. Pamela Stephenson, Sheila Steafel and Anna Dawson (in a tiny role) were regulars on Everett's shows, as was Cleo Rocos. Other familiar faces included Gareth Hunt, Don Warrington, John Fortune and Pat Ashton, as well as British cinema stalwarts Graham Stark and David Lodge.

Getting Vincent Price involved was an amazing coupe for Cameron. 'For a lunatic fan like me, it's really the icing on the cake.' Cameron also allowed Price to improvise his lines when required. The actor only had five scenes, none of which he shared with Everett. On viewing the film years later, it looks as though Price got added to the production after everything else was shot.

The filming on *Bloodbath at the House of Death* ran smoothly although Everett, whose character has a metal leg, would often forget which one he had to limp with. So much so, Cameron gave the clapper boy a sign to tell Everett which leg it was before he acted each scene.'

And that is where *Bloodbath at the House of Death* falters – with Everett himself. He only plays one character, and while he plays it very well, it goes against his traditional comic persona. The anarchy isn't there and the big screen treatment reveals his inadequacies as a leading man. In cinema terms he would be more effective playing supporting roles in ensemble pieces.

For Vincent Price, his role is an extended cameo. Resplendent in his bright satanic robes, he looks very gaunt. There is the novelty of hearing this most elegant of actors swearing like a trooper. In his broadest performance since *The Comedy of Terrors* (1963), Price, delivering the profanities with complete gusto, is having a lot of fun with the material at his disposal.

The film is hardly great, but it has enough funny moments to keep things ticking along. Ray Cameron's direction is competent and the performances are engaging. Despite moving away from his madcap image, Everett is acceptable and with a couple more film roles, he might have developed into a reasonably effective, if far more conventional comic actor. He is well complimented by Pamela Stephenson in a throwaway role of prim scientist turned sex addict. But even in their finest hour, they are upstaged by the grandiloquent Price.

Bloodbath at the House of Death is the least interesting of Price's indifferent trio of UK made comedy chillers; it was also the first time in a British horror film that he did not receive top billing. It marked the sad end to the actor's British horror connection, which is a shame because it's nowhere near as bad as the critics made it out to be.

Once completed, *Bloodbath at the House of Death* was supposed to be marketed as a family film. 'We aimed as a wide an audience as possible,' said Cryer. 'We're certainly not going to get ourselves out of the kids market which makes up such a wide part of Kenny's audience.' However horror films being what they are, even if it is a comedy for the kids, the end result doesn't always go well.

Laurence Myers arranged a special screening with censor James Ferman prior to putting the film on general release. 'It's a fairly terrible film,' said Myers. 'I recall showing it to James Ferman, who thought it was fine and funny enough, but thought we were showing him the reels in the wrong order. We weren't – the film just didn't make sense.'

Making matters worse, *Bloodbath at the House of Death* received an X certificate, alienating the audience it was marketed for. Released in the UK by Thorn EMI in March 1984, it followed on from Everett's notorious appearance at the Young Conservatives conference a year earlier, where, egged on by director Michael Winner, he turned up on stage with the oversize foam rubber hands he used for his TV character The Reverend Brother Lee Love, and shouted, 'Let's bomb Russia!' and 'let's kick Michael Foot's stick away!', the latter comment aimed directly at the aging Labour Party leader.

Everett's rant did a lot to damage his comic reputation, undermine his standing with the BBC and reduce his loyal fan base. This meant the critical reaction to *Bloodbath at the House of Death* would never be a positive one, with the press, especially the left wing tabloids, out for his blood.

The kindest comment came from *Screen International*, which isn't saying much. 'Audience rating: devoted addicts of Kenny Everett's television shows. Business prediction: average to good in down-market popular cinemas. Critical comment: Regrettably, and ironically, censorship for the cinema excludes the sub-teen and early teenage young audience that regularly watch Kenny Everett and could be expected to find this ratbag of overlong sketches hilariously funny.'

Time Out weren't too impressed either. 'The spoofings of so many genre films in a barrage of visual gags quickly becomes predictable; only Sheila Steafel's *Carrie* sketch is done with any imagination.' Film critic Martin Auty for the *Monthly Film Bulletin* wrote, 'Presumably intended as high camp; looks low grade *Carry On*,' while Leslie Halliwell decreed it as a, 'Spoof tailored for the requirements of a zany television comedian who never knows when enough is enough. Too much gore and far too much smut.'

Laurence Myers had his own views on the film's poor box office showing. 'We were dealing with single screens back then. There was always the next American blockbuster queuing up behind you. If your film didn't perform, then they'd pull it to make way for something more profitable.'

'It's not the film I want on my headstone or on my obituary when I die,' he added, 'but it's not without its fans. It doesn't matter if a film is regarded as part of our national heritage or some rubbish like that, audiences couldn't care less about that stuff. They either like it or they don't.'

Although it won the award for Best Science Fiction Film at the Brussels International Festival of Fantasy Film, *Bloodbath at the House of Death* went direct to video; its American VHS release featured Vincent Price on the cover, since Kenny Everett was unknown to Stateside audiences.

For many years, *Bloodbath at the House of Death* was considered lost. It never gets mentioned on the various webpages devoted to Kenny Everett or Vincent Price and is overlooked by horror fans. The eventual DVD release was sorted out by Marc Morris of Nucleus Films.

Following the completion of *Bloodbath at the House of Death*, there were celebrations in the Price household with November's BBC1 screening of *An Englishman Abroad*. The drama was later shown in America as part of *The Masterpiece Theatre*. Reviews were positive with Browne and Alan Bates receiving BAFTA awards. While it makes excellent viewing, it's fair to say Browne is miscast playing herself. Passing herself off as a younger woman is one thing, but it was over 20 years ago when she met Burgess, and she's simply far too old for a modern dramatization. However, as Bennett correctly stated, it would be difficult to find an actress to come close to such an individual woman, even if what she gave in the film was more of a vanity performance than an acting performance.

For Vincent Price, his British horror career came to an end. *Masque of the Red Death* began it with a massive bang and *Bloodbath at the House of Death* ended it with a damp squib. In between the two films there were four career defining performances, and great work alongside some of the best actors of the British cinema, one of whom he married! For all the highs and lows that came with his profession, he had carved out the unique position of being an American cultural icon held with equal respect in the UK.

The Final Years (1984 – 1993)

'I hate being old and ill! Don't get old if you can avoid it!' – Vincent Price

Price in *Edward Scissorhands* (1990)

Bloodbath at the House of Death may have ended Price's association with British horror, but the British connection carried on in one form or another, whether it was appearing on a talk show, presenting UK crime shows on *Mystery!*, or making the most of his product endorsements from television that enabled him to travel while his age and health allowed him to do so.

But acting remained his life, and ever the busy man, Price had to stay active for as long as he could. 'I can't afford to retire. I've got to keep working. I've got ex-wives and wives and mothers-in-laws and children to support.'

In December 1983, while *Bloodbath at the House of Death* was in post-production, Price received an offer from Disney (his first ever from the studio). It was an offer he cherished as it realised a lifelong ambition to voice a character in a Disney cartoon.

Price received two short scripts called *Basil of Baker Street*. 'It's about Sherlock Holmes, who is a mouse called Basil. I play – naturally – a villain – the rat, who is Moriarty, but he's called Rattigan. Strangely enough I seem to be overrun with *Sherlock Holmes* because every week I introduce the new episode of *Sherlock Holmes* in *Mystery!*'

'I've always been visually minded and a big fan of animation, so when they asked me to do it, I was thrilled! The thing was, they wanted me to audition! If anyone but the Disney people asked me I would have been offended. I was really in a state of terror, because I didn't know what they wanted. It turned out to be a very enjoyable experience, because the animators wanted my interpretation of the character. They showed me hundreds of character sketches that they had already done, and they gave me a free reign on that. So Rattigan's personality was based, in part, from my readings of the dialogue, and also from my gestures in the recording booth. Rattigan is really a larger than life villain, so I did the part by exaggerating it.'

Rattigan was initially written as a thin and rather weak bad guy (or bad rat!), but once Price got involved the sketches changed radically. 'Rattigan is the ultimate villain. He's got a huge sense of humour about himself, but he's dead serious at the same time about crime. When the actor gets there and the voice begins to happen, you begin to see the character – the animation – taking on your humanity, which of course is what they want. Because the more human the mouse or the rat is, the better for the picture.'

With the animation of *Basil of Baker Street* starting the following year, Price remained active in other areas. March 1984 saw him visiting Yale University for a retrospective of his life. Later in October he was awarded the Annual Life Achievement Award by the *Hollywood Press Club*. Retirement was not a word in Price's vocabulary ('I almost lost my marbles!'), so he grabbed whatever work came his way. There were few good film roles for an actor his age, but at least he kept busy with TV commercials and voice-overs that included a guest appearance as the voice of Vincent Van Ghoul in *The Thirteen Ghosts of Scooby Doo*.

Meanwhile Coral Browne followed her success on *An Englishman Abroad* with a superb performance as the aging Alice Hargreaves (the original *Alice in Wonderland*) in *Dreamchild* (1985). Unlike having to pretend to be her younger self in *An Englishman Abroad*, she had to be made up to look much older for this movie.

Around the summer of 1985, Price received an offer from a young filmmaker named Jeff Burr to star in his horror portmanteau *From a Whisper to a Scream* (1987). Along with producer Darin Scott, Burr turned up at Price's home with his script, and knowing that the actor was a wine connoisseur, he also brought with him a bottle of vintage red.

'We came bearing gifts,' said Burr, 'and wouldn't you know, he opened the door when we knocked on it! It was a flurry of, "Gee Mr Price, we're fans of your work, and we wrote this script," and he actually invited us inside. He had every reason to ignore us, and even if it was on a polite level, he could have said, "Okay boys, contact my agent," but he was just so gracious. He invited us in, sat and talked with us for about 15 minutes, took the script and that's how it all started.'

After listening to Burr's pitch, Price said he liked the script but admitted that being a horror film, he did not want to commit as it was a genre he wanted to distance himself from.

Burr filmed four terror tales between July and August 1985. Later, in February 1986 he screened one of the tales to Price, who finally agreed to star in the main story that links the segments.

Getting Price on board was a dream come true, so Burr decided to re-write the script to enlarge the actor's role and tailor it to his personality. On his return from a lecture tour in the Caribbean, Price felt the revised script was, 'boringly repetitive and nothing to do with what I agreed with,' further adding, 'I figure after all these years, I have earned the right to throw my weight around. I know why people want me. I have the name and the reputation so I figure I should have a say in the way my parts are written.'

The filmmakers reverted back to the original script and Price filmed his scenes in April 1986 at Roger Corman's Venice Studio in just two days. He plays Julian White, a librarian and resident of the creepy town of Oldfield. He relates four tales to a sceptical reporter who believes a recently executed murderess may have been in some way influenced by the town.

The first story features a nerdy office clerk obsessed by a beautiful co-worker. When she rejects his advances, he kills her and has sex with her while she's lying in the morgue. Nine months later, their offspring digs its way out of her grave to reunite with dad. The second tale concerns an ex-con who steals the secret of immortality from a voodoo priest. The third story has a carnival glass eater leaving his sideshow family to find love with a normal girl. The final tale takes place at the end of the American Civil War where several deserting soldiers are captured by a group of children.

From a Whisper to a Scream boasts an excellent cast of Susan Tyrell, Clu Gulager, Terry Kiser, Martine Beswick, Cameron Mitchell, and Laurence Tierney, with Price top billed in what was a cameo appearance. Unlike the Amicus pictures, which dealt with macabre fairy tales, this film is loaded with excessive gore and graphic nudity, perfect for a modern slasher movie, but not to Price's liking. 'I'm afraid they might have gone too far,' he lamented.

Renamed *The Offspring* (taken from the first story), the film was released in September 1987 and went straight to video. The changing times meant Price's name was no longer synonymous to the genre. It was his fourth horror anthology and his final chiller where he received star billing.

In July 1986, *Basil of Baker Street* was released under the new title *Basil – The Great Mouse Detective*. It met with a warm critical response and box office success worldwide, and Price's performance as Rattigan received the highest praise. It marked a final collaboration (of sorts) with Basil Rathbone, who also returned as the Great Detective. Rathbone's voice was taken from a spoken word recording he did a few months before his death called *The Adventure of the Red-Headed League*.

Price's next assignment turned out to be one of the defining moments of his long and distinguished career, a movie he joyfully described as, 'a very dear story about nothing.' That film was *The Whales of August* (1987).

Producer Mike Kaplan saw the stage version in 1981, and envisaged it as a possible star vehicle for the 'First Lady of American Film' Lillian Gish. The success of the American family drama *On Golden Pond* (1981) showed there was a market for a much gentler form of cinema entertainment.

Kaplan announced his project in April 1984, but even with Lillian Gish on board, funding remained elusive until June 1986. Oddly enough, the 93 year old actress turned down the role of Sarah Webber several times.

A number of veteran actresses were touted to play Sarah's sister Libby Strong in what was essentially a two-character drama. After considering Katherine Hepburn, Frances Dee and Barbara Stanwyck, Kaplan settled for Bette Davis, who was recovering from a stroke and was equally reluctant to take part.

This two-hander centres on one day in the life of Sarah and Libby as they spend what could be their last summer at Sarah's beach house in Maine. Also on the island is their friend and neighbour Tisha and local handyman Joshua, played by fellow movie veterans Ann Sothern and Harry Carey Junior.

While the sisters resolve to settle their differences, a charming Russian émigré (and alleged count) called Nikolai Maranov briefly comes into their lives. Several actors were considered for that role, among them Fred Astaire, Joel McCrea and Paul Henreid before the producers settled on Sir John Gielgud.

A long term dispute with director Lyndsay Anderson prompted Gielgud's early exit and Anderson's decision to hire Vincent Price to replace him caused something of a shock in Hollywood. *The American Cinematographer* describing the casting as 'daring.' 'In England,' said Anderson, 'we're not so completely blinkered by Vincent's horror reputation.' The British connection once again played an important part in Price's participation on the movie.

Price accepted the role with the same enthusiasm he had for Rattigan; '*The Whales of August* assignment seemed perfectly natural to me.' He based Maranov on his late brother Mortimer. '(Mort) was an enchanting man, but he never took advantage of all his opportunities. I used my memories of him to show a man who is very charming but in no way working toward anything. When I graduated, there was no jobs. The world was not our oyster, but a very small pebble you had to push around with your nose. So I realised you had to seize every opportunity that comes along.'

With a $3 million budget, production began towards the end of 1986, the eight week shoot commencing on Cliff Island, one of the Casco Bay islands just off the coast of Portland, Maine. It was a rather cold autumn and not surprisingly the aging cast had their own difficulties during filming.

'We were really very uncomfortable,' Price recalled. 'We couldn't get to the mainland without a 45 minute water-taxi ride. It wasn't the jolliest picture I've ever been on, but then the jolliest pictures are sometimes the ones that turn out to be the worst.'

There were further difficulties between the two leading ladies, neither of whom got on. In typical diva mode, Davis demanded top billing, which annoyed Gish, who wasn't interested in making a fuss. Eventually Davis got left hand billing in the credits with Gish billed slightly above her.

Davis grew agitated with Gish because she kept missing her cues due to her deafness. Away from work the two hardly spoke to each other. Gish, ever the trooper, was hurt by Davis' attitude, but remained understanding since the actress was recovering for a series of strokes.

Price on the other hand enjoyed working with Davis. 'Bette smoked about 18 million cigarettes and we giggled a lot. She kept calling it *The Whales of November*, because it kept getting colder and colder.' Working alongside the illustrious female trio of Gish, Davis and Sothern, Price joked, 'You could barely get on the set for all the crutches and canes in the way!'

Price kept away from his bickering co-stars and did his bit without a word of complaint, making the most of what was an extended cameo. 'You don't have to carry a picture. You walk in, play your little scene, and walk out with people remembering you.'

The critics certainly remembered him. Released in October 1987, *The Whales of August* received positive reviews with *Newsweek* commenting that 'Price, with his ravaged handsomeness, gives his best performance in years,' and *Variety* saying 'Price, in his first non-horror film in 25 years brings warm sophistication to his gentleman caller.' There was talk of a possible Oscar nomination for his performance, but only Ann Sothern received the accolade, losing out to Olympia Dukakis for *Moonstruck* (1987).

Price had the last word about *The Whales of August*. 'The film touches a number of points: a conflict of wills, the sense of family, the particular quality, which makes people from Maine absolutely a breed apart. The structure and language are beautiful and simple. Coral and I were amazed at how it held our attention. The characters are like figures in a Greek tragedy in a minor way, and have these mesmerising actresses playing them.'

After *The Whales of August*, Price continued working as much as he could, but as the decade came to a close, there were other less pleasant things on his mind – both personal and health-wise.

Although their marriage was a strong one, Browne was not an easy person to live with, and her declining health made her almost impossible. Worse still were her jealous rages. She resented Price's close relationship with his children and his many friends who were with him before they met. Thanks to Browne, they were alienated from their social circle. Price, an affable man who hated confrontation, usually gave in to her unreasonable demands.

'Coral's presence in my father's life irrevocably changed my own relationship with him,' said Victoria. 'Because she refused to embrace his family, he continually felt guilty about wanting to spend time with Barrett or me. It was as though, in marrying her, he had handed her the reins of his life. She was in control in an almost parental way, and so he snuck behind her back – calling us when she was out the house, arranging ways for us to meet him when he was working away from home. Our once easy companionship laboured under the weight of his guilt and Coral's jealousy.'

Browne's possessive rage grew worse the longer they were together. 'She kept everyone who liked him away from him,' recalled Adrienne Corri. 'I very rarely saw him alone apart from a couple of times when he came over to England without her. But when she was here, it was very much a case of only Coral's friends.' Thanks to Browne, many of Price's long term friendships ended bitterly; even Diana Rigg, who was instrumental in bringing them together, was given the short shrift years later.

Price still kept in touch with a few old friends, especially Peter Cushing and Christopher Lee, who he frequently corresponded with. Lee saw quite a lot of Price during his time in Los Angeles and continued to stay in contact when he returned to London. The camaraderie between the horror legends remained strong to the end.

By this time Cushing's health was beginning to fail him, but as far as the actor was concerned, it was a step closer to being reunited with Helen. According to Lee, 'Vincent once, in a phone call to me asked, "Is he still expecting Helen to be there to greet him?" And I said, "And looking forward to it." And Vincent said, "And what's if she's out?" I said, "I shall tell Peter what you said Vincent," and when I did, Peter laughed fit to despatch him immediately on his journey. When he'd recovered he said, "Only Vincent could say such a thing, and only you could pass it on."'

As Browne's behaviour got worse, the marriage went through a bad patch with Price getting involved with an unknown woman. Once Browne found out, she threatened a very public divorce and the affair ended. The stress of the situation affected Price's own fragile health.

Along with the respiratory problems that originated from his death scene in *Scream and Scream Again*, the arthritis, which crippled his father, also took effect rendering him less mobile. For a man who always kept busy, this was a dreadful blow. 'I see him leaving me day by day,' lamented Browne. 'He fell apart so suddenly.'

Price tried to keep positive about the situation. 'He never really moaned or groaned,' said Hazel Court, 'but he hated being old, hated it, more perhaps than anyone I've ever known. He was a prisoner. But his mind! His zest for life was so intense.'

'Vincent loved to work,' said Jane Russell. 'He wanted to keep doing something all the time, it was "Let's go lecture, let's do this, let's do that, I want to be active." Being in bed was just driving him crazy.' If there was any film work that came his way, he would take it regardless of quality.

Price accepted a small role in *Dead Heat* (1988) because he wanted to work with Treat Williams and Joe Piscopo, actors in his words were, 'very fine artists.' Production began in August 1987 with Price appearing at the start and end of the movie as Arthur P Loudermilk a billionaire financier of an invention that revives the dead. Despite a solid cast that included Darren McGavin, Keye Luke and Robert Picardo, *Dead Heat* hardly ranks as a classic chiller with everyone concerned looking ill at ease. It marked a sad end to Price's horror career.

Shortly after his participation in *Dead Heat*, Price had a pacemaker fitted to regulate his failing heart. With his wife's health just as precarious, they resorted to hired help to get them through the day.

In May 1988, Price appeared in the thriller *Backtrack* (1991), directed by old friend Dennis Hopper. Price is a strange choice for his cameo as Mafioso boss Lino Avoca. Even Hopper admitted, 'I don't know how I got the brilliant idea to have Vincent in *Backtrack*. He was wonderful. He did it as a favour to me. He didn't need to do that part.'

Hopper first met Price when he was 16, and they remained friends ever since; it was Price who developed the young man's appreciation of art. 'As far as art is concerned, my whole life would have been enormously diminished without having met Vincent Price.'

'Vincent was the most gentle, wonderful man I've ever met,' he added, 'so for me to think of him as a villain is impossible. He had an incredible voice, an incredible presence. I have dear and admirable thoughts of him. He was the genuine article.'

Despite an incredible cast that included Hopper, Jodie Foster, Dean Stockwell, John Turturro, Fred Ward, Charlie Sheen, Joe Pesci and the singer Bob Dylan, *Backtrack* is a strange thriller that isn't sure where it's going. It never received a theatrical release in the United States, and the severely edited version that came out in Europe in December 1991 under the title *Catch Fire*, so incensed Hopper that he had his name removed from the director's credits. Like most of Hopper's movies, it has surreal moments that make it interesting viewing.

Towards the end of 1988, Price's health forced him to step down as host of *Mystery!* 'I've never had a job I loved so much,' he commented sadly. 'I couldn't use my voice the way I wanted.' On his suggestion, Diana Rigg took over from him. Price's departure from *Mystery!* also marked an end to his lecture tours.

It was around this period that Price saw Christopher Lee one last time, and it was a very poignant occasion for both actors. 'I remember, dinning with him at Spago's in Los Angeles, a procession of people rising from their tables to greet him. He was already very ill, and when driving us home – Gitte in the back with Coral – he reached across and patted my leg, saying, "It's really wonderful to see you dear boy, and here's to the next time." We were shattered by the realization that there wouldn't be a next time, because always when our next meeting was mooted, he'd respond with a crack, such as "Not if I see you first!"'

In September 1989, Price was rushed to hospital where he was diagnosed with Parkinson's disease, which, on top of his arthritis reduced his mobility even further. He was placed on a drug that helped regain much of his strength – enough to take on another film role, and one that proved to be a poignant farewell to his cinema career.

Tim Burton, who paid homage to his boyhood hero and mentor in *Vincent*, had left Disney to become a director of some repute. Inspired by the classic gothic chillers, he often cast genre favourites Christopher Lee and Michael Gough in his films. For this particular production, he brought in Vincent Price.

Edward Scissorhands (1990) is Burton's tribute to the famous fairy tales of the Brothers Grimm and Ernst Hoffmann. It tells the story of a gentle, bio-mechanical boy named Edward (Johnny Depp, in the first of his many collaborations with Burton). Edward was created by an elderly Gepetto figure known as The Inventor, and both of them reside in a gothic castle overlooking a sterile all-American town.

Pre-production took place towards the end of 1989. After considering Tom Cruise and Tom Hanks for the title role, Burton settled on Johnny Depp, who made his name on TV in *21 Jump Street* and had recently scored a cult hit in John Waters' *Cry-Baby* (1990). For the tiny but important role of The Inventor, Burton had one choice – Vincent Price. 'His cameo had real emotional content. He was in the first film I ever made and was so supportive of me. He's an amazing guy, and I got through my childhood watching his movies.'

Price received his script in February 1990 with location work starting in Texas the following month. Burton was thrilled to have him on board. 'There was a connection, an emotional link for me, growing up and watching the Poe films. Vincent characters had a sensitivity; a heightened sensitivity, heightened awareness. There was an energy he had; it was evident in everything. The combination of his voice, the way he looked – there was always something going on under the surface. I liked believing Vincent: I believed him. Even though I know he was having a good time, I still believed him.'

'I think Vincent really found it with the horror stuff,' he added. 'I do think that's where he truly shone. And I don't know if it's because I loved him so much in it. He had that unique quality; other actors could do comedy, but only he could do what he did in the Poe films. Nobody wants to get pigeonholed, but you don't break through that by becoming bitter. Vincent broke through by embracing it – that's why I found him so inspirational.'

Price accepted the role without hesitation, and thanks to the new drugs, he had enough stamina to get through the production, his scenes being filmed in July 1990. More importantly the youthful exuberance of Tim Burton and Johnny Depp had a positive effect on him.

'One of the greatest things that Vincent ever told me was buy art,' said Depp. 'That's a good piece of advice I shall treasure forever. He called me every year on my birthday – he's was a Gemini too – and left me these beautiful messages. One of the most incredible moments I've ever had was sitting in Vincent's trailer, showing him this first edition I have of the complete works of Poe, with really amazing illustrations. Vincent was going nuts over the drawings, and he started talking about *The Tomb of Ligeia*; then he closed the book and began to recite it to me in this beautiful voice, filling the trailer with huge sounds. Such passion! I looked at the book later, and it was verbatim. Word perfect. It was a great moment and I'll never forget that.'

Price has three unforgettable flashback scenes in the film: his health preventing him from filming more. The first scene sees The Inventor proudly strolling about his laboratory. Now walking with the aid of a cane, Price looks extremely frail, yet he still cuts an elegant figure in the frock coat and cravat. It is this scene where he comes across the idea of creating a human being.

Scene two has The Inventor teaching the partially built Edward the rules of etiquette and making his creation laugh with a limerick. He seems frail and his once unique voice had lost much of its impact. But even then he makes the most of his scene, creating a warm and delightful figure.

But it's the final scene that's the most heart breaking. The ever-smiling Inventor presents Edward with his new hands. The smile then turns to an expression of pain as he falls dead leaving the incomplete Edward running one of his scissor fingers across his dead creator's cheek. It is a very sad moment, not just because of Price's excellent performance, but to the fans who were now experiencing the end of an era. It was a fitting finale to an amazing cinema career and his public was there to see it happen.

Edward Scissorhands was released in December 1990 to a warm critical response and public approval. For Vincent Price, the renaissance period that began with *Diversion and Delights* and *The Whales of August* had been rounded off with a touching performance in a high profile film.

Shortly after completing his stint on *Edward Scissorhands*, Price faced another personal challenge as his wife was diagnosed with breast cancer. With his own health problems to consider, it was a difficult time for the couple. After spending a quiet (and final) Christmas and New Year together, the Prices had no choice but to bring in a nurse to look after Coral.

Browne grew weaker through the start of 1991, but she wasn't giving up without a fight, even when she became bedridden. Finally, on 29 May 1991, only two days after her husband's eightieth birthday, the remarkable Coral Browne passed away. Price was not around at the time of her death as he was filming a documentary for Tim Burton; he told no one other than Burton about the tragic news. For the actor, work was the best therapy to help console his grief, although his children were also with him during this difficult time.

Browne's death prompted an outpouring of affection and respect from friends and colleagues in the acting world. She was cremated at the Hollywood cemetery and on 23 July 1991 (which would have been her seventy-eighth birthday), Price organised a celebration of her life at St Victor's Catholic Church, followed by a party in her honour.

In September 1991, John Schlesinger, who had filmed a documentary about the actress called *Caviar for the General*, organised a memorial for his friend at the Church of the Immaculate Conception in London. This was one trip to England Price could not go to because of his own health.

Price was devastated by her death. 'When I was courting Coral, the first gift she gave me was a photo of herself simply signed: "Remember Coral" – not really a challenge, as the problem was how to forget her. I've come to believe remembering someone is not the highest compliment – it is missing them. I find I miss every hour of Coral's life – I miss the morning cloudiness, noon mellowness, evening brightness. I miss her in every corner of our house, every crevice of my life. In missing her, I feel I'm missing much of life itself.'

In October 1991, Price gave his final film performance in *The Heart of Justice* (1993), a made-for-cable crime thriller that reunited him with Dennis Hopper, and a solid cast that included Eric Stoltz, Jennifer Connelly, Dermot Mulroney, Bradford Dillman, William H Macy and Felicity Huffman. The film, which was screened in February 1993, is a muddled affair where Stoltz's reporter investigates the murder of a novelist (Hopper) by a member of a prominent and incestuous family. While the film has potential, it is indifferently handled by director Bruno Barreto, leaving it a laboured effort that promises more than it delivered.

Price's role of wealthy homosexual Reggie Shaw is a cameo that consists of two scenes, the first he shares with the equally underused Hopper. Although still very frail, he looks healthier than he did in *Edward Scissorhands* and his voice has regained some of its power. While hardly memorable, it proved a fitting enough end to Price's film career.

In January 1992, *The Los Angeles Film Critics Association* paid tribute to Price. 'It was very exciting,' he recalled. 'Everybody was there, and they gave me a standing ovation. It was really very touching. It's pretty nice to be remembered when you're eighty years old! Well, you old fart, I see they got you just in the nick of time.'

Price became less able to move around, a nightmare for someone who prided himself on being constantly busy. 'He had predicated his entire existence on work, travel, action and accomplishment,' said Victoria about his final years, 'but the gradual dissolution of his abilities through illness eventually took away his will to live. For Vincent Price, a life of inactivity was no life at all.' Even his Catholicism gave him little comfort in his later years.

To keep the mind going, Price set about putting his affairs in order and re-establishing contacts with family members and old friends pushed aside by his wife's jealousy. He stayed in close contact with Hazel Court, Roddy McDowell and Dennis Hopper and enjoyed the company of his younger friends Tim Burton and Johnny Depp. As a man so well loved by his colleagues in the movie industry, he wasn't short of visitors, many of whom stayed away while Coral Browne was alive. 'With Coral gone,' said Victoria, 'my father lost no time reaching out to his children and to other members of his family with whom he had little contact in recent years.'

However, Price was incensed that his wife's will, for which he was co-executor, left an estate in excess of $6 million. For a man who always worried about money, and being married to a woman who often complained about his stinginess and her own financial problems, it came as quite a shock, especially when most of it was out his reach. All Price received from the will was personal property.

Once Price sorted out the conditions in the will, he set about getting rid of her personal effects. With the help of Victoria, he began cataloguing his art collection with the intention of writing a further book on art. But despite the initial enthusiasm, nothing came of it.

Now confined to a wheelchair, Price remained as sharp as a tack. 'Being elderly is a miserable period of life,' he told his daughter, 'from the physical standpoint, I mean. Mentally, there are great rewards. You have an entire lifetime during which, if you have spent your time on Earth profitably, you have accumulated enormous amounts of knowledge. You understand things now as you could not when you were younger. You gain wisdom and perspective. Now that I am coming to the end of my life, every day I think of something that's beautiful. The garden, the juxtaposition of leaves and plants, the variety of shapes of leaves and shades of green. Those are the things that are really worth cultivating in your life, and you must keep your eyes open for them and keep your imagination open to being surprised.' His moving words to Victoria sums up a man, who, in his final months, still loved and embraced life.

Vincent Leonard Price Junior died on 25 October 1993 from lung cancer, and complications of emphysema and Parkinson's disease. His death left family, friends and fans with a great sense of loss, especially in Britain where *The Times* obituary described him as 'the king of modern horror movies.'

'The world has lost a great actor and I have lost a wonderful friend,' said a deeply saddened Christopher Lee. 'During the years that my wife and I lived in Los Angeles, we were able to see a good deal of Vincent and his wife, Coral Browne, and it was one of the joys of our time there.'

Peter Cushing gave a far more upbeat response to his friend's departure. 'I do not mourn his loss, I rejoice in it. He had lost his wife some time ago and was a very lonely man.' Cushing's words about Price being reunited with Coral Browne in Heaven echoed his own desire to be reunited with Helen. His time finally came the following year when Cushing died from prostate cancer on the 11 August 1994. 'They were both grand masters of their art,' Lee said of Price and Cushing, 'but more importantly as human beings, wonderful people, wonderful actors and I miss them very much.'

After receiving a well-deserved knighthood, Sir Christopher Lee reunited with his old friends when he died on 7 July 2015 aged 93. No doubt Price, with typical good humour, would have complained about Lee being late!

After her divorce from Price, Mary Grant became a professional architectural designer, which took her around the country designing and refurbishing homes and buildings. Remaining friends with her former husband, she retired to Boston Massachusetts, where she died on 2 March 2012.

A small service and cremation was held for family and friends at the Hollywood Cemetery and the following day, the family hired a private boat to sail out to a spot near St Nicholas Beach. After the captain said the *Lord's Prayer*, Price's ashes were scattered into the sea along with a bouquet of red roses and his old straw hat. 'This hat,' said Victoria, 'its brim adorned with a heavy wooden African necklace, was so much a part of him that we felt it fitting to send it with him. As the hat bobbed away, a baby seal swam beneath it and began to play, almost swimming through the necklace. As the hat and necklace slowly sank, the seal gazed up at all of us on the boat with what seemed a smile, then swam away among the roses.'

On 21 November 1993, Victoria organised a private party at the Vincent Price Art Gallery, a fitting place for a man who had devoted his life to the world of art. Guests were invited to two exhibitions, followed by supper at his favourite LA restaurant, The City. 'I spoke at the gathering,' said Victoria, 'followed by the college president, and then by Roddy McDowell, who gave a eulogy that reduced everyone to tears. Michael Feinstein played two songs, after which we enjoyed Chef Susan Ferniger's wonderful food. It was the kind of party my father would have loved – great food, lots to drink, interesting people, loving friends and plenty of art on view.'

On 25 August 1995, Price's 100th film finally received its long overdue cinema screening.

Nasrudden had been held back for a variety of reasons, mostly involving funding since every scene was painstakingly hand drawn by Richard Williams. In the meantime, Williams continued his excellent animated work on several big budget movies. Thanks to the success of *Who Framed Roger Rabbit* (1988), he secured a lucrative deal with Warner Brothers to complete the film on a $25 million marketing budget.

Sadly *Nasrudden*, renamed *The Thief and the Cobbler*, went over budget and in 1992 Warners, fearing stiff competition from Disney's *Aladdin* (1992), took the project out of Williams' hands despite only 15 minutes of animation being left to complete.

Warners brought in new animators under the supervision of Fred Calvert. New scenes were added that included Disney-inspired songs and almost all the characters were re-voiced with only Price, Kenneth Williams, Windsor Davies, Donald Pleasence, Stanley Baxter and Eddie Byrne being retained from the original cast while Sarah Crowe, Felix Aylmer, Joan Sims and Sir Anthony Quayle were replaced by other actors: Clive Revill later stepped in for Anthony Quayle. The film finally got released through Allied Filmmakers in 1993 as *The Princess and the Cobbler*.

Disney subsidiary, Miramax Films, then acquired the rights, and carried out further re-writes and re-editing. Several cuts to lengthy sequences were made and a continuous dialogue track was added along with a new voice-over cast of Matthew Broderick, Jennifer Beals and Toni Collette in the lead roles. Eric Bogosian replaced Donald Pleasence while Price, Williams, Davies, Baxter, Revill and Byrne remained. Even the principle character of the Thief, who was silent throughout the film was voiced by Jonathan Winters.

Miramax finally released the film under the uninspired title of *Arabian Nights* in 1995. The critical reaction was negative, with many complaining about the studio interference. Williams was so bitter about the end result he refused to talk about the movie.

In 2006, filmmaker Gene Gilchrist set about an extensive and complex restoration entitled *The Recobbled Cut*. Gilchrist followed most of Williams' narrative and avoided a lot of the changes made by Fred Calvert, although he kept some animated sequences to advance the story. Other animators were also commissioned to add several scenes in the Williams' style. The end result brought a positive reaction from critics and while Williams wouldn't watch *The Recobbled Cut*, he praised Gilchrist in enhancing the film's reputation. It has since been revised in 2008 and 2013 to a much higher quality.

The Thief and the Cobbler, is a flawed work. Williams' surreal and imaginative animation is undermined by flat studio sequences that destroyed what could have been a masterpiece. Price's first rate vocal performance as the Grand Vizier Zigzag is on par with Rattigan in *The Great Mouse Detective*. For all its faults, *The Thief and the Cobbler* is a fitting end to the remarkable career of Vincent Price.

Epilogue

'I have great admiration for the motion picture as a profession.
I think it's a great art form.' – Vincent Price

Vincent Price and Coral Browne

On 14 November 2018, I bought a ticket for an evening event that was too good to miss; In fact, I would have been completely bonkers if I didn't go!

Always looking out for potential book talks, I checked out the list of events organised by the Darlington Film Club. One event that really stood out was a retrospective on Vincent Price. The guest speaker was none other than Victoria Price. It was an amazing opportunity for a fan like me to meet the great man's daughter!

The audience was treated to a screening of *The Pit and the Pendulum* and after the screening, there was a brief recess, and that was when I got to meet Victoria, who was signing copies of *Vincent Price: A Daughter's Biography*, and her father's book *Cooking Price-Wise*. A darling lady who had time for her father's fans, meeting and chatting with her for a few minutes was more than I could ever wish for. When I told her I was working on a book about her dad, and his links to Britain, she was thrilled to bits!

Victoria's talk about Vinnie was informative, enlightening and entertaining. Full of warmth and humour, and more importantly, a great love and respect for her father, and the legacy he left to his fans, she is very much a 'Daddy's Girl,' and proud of it! After the talk, she graciously answered questions that included her dad's use of a washing machine to prepare fish for cooking, and having tea with Christopher Lee and Peter Cushing!

I've always been fascinated by the falling out between Vincent Price and Robert Quarry during the making of *Dr Phibes Rises Again*. To satisfy my own curiosity, I asked her what she thought about their fractured relationship. Victoria felt, and I would agree, that her father was more distressed by what had happened, and showed no real hatred towards Mr Quarry.

Victoria's love and devotion to her father is something to behold, especially when she told the audience she sold everything to spend her time travelling the freeways, motorways and autobahns to share the great man's legacy. She is as remarkable as her old man!

Vincent Price is no longer with us, but his films are, whether screened on television somewhere in the world or available on DVD or Blu-Ray. In an infamous and seldom refined genre, Price has carved his own piece of cinema immortality, and not just because of his obvious talent. He created a distinctive persona that brought smiles and chills in equal measures to his many fans.

Vincent Price was many things: classical actor; art expert; writer; philosopher; philanthropist; bohemian; lecturer. A much travelled man who embraced life and the world around him, and he achieved this through hard work and a combination of dedication and determination. He valued his friendships and saw so much good in everyone. His wonderful qualities as a human being made him an old and valued family friend to the fans who have never met him. He will still be remembered for many years to come, while bigger Hollywood stars fade into the showbiz ether.

Price's time in Britain was a creative and influential time. One only has to mention Matthew Hopkins or Edward Lionheart to know his outstanding work in British horror. Even *Cry of the Banshee* and *Madhouse* had a quality about them that made them superior to a lot of his American chillers. From his childhood onwards, his life had a strong British connection with his magnificent speaking voice and sophisticated manner often mistaking him for being English. He had the best of both worlds.

Vincent Price was the king of horror – on both sides of the Atlantic.

Bibliography

Baker, Roy Ward: *The Director's Cut*

Boot, Andy: *Fragments of Fear*

Bradley, Doug: *Sacred Monsters: Behind the Mask of the Horror Actor*

Brosnan, John: *The Horror People*

Bryce, Allan: *Amicus: The Studio That Dripped Blood*

Chibnall, Steve: *White Mischief: The Cult Films of Peter Walker*

Cushing, Peter: *Past Forgetting*

Del Vecchio, Deborah and Johnson, Tom: *Hammer Films: An Exhaustive Filmography*

Del Vecchio, Deborah and Johnson, Tom: *Peter Cushing: The Gentleman of Horror and His 91 Films*

Fryer, Ian: *The British Horror Film*

Hamilton, John: *Beasts in the Cellar: The Exploitation Career of Tony Tenser*

Iveson, Mark: *Cursed Horror Stars*

Lee, Christopher: *Lord of Misrule: The Autobiography of Christopher Lee*

McCann, Graham: *Bounder! The Biography of Terry-Thomas*

Meikle, Denis: *Vincent Price: The Art of Fear*

Miller, David: *Peter Cushing: A Life in Films*

Miller, Mark: *Christopher Lee and Peter Cushing and Horror Cinema: A Filmography*

Newman, Kim: *Nightmare Movies*

Ogilvy, Ian: *Once a Saint: An Actor's Memoir*

Price, Victoria: *Vincent Price: A Daughter's Biography*

Rigby, Jonathan: *American Gothic*

Rigby, Jonathan: *Christopher Lee: The Authorised Screen History*

Rigby, Jonathan: *English Gothic*

Rigby, Jonathan: *Euro Gothic*

Southcott, Jonathan: *The Cult Films of Christopher Lee*

Svelha, Gary & Susan: *Vincent Price*

Williams, Lucy Chase: *The Complete Films of Vincent Price*

Wright, Bruce Lanier: *Nightwalkers*

Name Index

Title Index

About the Author

Mark Iveson is the author of *Cursed Horror Stars*, also published by Telos. Born in Gateshead, he spent his early years in London before returning to the North-East as a teenager. Mark currently works as a civil servant for the Department for Work and Pensions.

A horror movie buff from childhood, Mark has a near photographic knowledge of the genre. A lifelong movie fan, he especially loves science fiction, British film comedy and James Bond; the only films he doesn't care for are musicals!

Mark began writing film, theatre and gig reviews for several work related magazines and periodicals. He wrote for the vampire magazine *Bite Me*, theatre reviews for the arts magazine *Up Front*, and non-film related articles for the *Geneva Times*.

Mark made his name as a principle writer for the movie webmag *Shadowlocked*. He contributed over thirty articles and reviews during his time at the webmag.

Mark's other passion is music. He plays guitar, mandolin and banjo, and is a regular performer at several buskers' nights around Newcastle. He also spent two years as bass guitarist with the popular North-East rock band *Old Man Goat*.

Since the publication of *Cursed Horror Stars*, Mark has done several book talks across the North-East, a number of which were at the celebrated Castle Keep in Newcastle's city centre. He has been guest speaker at the 2016 *Whitley Bay Film Festival* and the 2016 *Newcastle Book Festival*. Mark has also run several book stalls in Newcastle and Whitby.

Mark attends the Swanwick Writers' Retreat at the Hayes Conference Centre in Swanwick, Derbyshire, a great inspiration to his writing career.

The author with Victoria Price.

Other Titles
From Telos Publishing

Taboo Breakers
Calum Waddell

Hulk
Tony Lee

Still the Beast is Feeding: Forty Years of Rocky Horror
Rob Bagnall and Phil Barden

The Making of Casino Royale (1967)
Michael Richardson

Cursed Horror Stars
Mark Iveson

Rubber Sharks and Wooden Acting: The Ultimate Bad Movie Guide
Nico Vaughan

Infogothic: An Unauthorised Graphic Guide to Hammer Horror
Alastair Hughes

It Lives Again: Horror Movies in the New Millennium
Axelle Carolyn

All available online from
www.telos.co.uk

Made in the USA
Monee, IL
02 August 2021

74805404R00138